G000123378

NAMES, TIME AND PLACE

Essays in memory of Richard McKinley

NAMES, TIME AND PLACE

Essays in memory of
Richard McKinley

Edited by
Della Hooke and David Postles

LEOPARD'S HEAD PRESS
2003

First published in 2003 by
Leopard's Head Press
1-5 Broad Street, Oxford, OX1 3AW

© D. A. Postles 2003

ISBN 0 904920 46 1

Typeset by Denham House, Yapton, West Sussex
and printed in Great Britain by
Halstan & Co., Ltd., Amersham, Buckinghamshire

Contents

———————— ✦❖✦ ————————

List of Illustrations and Maps

List of Contributors

---

† CECILY CLARK (Cambridge). The late Cecily Clark was the doyenne of English anthroponymy. Her collected papers were published as *Words, Names, and History: Selected Writings of Cecily Clark*, ed. P. Jackson, (Cambridge, 1995).

† JOHN DODGSON (University of London). One of the late John Dodgson's monumental contributions to onomastics comprised the multi-volume *Place-names of Cheshire* which the English Place-name Society published between 1970 and 1997. He was also a renowned Domesday scholar.

GILLIAN FELLOWS-JENSEN (Københavns Universitet) has, through the Institut for Navneforskning, produced the authoritative books, materials and papers on Scandinavian influence on English place- and personal names, through a succession of books and articles starting with her explanation of Scandinavian personal names in Lincolnshire and Yorkshire in 1968.

HAROLD FOX (University of Leicester) is Senior Lecturer in Topography in the Centre for English Local History, School of Historical Studies. He has been Head of the Department of English Local History. Amongst his many important publications, the most recent is *The Evolution of the Fishing Village: Landscape and Society along the South Devon Coast, 1086–1550*, (Oxford, 2001) reflecting his long-term research into the South-West and Devon in particular.

MARGARET GELLING (University of Birmingham). For many years, Margaret Gelling has been established as the leading authority on place-names in England. The author of numerous books on the origin and significance of place-names in their geographical and historical contexts, she received the M.B.E. in 1995 for her contribution. She has contributed volumes to the English Place-name series and to the regional volumes of Anglo-Saxon charters. Her most well-known work, *Signposts to the Past: Place-names and the History of England*, has extended through three editions illustrating its communication of scholarly research to a wider audience.

DAVID HEY (University of Sheffield). Although he has now retired, Professor David Hey remains an inspirational teacher of local history. His early academic career evolved in the Department of English Local History with his thesis on Myddle, Shropshire, and his post there as a research fellow. He has been a prodigious author, one of whose most recent volumes is *Family Names and Family History*, (London, 2000).

DELLA HOOKE (University of Birmingham). Over many years, through her numerous scholarly volumes, Della Hooke has become the authority in the reconstitution of early landscapes from lexical evidence in Anglo-Saxon charters and diplomas. In particular, her familiarity with the West Midlands has resulted, in the 1990s, in two books on boundaries described in charters relating to Worcestershire and Warwickshire.

EVELYN LORD (University of Cambridge) was formerly a post-graduate researcher in the Department of English Local History and is now on the academic staff of the Institute of Continuing Education, University of Cambridge. Her doctoral thesis on the boundary areas of Surrey and Sussex was undertaken with an E.S.R.C. postgraduate award at the Department of English Local History.

PRYS MORGAN (University of Wales, Swansea). Although the primary research area of Prys Morgan is modern Glamorgan and Welsh history since the eighteenth century, he is also the acknowledged expert on Welsh names and naming processes, his published work including, with T. J. Morgan, *Welsh Surnames*, (Cardiff, 1985).

OLIVER PADEL (University of Cambridge) was formerly Editor of *Nomina*, the journal of the Council (later Society) for Name Studies in Great Britain and Ireland, and is Lecturer in the Department of Anglo-Saxon, Norse and Celtic in the University of Cambridge.

DAVID POSTLES (University of Leicester) is Marc Fitch Research Fellow in the Centre for English Local History in the School of Historical Studies and leads the English Surnames Survey for the Marc Fitch Fund.

SUELLA POSTLES is Community Historian and formerly Keeper of Social History, Nottingham City Museums Service, and developed the Brewhouse Yard Social History Museum. She completed an M.A. in the Department of English Local History on local social organization in early-modern Barkby, Leicestershire.

MARGERY TRANTER (University of Leicester) is an Honorary Research Fellow in the Centre for English Local History in the School of Historical Studies where she has pursued over many years her research into the amorphous boundary between Leicestershire and Derbyshire and her interest in Derbyshire local history, including an edition of the 1851 religious census for the Derbyshire Record Society.

Introduction

———————— ·ᴥ·ᵴ·ᵴ·ᵴ· ————————

Aᴌᴛʜᴏᴜɢʜ ɪᴛ ʜᴀs ʙᴇᴄᴏᴍᴇ a volume *in memoriam*, this volume had its genesis in 1989 when Richard McKinley remained one of the formative influences on English anthroponymy — the social and cultural implications of personal names — along with Peter McClure and the late and much missed Cecily Clark. Richard had, indeed, occupied a seminal place in English anthroponymy since 1965. As, in 1989, Richard approached his 70th birthday, Charles Phythian-Adams, then Head of the Department of English Local History, suggested that a *festschrift* for Richard would be appropriate. Two constituencies (at least) had a close interest in contributing: his present and former colleagues at the Department; and his friends in the Society for Name Studies (as it has since been reconstituted). A circular was thus distributed through these two groups to raise the prospect of a *festschrift* and inviting papers should the project come to fruition. A number of offers having been received, Roy Stephens, Secretary to the Marc Fitch Fund and Director of Leopard's Head Press, was approached as to whether the volume might be published by Leopard's Head Press in acknowledgement of Richard's contribution to the remit of the Fund as its Research Fellow for the English Surnames Survey for over twenty years. As a result of this discussion, the idea was placed before Council of the Marc Fitch Fund which kindly agreed to the proposal. Considering, however, the programme of work of the Fund's Research Fellow, David Postles, Susan Reynolds, then a member of the Council, suggested that a joint editor ought to be co-opted. Since the Department was already editorially represented, an open invitation was extended to the other constituency, the (now) Society for Name Studies. In response, Della Hooke offered to co-edit the volume.

During the early part of 1990, many of the papers were promptly received, including papers from David Hey, John Dodgson, Cecily Clark, Gillian Fellows-Jensen and Margaret Gelling. All therefore seemed set very fair. As seems inevitable with a *festschrift*, however, delays interfered with progress. Two contributors withdrew at a fairly early stage, one because of substantial changes to career and life. Progress was then further postponed as a small number of contributors failed to submit their papers. Finally, one of the contributors, finding it difficult to meet the commitment, agreed to withdraw.

Unfortunately, that agreement did not conclude the difficulties of the volume as a few other contributors delayed the return of proofs and, not least, refinements were required to the appreciation of Richard which have taken a considerable, perhaps unconscionable, time to be finalized. The volume has therefore stalled in the early galley proofs of most of the contributions — for over a period of several years. During that intermission, two of the contributors have sadly died, but it was felt important to retain their homage to Richard, as they surely would have wanted and as, indeed, the surviving partner of one has agreed. Most sadly, the honorand himself died and this volume has become by circumstance a gift *in memoriam*.

The result remains, however, a respectful submission of our esteem for Richard. Whilst it could never encompass all of the remarkable range of his interests and knowledge, the volume does focus on the issues which continued to be close to the final stage of his academic career. Indeed, the very distinguished place-name scholars who have produced papers for this volume have very effectively associated their research with anthroponymy: thus the papers of Gelling, Padel, Dodgson, Morgan and Fellows-Jensen. Fox essentially complements these papers by considering the context for the continuity of surnames in late medieval England.

Postles and Postles extend from the late middle ages into the early-modern period in a case study of a particular parish which establishes contact with David Hey's more conceptual and general paper on the significance of surnames for the stability of local populations and 'core' families in early-modern England. Whilst Hey's paper was amongst the first published formulations of his ideas on surnames and stable families, his published explanations of those connections have subsequently 'ramified' (to use a verb made familiar by Richard in his volumes for the English Surnames Survey) and he has established an important literature for the post-medieval importance of surname studies. In like manner, Evelyn Lord explores the role of surnames in a context only recently approached — the nineteenth century. In most of his county volumes in the

English Surnames Survey, Richard examined the early-modern distribution of surnames, from Hearth Taxes in particular, and their nineteenth-century concentrations from the 1851 census enumerators' returns, through case studies of sample areas in respective counties. The contributions to this volume by Hey and Lord provide a conceptual framework for surname studies in post-medieval English local societies.

One important 'society' with which Richard only tangentially engaged was the Welsh. As far as they intruded into English surname studies, he commented on Welsh names. The significance of Welsh naming patterns is, however, extremely important, in its own right as well as comparatively. We are therefore extremely pleased to have the erudite contributions of Prys Morgan and Oliver Padel which rectify this lacuna in Leicester's examination of surnames. Moreover, whilst one is a general conceptualization, the other is an intensely localized and contextualized account which has immense significance.

From 'habitative' surnames (Gelling) to surnames in local societies on the Surrey/Sussex borders (Lord), the last touching on one of the last of Richard's county volumes (Sussex), we feel sure that Richard would have felt a close and tender association with all the contributions in this volume — and we hope that he would have been delighted with them. In the circumstances that have arisen we can only hope that these studies go someway towards being a fitting tribute in his memory.

Our thanks are owed to Charles Phythian-Adams for initiating the idea, to Roy Stephens not only for agreeing to the project for the Press but also because of his fond admiration for Richard (and, indeed, for bearing most of the frustration of bringing this volume to fruition), and not least to all the contributors, most of whom have also exercised enormous patience and forbearance. In terms of dedication, we ought to include Marc Fitch, for his close involvement and interest in Richard's work and his personal support. This introduction was in the original scheme to have been a Foreword by the late Dr Fitch. Finally, we ought also to remember the late Cecily Clark who knew Richard so well and stimulated all our work on anthroponymy, and also the late John Dodgson.

David Postles
Leicester

October 2002
(as the volume approaches conclusion).

Richard McKinley: An Appreciation

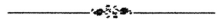

RICHARD McKINLEY SPENT most of his working life at the University (formerly University College) of Leicester, although there was a short break in the 1950s and 1960s when he held posts at the Exeter City Library and the Staffordshire Record Office. He came to Leicester in 1949, shortly after the foundation of the Department of English Local History, and was given working space in the Hatton Room, located in the College's principal building (once a lunatic asylum) and containing a fine and rare collection of works relating to local history throughout England. There, the young Manchester graduate, with several years of war service behind him, worked as Local Assistant Editor for the *Victoria County History of Leicestershire*, under the direction of W. G. Hoskins. The Department of English Local History at that time was largely a research unit, so Richard's teaching was to students in the Department of History. When the local funding for the Victoria County History ran out, he moved away from Leicester to take up the posts in archives services referred to above. He returned in 1963 in order to establish the English Surnames Survey within the Department of English Local History and from then until his retirement he contributed classes on a variety of topics (but especially palaeography) to the Department's M.A. programme.

Richard was always the Department's foremost scholar. All of his colleagues recognized that without any sense of envy; it was an established fact, Herbert Finberg (himself a great scholar) describing Richard as 'the most learned man he had ever met'. A rigorous training in the renowned Manchester school, under Namier, Jacob, Redford and Cheney, work for the ever vigilant Pugh, his years as an archivist and his scrutiny of so many counties for the English Surnames Survey — all gave him an unrivalled insight into British history at all levels. What I used to fear when asking him for help with some historical query was a negative answer, for that usually meant that the problem was without any solution. Colleagues in the

Department of English Local History, other enquirers from within and without the University, and many generations of students were guided towards happy solutions to their historical problems by his profound knowledge of the Middle Ages. But more than that, he could usually assist if the query was about twentieth-century local government, the Victorian city, the poor law or Tudor taxation . . . the range was enviable and the recall instantaneous. One colleague, at a party, tried to disarm him by asking, in small talk, if he knew the date at which the big-dipper was installed at Blackpool, but the joke was not on Richard because he immediately gave the answer — in his usual precise, matter-of-fact way. I have been told that he was an excellent guide to urban landscapes because of his intimate knowledge of the history behind almost every building.

One cannot write of a Manchester medievalist without recalling the sombre features of Tait and Tout who peer at us rather awkwardly from their *Festschrift* frontispieces. Richard McKinley was not at all like that, for a good deal of humour lay just below the surface of his benign appearance. Although they might not be offered without a little prompting, a fund of humorous anecdotes and a wry chuckle could be drawn from him without much difficulty and he was not averse to telling a story against himself. If asked he would talk about his service years in Burma, about his travels in Europe and beyond, and about his current reading which ranged far beyond the subjects of his historical research. His collection of books — generously donated to the Department by his sisters — confirmed an abiding academic interest in the Middle Ages but there were many items which reflected far wider interests: for example about people and places in prehistory and early history (the Etruscans, the Minoans and others) and about the history of tactics in warfare (an interest which perhaps stemmed from his army service), including one (in French) on the military importance of the elephant and no less than three on the defence of Gibraltar by George Augustus Eliott. After Richard's death, we learned from relatives of his boyhood passion for history, kindled in part perhaps by the scholarly atmosphere in the clerical household in which he was brought up, certainly by a large encyclopedia containing the histories of out-of-the-way and exotic places.

Richard left behind him two monumental historical works, the first being the *Victoria County History of Leicestershire*. William Hoskins to a large extent planned the thematic volumes, but it was left to

Richard to bring those plans to fruition and to carry the series forward with topographical volumes on the City of Leicester (and its surrounding parishes) and on Gartree Hundred. He admitted to me that when he first came to Leicester his task initially was to infill the vacant spaces in the design. The section on 'Religious Houses' came naturally to him, for he had recently completed work on the cartulary of Breedon Priory (in a Manchester M.A. dissertation of some length which would surely warrant the degree of M.Phil. or Ph.D. today); but characteristically he turned his hand to chapters on subjects more foreign to him, for example on modern political history, on the royal forests of Leicestershire, and on mining, quarrying and banking — and made them his own. Moreover, his sections took their place alongside the work of a glittering collection of other scholars who agreed to write on aspects of Leicestershire's history, including Simmons, Thirsk, Plumb and Hilton. Richard's two topographical volumes belong to a new generation of V.C.H. writing: for each parish new sections — on nonconformity and economic history, for example — were added to the old sections on manorial descent and the (established) church. This *genre* of historical writing — painstaking assembly of information parish by parish — is still maligned in some circles, but how wrongly, for is not many an historian's work initiated and guided by the standardized, complete V.C.H. coverage of topics such as medieval market grants, field systems, parish schools and Methodist meetings? Those who use the Leicestershire topographical volumes researched and edited by Richard McKinley will know that they can rely on them without fail.

Richard's second great achievement is the English Surnames Survey, a project which originated in the interest which Hoskins had in local Leicestershire farming families and in their names and migration and which flourished as a result of a friendship between Hoskins and Marc Fitch (the latter fascinated by the origin and spread of his own family and by other Essex surnames) and through the generosity over many years of the Marc Fitch Fund. Richard, with a specialist knowledge of so many local sources, was an obvious choice as the Survey's director. He researched and wrote four volumes (*Norfolk and Suffolk Surnames in the Middle Ages*, 1975; *The Surnames of Oxfordshire*, 1977; *The Surnames of Lancashire*, 1981; *The Surnames of Sussex*, 1988) and he contributed a chapter on the evolution of hereditary surnames to *The Surnames of Devon* (1995), by David Postles. Richard therefore laid the methodological foundations of a continuing project which will always be indispensable as a reference work. But, far more than that, as the Survey proceeded, it began to tell us much about naming processes themselves and to unlock and illuminate many related areas of social and economic development. For example, Richard's study of Norfolk and Suffolk found that hereditary surnames (passed down from generation to generation) seem to have evolved earlier in East Anglia than in some other parts of England, notably the North, and he related this precocious trend to the early commercial and urban developments of the former region and with the extensive migration associated with them. His work on Lancashire led to the finding that local 'ramification' of individual names (their growth and spread from a single original source) was far more strongly developed in that county than in some others, and to the surprising conclusion that industrialization in the eighteenth and nineteenth centuries did not appear to have much affected the stock of Lancashire's names.

At Leicester, Richard's colleagues and students valued his scholarship and, equally, in an age in which it is no longer possible to assume that all academics and administrators in universities are entirely sincere and without self-interest, they valued his complete integrity: you knew where you were with Richard McKinley. In the world of scholarship more generally, his primacy in his field was recognized when in 1989 he became Chairman of the Council for Name Studies in Britain and Ireland. All will agree with the author of the obituary in the Council's periodical, *Nomina*, who wrote of Richard's erudition in so many fields and described his four volumes in the Surnames Series as 'an impressive intellectual achievement and fitting memorial to a remarkable scholar'.

Harold Fox
Centre for English Local History
University of Leicester

Richard McKinley

Marc Fitch Research Fellow and director of the English Surnames Survey in the Department of English Local History, University of Leicester, 1965–1986.

A Bibliography

1950 — The cartulary of Breedon Priory, with introduction and critical apparatus, M.A. thesis, University of Manchester.

1954 — Editor (with W. G. Hoskins), *The Victoria History of the County of Leicester*, II, London, 270pp.
'Religious Houses', *ibid.*, pp.1–54.
'Political History, 1885–1950', *ibid.*, pp.135–45.
'The Forests of Leicestershire', *ibid.*, pp.265–70.

1955 — Editor (with W. G. Hoskins), *The Victoria History of the County of Leicester*, III, O.U.P., 338pp.
'Industries of Leicestershire: Mining, quarrying, banking', *ibid.*, pp.30–46, 50–6.
'Education in Leicestershire: Charity schools, elementary education in the nineteenth and twentieth centuries', *ibid.*, pp.243–51.

1958 — Editor, *The Victoria History of the County of Leicester*, IV, *The City of Leicester*, O.U.P., xx + 484pp.
Contributions to 'The Topography of Leicester', *ibid.*, pp.338–458.
'Social and administrative history since 1835', *ibid.*, pp.251–302, (with C. T. Smith).

1964 — Editor (with J. M. Lee), *The Victoria History of the County of Leicester*, V, *The Gartree Hundred*, O.U.P., 367pp.

'The Foundation of the Staffordshire General Infirmary', *Transactions of the Old Staffordshire Society*, 1963–65, pp.14–26.

1969 — *Norfolk Surnames in the Sixteenth Century*, Leicester, Department of English Local History Occasional Papers, 2nd series, 2, 60pp.

'The Survey of English Surnames', *The Local Historian*, VIII, pp.299–302.

1972 — 'The Extractive Industries', in N. Pye, ed., *Leicester and its Region*, Leicester, pp.340–62 (with J. J. Fagg).

1975 — *Norfolk and Suffolk Surnames in the Middle Ages*, Chichester, 153pp.

Reviews — G. A. Chinnery, ed., *Records of the Borough of Leicester*, VII, in *Urban History Year Book*, Leicester, pp.95–7.

M. James, *Family, Lineage and Civil Society*, in *Midland History*, III, pp.152–3.

1976 — 'The Survey of English Surnames', in H. Voitl, ed., *The Study of Personal Names of the British Isles*, University of Erlangen, pp.119–25.

'The Distribution of Surnames derived from the names of some Yorkshire towns', in F. Emmison and R. Stephens, eds., *Tribute to an Antiquary*, London, pp.165–75.

1977 — *The Surnames of Oxfordshire*, Oxford, 212pp.

1979 — 'Hereditary surnames and the chronology of their evolution', in *Proceedings of the XIIIth International Congress of Genealogical and Heraldic Sciences*, pp.347–88.

'Research into Lancashire Surnames', *Genealogists' Magazine*, XIX, pp.393–5.

Review — K. Foster, *Englische Familiennamen aus Ortsnamen*, in *Nomina*, 3, p.117.

1980 — 'Social Class and the Origin of Surnames', in *Genealogists' Magazine*, XX, pp.103–10

1981 — *The Surnames of Lancashire*, Oxford, 501pp.
'British Surnames', in M. Rubincam, ed., *Genealogical Research: Methods and Sources*, I, American Society of Genealogists, pp.555–64.

1988 — *The Surnames of Sussex*, Oxford, 483pp.
Reviews — Gabriel Ward Lasker, *Surnames and Genetic Structure*, Cambridge, 1985, in *English Historical Review*, 103, p.279.

1990 — *A History of British Surnames*, Longman, 230pp.

1991 — 'Medieval Latin translations of English personal by-names: their value for surname history', *Nomina*, XIV, 1990–1, pp.1–6.
Reviews — S. Carlsson, *Studies on Middle English Local By-names in East Anglia*, in *ibid.*, pp.125–7.
Robert Bell, *The Book of Ulster Surnames*, in *ibid.*, pp.131–2.

1995 — 'The evolution of hereditary surnames in Devon', in D. Postles, *The Surnames of Devon*, Oxford, xx + 332pp.

Margery Tranter
Centre for English Local History
University of Leicester

Part One

———————————————·⋙⋘·———————————————

Essays by colleagues
associated with
Name Studies

I

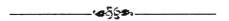

Alfordruncen, Brenebrec, Cattesnese:
some early-twelfth-century Suffolk by-names

† CECILY CLARK

RICHARD MCKINLEY'S great achievement lies in the four county surveys, treating respectively of Norfolk and Suffolk, Oxfordshire, Lancashire, and Sussex, that he has contributed to the English Surnames Series: surveys setting English surname-studies within historical and socio-economic frameworks.[1] There nevertheless remains, within these frameworks, detail needing to be bought into sharper focus, especially concerning the early 'by-name' usages that preceded the adoption of hereditary family-naming.[2] By definition, such detail must be studied microscopically, rather than with the panoramic sweep appropriate to a county-wide survey.

The present essay therefore focuses upon a single document of only 19 folios: a fiscal roll, datable 1097x1119, listing free tenants on manors held by the abbey of Bury St. Edmunds.[3] Despite having

---

1 *Norfolk and Suffolk Surnames in the Middle Ages*, English Surnames Series [hereafter ESS], 2, Chichester, 1975; *The Surnames of Oxfordshire*, ESS, 3, London, 1977; *The Surnames of Lancashire*, ESS, 4, London, 1981; *The Surnames of Sussex*, ESS, 5, Oxford, 1988.

2 The term 'by-name' indicates any identificatory term or phrase, Latin or vernacular, appended to a baptismal name or an 'idionym' (see n.15).

3 D. C. Douglas, ed., *Feudal Documents from the Abbey of Bury St. Edmunds*, London, 1932, pp.25–44 [hereafter *FDB*]. The printed text, marred by misprints, has been checked against C.U.L. MS. Mm.iv.19, ff.134v–43v, for which see R. M. Thomson, *The Archives of the Abbey of Bury St. Edmunds*, Suffolk Record Society, 21, Woodbridge, 1980, pp.119–21, also p.16. Except when involving recognized proper names, by-names will normally be given here, as in the manuscript, without capitalization.

been in print for almost 60 years and during that time much cited, this document is far as yet from having been fully exploited. Extant only in an early-thirteenth-century cartulary copy, it is as it stands fragmentary, covering merely two and a half of the eight and a half hundreds within the Bury jurisdiction: a coverage that overlaps only partly with that of the likewise fragmentary late-twelfth-century survey of the abbey's holdings.[4] Although many features of this document, not least its baptismal-name patterns,[5] require its compilation to have antedated by roughly a century the copy extant, its precise date remains uncertain; for, though all concur in setting the *terminus ad quem* no later than 1119, by no means all accept the closer dating to *c.*1097 sometimes proposed.[6] Possible dates of birth for those listed range, if a date *c.*1097 be accepted, from *c.*1035 to *c.*1080 or else, should one of *ante* 1119 be preferred, from *c.*1055 to *c.*1100.[7]

More pertinent than the document's exact date are the onomastic patterns it reveals. Roughly 680 individuals are named here (a risk of unmarked duplication puts a precise total out of the question), some 643 men and 37 women; and, of these, only some 35 at most, all men — little more than 5 per cent, that is — bear baptismal names apparently introduced into Suffolk by post-Conquest settlers.[8] The population concerned can thus be identified as a native English one only lightly touched by Continental influences. Pertinent too is the social group represented: free tenants holding plots that vary in size from a quarter of an acre to 80 acres — a class which, for all that

---

4 R. H. C. Davis, ed., *The Kalendar of Abbot Samson of Bury St. Edmunds*, Camden Third Series, 84, London, 1954. The late-thirteenth-century manuscript text (C.U.L. Additional MS. 6006, ff.81–105, for which see R. M. Thomson, *Archives*, pp.139–41, also pp.16–17) is poor, and the printed version further marred by misprints and by occasional misrepresentation of Old English names.

5 See C. Clark, '*Willelmus rex? Vel alius Willelmus?*', *Nomina*, 11, 1987, pp.7–33.

6 See the summary references given in '*Willelmus*', p.20, n.5. A recent opinion, that of A. Gransden, expressed in her article 'Baldwin, abbot of Bury St. Edmunds, 1065–1097', *Proceedings of the Battle Conference on Anglo-Norman Studies*, 4, 1982 for 1981, pp.65–76 and pp.187–95, at p.68, agrees with Doulgas (*FDB*, pp.xlvi–xlix, lvii–lxvii) in seeing the survey as consonant with Abbot Baldwin's known politics.

7 '*Willelmus*', p.24, n.29.

8 '*Willelmus*', *passim*.

it constituted, in East Anglia especially, an important element of the population, is barely represented in any extant pre-Conquest record at all,[9] and thus one whose emergence into visibility gives a new dimension to onomastic as well as socio-economic history.

The mode of compilation, vill by vill, gives these lists great anthroponymical value, in so far as it in some measure allows of seeing onomastic behaviour as it should be seen (and in the *English Surnames Series* always has been seen), that is, in local and social terms rather than formal and linguistic ones.[10] That the date of compilation happened to coincide with a turning-point in the history of baptismal-naming has been noted.[11] How far this same document may throw light also upon the history of by-naming, and ultimately therefore of family-naming, remains to be determined.

1 — Naming structures

Of the persons listed here, just under half (310 out of 680) are accorded what may, in the broadest acceptance of the term, be called 'by-names'.[12] The primary means of identification thus remains the baptismal name.

The baptismal-name stock current in this community — or, rather, group of communities — was still a pre-Conquest one, predominantly Old English, but with an Anglo-Scandinavian admixture for about a fifth of the names found, and also with a scattering of naturalized Continental-Germanic forms.[13] The custom, normal amongst all early Germanic peoples, of marking familial relationships by repetition and permutation of name-elements was still to some extent observed;[14] and this might seem to justify assigning the basic

---

9 *Cf.*, e.g., D. E. A. Pelteret, 'Two Old English lists of serfs', *Mediaeval Studies*, 48, 1986, pp.470–513.

10 *Cf.*, '*Willelmus*', pp.10–11; also C. Clark, 'Socio-economic status and individual identity: essential factors in the analysis of Middle English personal-naming', forthcoming in D. A. Postles, ed., *Naming, Society and Regional Identity*.

11 '*Willelmus*', *passim*, esp. pp.10–11.

12 *Cf.*, n.2 above. The present section elaborates the definition.

13 See '*Willelmus*', pp.11, 14, also pp.22–3, nn.26 and 27.

14 '*Willelmus*', p.12.

system to the so-called 'one-name period' when identification
depended upon distinctiveness of 'idionym',[15] not upon qualifying
by-name. Such a classification would, however, be over-simplified; for,
although over half the individuals enrolled figure indeed under simple
'idionyms' evidently in their cases adequate for fiscal identification,
for the remainder the primary name is, as noted, supplemented by
some sort of postposed identificatory phrase — by a 'by-name', in
short. Upon inspection, the reason is clear: the idionyms supplemented were ones duplicated within the record for the same vill,
and thus on their own ambiguous. Supplementation was not entirely
systematic; and so in some lists, notably that for Troston,[16] it remains
unclear whether some individuals were holding more than one plot
— in which case their names ought properly to have been on each
reappearance preceded by *Item* — or whether distinctive by-naming
had simply been overlooked. At all events, the system was no longer
a pure 'one-name' one.

The reason for this shift was that in England, as in the rest of the
Germanic world, the infinite variety of which the permutational
name-system was inherently capable had by the eleventh century
been curtailed through growth of disproportionate preferences for
just a few of the many compounds possible: at Hinderclay, for
instance, four out of the 11 men listed were called *Godric*,[17] and who
knows how many more might not have come to light had men other
than heads of free households been taken into the reckoning. With
such patterns of baptismal-naming, even small communities must
have needed everyday means (not necessarily, of course, by-naming)
for distinguishing one namesake from another.

So, our document identifies some 45 per cent of the individuals
listed by means of postposed phrases of various sorts, some Latin,
some vernacular. How typical was this of early-twelfth-century

15 The term 'idionym' is sometimes preferable in so far as applicable (a) to pagan
    usages no less than to Christian ones and (b) to 'original nicknames' used
    independently (as occasionally in our present text) as well as to true 'baptismal'
    names. For the basic Germanic personal-name system, see, e.g., the present
    writer's chapter on Onomastics in the forthcoming R. M. Hogg, ed., *Cambridge
    History of the English Language*, I.

16 *FDB*, p.37.

17 *FDB*, pp.40–1.

usages? The *Liber Vitae* of Thorney Abbey, compiled sporadically from the first decade of the twelfth century until well into its third quarter, accords notoriously few by-names to those of less than under-tenant status; as a record intended for God rather than for bureaucrats, it may be untypical of the age.[18] What was typical is hard to say. There was, at all events, only limited linkage between modernity of baptismal-naming and high frequency of by-naming. Thus, in baptismal-naming the two Burton surveys datable (B) to *c.*1115 and (A) to *c.*1126 — and so either roughly contemporaneous with our Bury record datable *c.*1097x1119 or else, and more probably, about a generation later — show advanced fashions, with Continental-type names running for men at 18 per cent and 24 per cent respectively, against the 5 per cent in the Bury record; but, against the latter's 45 per cent incidence of by-naming, they show only 30 per cent to 35 per cent and, to make the discrepancy wider, such by-names as they offer consist predominantly of Latin occupational terms, with only a few vernacular forms of any sort.[19] No figures for incidence of by-naming relate, of course, directly to everyday usage; for primarily all reflect scribal practices, mainly as triggered by occurrences of homonymous individuals within a single vill. To suppose styles of recording partly influenced by colloquial usages would not, on the other hand, be unreasonable, as the sporadic recourse in all records to vernacular forms confirms. The Bury patterns of *c.*1097x1119 may further be compared with those found in Abbot Samson's *Kalendar* of *c.*1190: for baptismal-naming, this shows some three-quarters of the male peasants listed as bearing ones of Continental type, so revealing a vast change in fashions over the three or four generations separating it from our chosen document with its 5 per cent; but in frequency of by-naming the change is slighter, with the *Kalendar* showing incidences that vary around 60

---

18 See, e.g., C. Clark, 'The *Liber Vitae* of Thorney Abbey and its "catchment area" ', *Nomina*, 9, 1985, pp.53–72, at p.53.

19 C. G. O. Bridgeman, ed., 'The Burton Abbey twelfth-century surveys', *Collections for a History of Staffordshire edited by the William Salt Archaeological Society*, 1916, pp.209–300, at pp.212–47, the sections tested being pp.212–25. Sporadic recourse to expressions such as *Godricus ad barbam . . . alter Godricus, Ailwinus, alter Ailwinus, Edricus . . . Alter Edricus scilicet forestarius* (pp.212, 213, 222) suggests some lack of recognized everyday *cognomina*.

per cent, against the earlier record's 45 per cent.[20] Lack of space forbids more than token exemplification of these patterns here; but the topic deserves exploration.

In assessing the nature and the styles of twelfth-century by-naming, it must be borne in mind that only such vernacular forms as found favour with local administrators — or, perhaps, defeated their capacity for Latinization — are now accessible. So, although the categories into which recorded instances fall are necessarily the universal ones (familial; occupational; locative; characteristic), the only forms available are documentary ones, some of them neither adopted nor adapted from colloquial usage but devised *ad hoc* on bureaucratic principles.

Of the 680 or so individuals listed here, some 310 (296 men; 14 women) are identified by means of postposed phrases of various sorts. Of these phrases, 126 are explicitly patronymic or metronymic (113 formulas with *filia* or *filius*; 13 vernacular phrases with *dohter, stepsune*, or *sune*[21]), five consist of an idionym or nickname given in an English genitive case but without indication of relationship,[22] and between 22 and 26 might reasonably be construed as asyndetic patronyms;[23] there are also some 20 instances specifying other sorts of relationship.[24] Here, that is, vernacular patronyms and

---

20 *Kalendar* (n.4 above).

21 *Ade sune, Ædesdohter, Ællice sune, Brune sune 2x, Brune stepsune, Cocce sune, Cole sune, Hune sune 2x, Hunte sune, Moce sun, Puse sune, Teperesune,* and 1x of the ambiguous *Blace sune* used independently; see further C. Clark, 'Willelmus', p.23, n.27 (at this date the weak gen. sing. inflection *-an* would normally have developed to *-e* = [ə] and the strong *-s* be merged with the initial of *-sune*).

22 *Æltredes* (OE *Ealdrǣd*), *Dages, Doddes, Oswennes* (OE *Oswynn* fem.), *Tates;* for the three single-element names, see 'Willelmus', p.23, n.27. For the patronymic and metronymic use of plain genitives, *cf.* R. McKinley, *Norfolk and Suffolk* [hereafter *N&S*], pp.131, 140.

23 *Ælfwine, blurf* (8 for **Brūnwulf*), *Brihtmer* (OE *Beorhtmǣr*), *Celing,* perhaps *Chebbel* (see n.32 below), *[Chi]luert,* perhaps *Cobbe, Crite, Dod, Dode,* perhaps *Frost* (see n.33 below), *Glauard, Gott,* perhaps *Grelling,* perhaps *Hert* (see n.34 below), *Leuedey* (OE *Lēofdæg*), *Mum,* perhaps *Stettel, Tederi, Tiltac, Torce, Trege, Tuittel, Udelac* (OE *Wudulāc*), *Wihgar* (OE *Wihtgār*), *Uunric* (OE *Wynnrīc*); for some of the names listed but not annotated above, see 'Willelmus', p.23, n.27, also p.27 (*blurf, [Chi]luert*), p.30 (*Tederi*).

24 *frater* 3x, *nepos* 2x, *pater, soror, sororius, uidua* (normally without late husband's name) 12x.

metronyms seem current in all three possible forms: phrasal, genitival, and asyndetic; in later East Anglian usages, however, phrasal forms in *-son* and *daughter* were to be rare.[25] A further 27 by-names involve locative phrases, consisting of Latin *ad* or *de*, more rarely English *at* or *of*, followed by either a Latin or an English topographical term[26] or, more often, by a proper place-name.[27] Unambiguously occupational by-names occur 55 times, comprising 12 vernacular forms (using eight different terms, for several of which this is the earliest record extant)[28] and 43 Latin ones (using 15 different terms).[29] The remaining 50 or more by-names seem, provisionally, best classified as 'nicknames'; these furnish this essay's main theme.

25 R. McKinley, *N&S*, pp.129–31. The discussion of *filius*-formulas in B. Seltén, *The Anglo-Saxon Heritage in Middle English Personal Names: East Anglia 1100–1399*, I, Lund, 1972, pp.46–50, takes inadequate account of scribal convention.

26 *de silua* 2x (*FDB*, pp.31, 34); the perfunctorily half-Latinized *de mor* (*FDB*, p.31); *ate slo* (*FDB*, p.43) 'by the slough' (an instance missed by S. Carlsson in his *Studies on Middle English Local Bynames in East Anglia*, Lund Studies in English, 79, Lund, 1989, p.96), a form for which see in general R. McKinley, *N&S*, p.111; also perhaps *oftun* (*FDB*, p.25), although there is a proper place-name *Offton* in Bosmere Hundred.

27 *de Aessefelde* (Ashfield), *de Brademere* (Bradmere), *de Culeford* (Culford), *de Fornham* (Fornham), *ad Galhho* (Galhoe), *de Grisetoft, de Haldham* (Aldham), *de Hertherst* (Hartest), *de Hyldrecle* (Hinderclay), *de Laueshel* (Lawshall), *de Lithleburi* (Littlebury), *de Liuremere* (Livermere), *de Osham, de priditune* (?) *de smalende* (?) *de smidere* (?) *de Trostune* (Troston), *de Trugetune* (?) *ad Westmere, ad Westbrom* (Westbroms).

28 OE *blōdlǣtere* (*cf.* P. H. Reaney, *Dictionary of British Surnames*, 2nd edn. rev., R. M. Wilson, London, 1976 [hereafter *DBS*], s.n. *Blood*); ME *cropper(e)* 'one who prunes trees' (H. Kurath *et alii*, eds., *Middle English Dictionary*, Ann Arbor, 1954 (in progress) [hereafter *MED*] dates the earliest example given to 1221; *cf. DBS*, s.n. *Cropper*); *daia* < OE *dǣge* 'dairymaid' (*cf. DBS*, s.n. *Day*); OE *dēmere* 'lawman' (*cf. DBS*, s.n. *Deemer*); OE *hǣgweard* 5x (*cf. DBS*, s.n. *Hayward*); OE *horspegn* 'groom'; ME *whelwright* (G. Fransson, *Middle English Surnames of Occupation*, Lund Studies in English, 3, Lund, 1935, p.162, dates the earliest example 1274; *cf. DBS*, s.n. *Wheelwright*); **inngerefa* 'warden of lodgings' (see O. von Feilitzen, 'Notes on Old English bynames', *Namn och Bygd*, 27, 1939, pp.116–30, at p.130); plus 1x of OE *tæpere* 'tapster' as patronym (n.21 above; *cf. DBS*, s.n. *Tapper*) and one, apparently in a patronym, of either OE *bēatere* 'flogger' or OE (*bētere* 'mender' (*FDB*, 26; for ME *betere* '(metal-)beater', see G. Fransson, *op. cit.*, pp.102, 134.

29 *aurifaber* 2x, *bercarius, clericus* 2x, *diaconus* 3x, *equarius, faber* 7x (plus 1x as patronym), *mango* 2x, *mercator, molendinarius* 2x, *pelliciarius* 2x, *pistor, porcarius, prepositus* 2x, *presbiter* 14x, *sutor* 2x.

This document's value lies not just in its early date but particularly in the proportion of vernacular forms it offers, and the consequent implication of a vernacular as well as bureaucratic basis for recorded by-naming. Of the identificatory phrases given, about a third are in vernacular form: whether or not this was because the clerk(s) responsible had limited Latin, it reveals the vigour, at this time and in these districts, of colloquial by-naming. A fair number of the forms attested here correspond to modern surnames; and further scrutiny reveals even more of them as conforming to widespread Middle English patterns of by-name formation.[30] This reinforces belief in our record as partly reflecting vernacular usages, and so a principal question to be considered, as far as evidence allows, concerns the degree of such reflection. For by-naming the matter is more delicate than for baptismal-naming, because uncertainties over the latter are limited by the quasi-finite stock of forms available

---

30 Many of the present forms are cited in *DBS*; see further below. For Middle English by-naming in general, the limited number of studies so far published includes: G. Tengvik, *Old English Bynames*, Nomina Germanica, 4, Uppsala, 1938, for criticism and supplementation of which see O. von Feilitzen, 'Notes' (n.28 above); B. Seltén, *Early East-Anglian Nicknames: 'Shakespeare' Names*, Scripta Minora Regiae Societatis Humaniorum Litterarum Lundensis, 1968–1969, 3, Lund, 1969 [hereafter *SN*], and *idem, Early East-Anglian Nicknames: Bahuvrihi Names*, Scripta Minora, 1974–1975, 3, Lund, 1975 [hereafter *BN*]; J. Jönsjö, *Studies on Middle English Nicknames: I – Compounds*, Lund Studies in English, 55, Lund, 1979 [hereafter *MEN*], for which see, e.g., the review by C. Clark in, *English Studies*, 63, 1982, pp.168–70 and the article by P. McClure cited below; and I. Hjertstedt, *Middle English Nicknames in the Lay Subsidy Rolls for Warwickshire*, Acta Universitatis Upsaliensis: Studia Anglistica Upsaliensia, 63, Uppsala, 1987 [hereafter *NW*], for which see the reviews by e.g., J. Insley in *Studia Neophilologica*, 62, 1990, pp.115–19, and C. Clark in *Nomina*, XIII, 1989–90, pp.143–5. As Peter McClure in particular pointed out in his percipient and seminal review-article based upon J. Jönsjö's work (Nomina, 5, 1981, pp.95–104), these monographs, lexicographically conscientious though they are, are all — in so far as Hjertstedt's later-published work has not benefited from and does not even cite McClure's criticism — vitiated by disregard both of socio-economic background and of psychological motivation; they are none the less useful as repertories of recorded forms, and will be used as such below. For the Early Middle English period we can, however, rely on O. von Feilitzen, 'The personal names and bynames of the Winton Domesday', in M. Biddle *et alii*, eds., *Winchester in the Early Middle Ages*, Winchester Studies, 1, Oxford, 1976, pp.143–229, by-names being treated at pp.192–221.

as well as by the conventionality of their rendering. The resort here to by-names, whether vernacular or Latinized, only when needed for identification (and not always, perhaps, even then) implies that bureaucratic intervention in naming-patterns was as yet less systematic than it later became.

The particularity of the record and of the population represented will be stressed throughout (to say this is not at all to deny the worth, especially for the pioneering stages of anthroponymics, of the classic surveys and repertories treating single categories of name and based on wide-ranging source-material). Each document has its own background and its own line of transmission, and each therefore its own orthographical as well as dialectal characteristics. Each population, whether geographically or socially defined, must be allowed to have had its own usages and traditions, socio-onomastic as well as dialectal. Names — or, better, bodies of names — must never therefore be examined *in vacuo* but always in their historical, social, geographical and, when possible, prosopographical contexts.

2 — Some by-names and their implications

As some phraseology used above in categorizing the by-names has implied, such categorization — and, with it, any statistics thereon based — is often insecure. Some forms are, to modern eyes at least, inherently ambivalent. Certain types of formation in -*er* or in -*man* may, as has long been recognized, be taken either as topographical or as occupational: present instances (both, as it happens, from the same vill) include *Ælfled cerceman* and *Æluric halleman*, the by-names in question being interpretable either as 'living beside the church/the hall' or else as 'employed at the church/hall', with here the further twist that *cerceman* applies to a woman and so might prehaps constitute either a virtual asyndetic patronym ('[daughter of] the man who lived beside/worked at the church') or else a very early instance of matrimonial naming, rather than a description proper to the person listed.[31] Deeper ambiguities beset certain by-

---

31 *FDB*, p.28 (Rougham, 1 acre) and (Rougham, 4 acres). *Cf. DBS*, s.nn. *Churchman, Hallman*; and, for further examples of *Churchman*, see I. Hjertstedt, *NW*, pp.215, 219, 220. For the type of compound, see G. Fransson, *Surnames of Occupation*, pp.190–2, 203–8 (the present forms not being listed); also R. McKinley, *N&S*, p.119, and *Sussex*, pp.147, 173–80.

names — such as, for instance, those seen in *Æluric chebbel*,[32] *Lefstan frost*[33] and *Goduine hert*[34] — that might, at all events by modern eyes, be taken either as patronyms based upon idionyms derived from 'original nicknames' (OE **Cybbel*, Scand *Frosti*, OE *Heor(o)t*) or else as live nicknames, employing the corresponding items of common vocabulary, proper to their present bearers; the modern family-names *Ke(e)ble*, *Frost* and *Hart(e)*, although confirming currency of the by-names concerned, throw no light upon either their status or their aetiology. As the latter examples suggest, the chief vehicles of ambivalence are those by-names provisionally classed as 'nick-names': a handy catch-all category for the otherwise indefinable.

True, some epithets, substantival no less than adjectival, can hardly not be accepted at face value: in particular, those represented in the record by Latinizations such as *caluus, longus, niger* and *ruf(f)us*[35] and also perhaps some frankly unflattering ones, as in *Æduui alfordruncen*,[36] *Lefui bastard*[37] (where the Gallicization might be scribal), and *Uluric*

32 *FDB*, p.33 (Woolpit, 3 acres). See O. von Feilitzen, 'Winton Domesday', p.205, n.5, and references there given; also G. Tengvik, *Bynames*, p.301, and *DBS*, s.n. *Keeble*. For some further examples, see C. Clark, 'Battle *c*.1110: an anthroponymist looks at an Anglo-Norman new town', *Proceedings of the Battle Conference on Anglo-Norman Studies*, 2, 1980 for 1979, pp.21–41, 168–72, at p.38 (an idionym *Chebel*), and I. Hjertstedt, *NW*, s.n. *Cubbel*.

33 *FDB*, p.25 (Barton, 4 acres). See G. Tengvik, *Bynames*, p.376, and *DBS*, s.n. *Frost*. For ON *Frosti*, see G. Fellows-Jensen, *Scandinavian Personal Names in Lincolnshire and Yorkshire*, Navnestudier, 7, Copenhagen, 1968, pp.87–8, s.n. *Frosti*.

34 *FDB*, p.25 (Barton, 6 acres). See G. Tengvik, *Bynames*, p.362, and *DBS*, s.n. *Hart*. For *Heort* as an idionym, see O. von Feilitzen, 'Some Old English uncompounded personal names and by-names', *Studia Neophilologica*, 40, 1968, pp.5–16, at p.8. For a further contemporary example of a by-name *hert*, see C. Clark, 'Battle', p.37.

35 *Æilric caluus, FDB*, p.35 (Hampton, 15 acres); *Ælfuine longus*, p.27 (Pakenham, 26 acres), also [the same or another?], p.36 (Great Livermere, 3 acres), and *Godui Longus*, p.30 (Hessett, 7½ acres); *Godric niger*, p.30 (Hessett, 8 acres), and *Ulfuuine niger*, p.32 (Woolpit, 4 acres); *Aluard rufus*, 37 (Troston, 18 acres), *Osbern rufus*, p.38 (Langham, 9 acres), *Syricus fuffus*, p.27 (Pakenham, 15½ acres), and *Siric rufus* [the same or another?], p.36 (Great Livermere, 3 acres).

36 *FDB*, p.30 (Hessett, 3 acres). See G. Tengvik, *Bynames*, p.340; *cf.* J. Jönsjö, *MEN*, s.n. *Aydrunken*.

37 *FDB*, p.25 (Barton, 3 acres). See G. Tengvik, *Bynames*, p.373 (with further early instances of *bastard[us]*), and *DBS*, s.n. *Bastard*; also I. Hjertstedt, *NW*, s.n. *Bastard*.

cucuold.[38] On the other hand, in *Lefuine barun, Lefuin eorl*, and *Goduine teng* (this last being taken as *þegn*) epithets cannot be taken literally.[39] Risks of irony are, moreover, seldom far around the corner. Were the men set down as *Gode cild* and as *Lefui fæger cild* named with quite a straight face?[40] Did the name *Lefstan litle* indicate a dwarf or a giant, was the man designated simply as *Strangman* a mighty hero or an undersized wimp, and was the Cenric called *cres* 'the elegant' a dandy or a bundle of filthy rags?[41]

With substantives serving otherwise than as epithets uncertainties multiply. Some problems, as illustrated, stem from our inability to tell common noun fron proper name; others, from our inablility to interpret early spellings: thus, in *Vluric pec* the by-name form might represent either OE **pēac*, ME *pēk*, 'pointed hill' (in Suffolk surely in some transferred sense) or ME *pek(ke)* 'measuring vessel',[42] and that in *Æluric ches* might represent either *keech* 'lump of fat' (first recorded in *OED* 1613) or the widespread dialect adjective *kedge* 'lively'.[43]

---

38 *FDB*, p.27 (Pakenham, 6 acres). See G. Tengvik, *Bynames*, p.375; perhaps also *DBS*, s.n. *Cuckow*, and I. Hjertstedt, *NW*, s.n. *Cockou*.

39 *FDB*, p.40 (Hepworth, ¾ acre); p.38 (Elmswell, 2 acres); p.33 (Woolpit, 2 acres). Tengvik's preferred interpretation of *teng* as *tang* 'something pointed' (*Bynames*, pp.381–2) was corrected by O. von Feilitzen, 'Notes', p.130. *Cf. DBS*, s.nn. *Baron, Earl, Thain*, and I. Hjertstedt, *NW*, s.nn. *Baron, Erl*. For the frequency as peasant nicknames of titles for secular and ecclesiastical offices, see in general R. McKinley, *N&S*, pp.31, 54–5.

40 *FDB*, p.37 (Troston, 8 acres); p.33 (Woolpit, 3 acres). See G. Tengvik, *Bynames*, p.312, and *DBS*, s.nn. *Fairchild, Goodchild; cf.* C. Clark, 'Battle', p.36 (*gotcild*), J. Jönsjö, *MEN*, s.nn. *Fayrchyld, Godchild*, and I. Hjertstedt, *NW*, s.n. *Fayrechyld*. For irony in nicknaming, see, e.g., P. McClure, 'Nicknames', p.100.

41 *FDB*, p.29 (Rougham, 8 acres); p.39 (Elmswell, 2 acres); p.25 (Barton, 4 acres). See G. Tengvik, *Bynames*, pp.321, 343, and *DBS*, s.nn. *Little, Strangman, Crease* (this last < OE *crēas* 'elegant').

42 *FDB*, p.39 (Walsham, 9 acres). See G. Tengvik, *Bynames*, p.325 (comment tortuous and unhelpful), O. von Feilitzen, 'Winton Domesday', p.215, s.n. *Piec*, and *DBS*, s.nn. *Peak, Peck*, (although the spelling *pec* might equally represent [petʃ], the surnames listed here s.n. *Petch* may be irrelevant in so far as these latter seem derived from the disyllabic OFr *péché* < Latin *peccātum*). Material cited by R. McKinley, *N&S* pp.17, 28–9, suggests that in Suffolk *Pecke* was frequent but *Peake* rare if not absent.

43 *FDB*, p.33 (Woolpit, 1 acre). See G. Tengvik, *Bynames*, pp.301–2 (multiple options, none convincing), and, more helpfully, *DBS*, s.nn. *Kedge, Ketch; cf.* J. Wright,

Likewise with *Æluric paner*, it is hard to be sure whether the by-name represents an early instance of ME *pan(i)er* 'basket' (an Old French loanword), in which case it might mark its bearer as weaving baskets or as hawking wares in them or else, perhaps, as being built like one, or whether it represents a native occupational term **pannere* 'maker of pans'.[44] Even with a term identifiable unambiguously, implications may escape us: thus, in *Ailuuin candela* the by-name undoubtedly represents a re-Latinization of OE *candel* < Lat *candela*, but whether it was meant literally to mark its bearer as trading in candles or playing some ecclesiastical rôle involving them or else in some figurative sense not now recoverable we cannot tell.[45] Perhaps the Leofmær called *citere*, from an Old English word for 'harp', was a part-time minstrel,[46] and the Ælfric called *uuort* 'wort, plant' (OE *wort*) a herbalist (hardly, in an agricultural community, a greengrocer),[47] but we cannot be certain. As for the Ælfwine called *prisun'* whether he were an ex-convict (OFr and ME *prisun* can mean 'prisoner' as well as 'prison') or the local gaoler we can only guess.[48]

The unquantifiable frequency of irony in nicknaming we have noted; other figures of speech often invoked include metaphor and metonymy. True, we can be little surer of the incidence of either of

English Dialect Dictionary, 6 vols., Oxford, 1898–1905, s.vv. *kedge* adjective 'lively', *keech* 'lump of congealed fat'. I. Hjertstedt, *NW*, cites our form s.n. *Kek*, referred to ON *keikr* 'bent backwards'.

44 *FDB*, p.32 (Woolpit, 1 acre). G. Tengvik, *Bynames*, p.262 (giving alternative explanations). For OE **pannere* 'pan-maker', see further G. Fransson, *Surnames of Occupation*, p.138. For the ME *pan(i)er* borrowed from Old French, see *MED*, s.v. *panier(e)*, *DBS*, s.n. *Panner*, and I. Hjertstedt, *NW*, s.n. *Panyer*; *cf.* G. Fransson, *op. cit.*, p.54, s.n. *Panierman* 'hawker', and p.171, s.n. *Paniermaker*.

45 *FDB*, p.26 (Barton, 4 acres). See G. Tengvik, *Bynames*, p.374, and *DBS*, s.n. *Candle*.

46 *FDB*, p.31 (Hessett, 15 acres). See G. Tengvik, *Bynames*, p.374. For nicknames indicating musicians, see in general R. McKinley, *N&S*, p.52.

47 *FDB*, p.33 (Woolpit, 1 acre). See G. Tengvik, *Bynames*, p.340 (etymology unlikely), also *DBS* and I. Hjertstedt, *NW*, both s.n. *Wort*. The Thorney *Liber Vitae* offers a further example almost contemporary with the present one, *Ælmer wort* (BM Additional MS 40,000, f.3r).

48 *FDB*, p.26 (Barton, 1 acre). See O. von Feilitzen, 'Winton Domesday', p.215, also G. Tengvik, *Bynames*, p.379 (no corresponding entry in *DBS*); *cf.* A. Tobler and E. Lommatzsch, eds., *Altfranzösisches Wörterbuch*, Berlin and later Wiesbaden, 1936 – in progress, s.v. *prison* s.m. 'Gefangener', and *MED*, s.v. *prisoun*, sense p.7.

these figures than we can of that of irony; but the possibility of one or other must be borne in mind. Someone may, for instance, be characterized in terms of a single bodily feature: thus, *Ælfstan ære* 'the Ælfstan with the [malformed] ear' (with OE *ēare* 'ear' rather than the rare adjective *earu* 'active'),[49] *Lefuine scanches* 'the Leofwine with the [odd] legs' (OE *sceanca*).[50] Identification may rest, as with *citere* and *uuort*, on mention of a characteristic instrument or item of trade. Alternatively, it may invoke metaphor, often an emblematic comparison between human being and animal, and then the best clues may be found in catchphrases, proverbs and poetry: thus, *Æilmer bar* 'the Æðelmær fierce and formidable as an enraged boar' (OE *bār*),[51] *Ædui mus* 'the Eadwig whose ?pusillanimity/?drunkenness rivals that of the proverbial mouse' (OE *mūs*),[52] *Ulfui ra* 'the Wulfwig swift and nimble as a roebuck' (OE *rā*);[53] the same might apply to

49 *FDB*, p.33 (Woolpit, 1 acre). See G. Tengvik, *Bynames*, p.284; no corresponding entry in *DBS* or in any of the monographs consulted.

50 *FDB*, p.40 (Hepworth, ½ acre). See G. Tengvik, *Bynames*, pp.332–3, and *DBS*, s.nn. *Shank*, also *Cruickshank, Sheepshanks* (no entry corresponding to 'ear'); for further ME compounds with *-shank(s)*, see B. Seltén, *BN*, pp.55, 64.

51 *FDB*, p.33 (Woolpit, 4 acres). See G. Tengvik, *Bynames*, p.359, O. von Feilitzen, 'Winton Domesday', p.207, and *cf. DBS*, s.n. *Boar*. For the importance of proverbs and catchphrases, see, e.g., C. Clark and D. Owen, 'Lexicographical notes from King's Lynn', *Norfolk Archaeology*, 37, 1978, pp.56–69, at pp.57, 61, and R. McClure, 'Nicknames', pp.97–8, 99. Preliminary guidance in this matter may be found among the citations in *MED*, s.v. *bōr*, esp. sense, p.4 (a). See further: B. J. and H. W. Whiting, *Proverbs, Sentences, and Proverbial Phrases from English Writings mainly before 1500*, Cambridge, Mass., 1968, pp.49–51 (the boar as fierce), and M. P. Tilley, *A Dictionary of the Proverbs in England in the Sixteenth and Seventeenth Centuries*, Ann Arbor, 1950, p.56 (fierce; greedy).

52 *FDB*, p.26 (Barton, 4 acres). See G. Tengvik, *Bynames*, p.364, and O. von Feilitzen, 'Winton Domesday', p.214 and *cf. DBS*, s.n. *Mowse*. See further *MED*, s.v. *mous*, esp. senses p.1 (c) and (d), B. J. and H. W. Whiting, *Proverbs*, pp.416–17 (the mouse as drunken; weak and fearful; sly), M. P. Tilley, *Dictionary*, pp.479–81 (drunken; snug in cheese/malt-heap/mill; sly), and F. P. Wilson, *The Oxford Dictionary of English Proverbs*, 3rd edn., rev., Oxford, 1970, pp.206, 347–8 (in present-day usage, it may be noted, a nickname 'Mouse' is sometimes given to jockeys).

53 *FDB*, p.36 (Timworth, 5 acres). See G. Tengvik, *Bynames*, p.365, and *cf. DBS* and I. Hjertstedt, *NW*, both s.n. *Roe*. See further *MED*, s.v. *rō*, esp. sense (c), B. J. and H. W. Whiting, *Proverbs*, pp.490–1 (the roebuck as sprightly; swift; wild), and M. P. Tilley, *Dictionary*, p.574 (swift).

Goduine dernel, if this is rightly taken as 'the Godwine false and insidious as corn-cockle' (ME *dernel, darnel*), the allusion being a familiar Biblical one (Matthew 13:24–30).[54]

Some to-do has been made about the so-called 'bahuvrihi' compounds and their interpretation.[55] Such a form, consisting of a substantive preceded by a qualifier, is defined by being metonymic, that is, specifying only a single attribute of the complex entity it denotes: e.g., the common noun *paleface* '[a person with a] light-skinned face' and the nickname *Longshanks* '[the man with] long legs'. It is common ground that it is as nicknames that formations of such type especially often occur, and our Bury survey offers some of the earliest examples in English: *Osbern cattesnese* 'the Osbern with the nose like a cat's' (OE *catt* + ME *nēse* < OE **neosu*), *Aluric godhand* 'the Ælfric with the good (?skilful, ?generous) hand', *Leouuine holege* 'the Leofwine with the sunken eye(s)' (OE *holh* + *ēage*), *Vlfuine huitfot* 'the Wulfwine with the white foot/feet' (OE *hwit* + *fōt*), *Godric langhand* 'the Godric with the long hand'.[56] The recorded bearers of such names are here humble men, the largest among their holdings amounting to only six acres. Not unexpectedly, given the date, their idionyms are all of pre-Conquest types and the elements involved in their by-names native ones. The 'bahuvrihi adjective' was, we must remember, frequent in Old English poetry, e.g., *blīðheort* 'glad-heart[ed]', *blōdigtōð* 'gory-fang[ed]', *fāmigheals* 'foamy-neck[ed]'. Nickname material not only here but also in the Winton Domesday shows it as characteristic too of rustic and urban colloquialism alike.[57] In that light, the forms seem unproblematic. The agonizings

---

54 *FDB*, p.31 (Hessett, 2 acres). See G. Tengvik, *Bynames*, p.369, and *cf. DBS*, s.n. *Darnell*. See further *MED*, s.v. *darnel*, and B. J. and H. W. Whiting, *Proverbs*, p.117 (darnel as worthless); *cf.* M. P. Tilley, *Dictionary*, p.149 ('He that is dim-sighted has eaten darnel').

55 See, e.g., B. Seltén, *BN*, esp. pp.8–10; although taking a few examples from the present document, he makes but limited use of it. H. Marchand, *The Categories and Types of Present-Day English Word-Formation: A Synchronic-Diachronic Approach*, 2nd edn., Munich, 1969, treats bahuvrihi compounds at pp.368–9, also pp.13–14, but without taking adequate account of early name-evidence.

56 *FDB*, p.38 (Langham, 3 acres); p.25 (Barton, 3 acres); p.30 (Rougham, 6 acres); p.30 (Hessett, 3 acres); p.43 (*Huntefelde*, 3 acres jointly with others).

57 See O. von Feilitzen, 'Winton Domesday', pp.218, 220–1.

over their definition may arise from the practice, prevalent among certain types of linguist, of basing classification upon formal criteria and semantic theory rather than upon function, context, and common-sense. Once forms like those cited are considered as nicknames, they appear no more (if also no less) difficult of interpretation than simplex metonymic forms such as *Ælfstan ære, Lefuine scanches*, and so on.[58]

Preoccupation with morpho-syntax has diverted attention away from more relevant questions of connotation. Some forms here, such as *cattesnese* and *holege*, seem to refer straightforwardly to physiognomy. With others matters are less clear: *huitfot*, for instance, can scarcely allude to a working peasant's lily-white feet (in the way that French *aux blanches mains* seems to do to the pale hands of aristocrats); but it might refer to boots dusty from working chalky soil or from trudging constantly, perhaps as packman or messenger, along dry trackways. Again, *godhand* pretty certainly and also probably *langhand* connote moral rather then physical characteristics (compare present-day expressions such as *light-fingered, sticky fingers, the long arm of the law*); but just what implications were intended, and whether they were complimentary or ironical, we cannot be certain. The name *Vlnod uuodhorn* is at least equally obscure: in Sussex similar by-names are taken by Mr McKinley to represent a minor place-name but here, where OE *hyrne* 'nook' gives *herne* or *hirne* rather than *hurne*, one might (with Tengvik) be tempted to see reference to a horn as adjunct to the forester's or huntsman's trade; more probably, this nickname is to be classed with the numerous others in *-horn*, variously taken as metaphorical for 'head' or for an obscenity, in either of which cases the first element must represent OE *wōd* 'crazy', thus furnishing a semantic parallel to the recorded *Gydyhorn*.[59]

---

58 Although acknowledging the kinship between compound and simplex metonymic forms, B. Seltén, *BN*, p.8, chose to disregard the latter; a similar omission mars Marchand's treatment (see n.46 above). O. von Feilitzen, by contrast, focuses on function and on sense rather than on form, e.g., in the classifications at 'Winton Domesday', pp.220–1.

59 *FDB*, p.41 (Coney Weston, 2 acres). G. Tengvik, *Bynames*, p.357, preferred 'wood-horn'. For the interpretation *-horn* = '-head', see B. Seltén, *BN*, pp.56–7; but, for the likelihood of an obscenity, *cf.* P. McClure, 'Nicknames', p.99. For *Gydyhorn*, see B. Seltén, *BN*, p.24, and for some further compounds in *-horn*, J. Jönsjö, *MEN*, p.210.

3 — The 'pickpocket' or 'Shakespeare' names

A notable feature of this by-name corpus is the proportion of phrasal nicknames, *Satznamen*, that it contains:

Ailric brenebrec, FDB 25 (Barton, 10 acres).

OE *Æðelric; brenebrec* < OE *beornan*, ME *brennen* 'to burn' + OE *brǽc* 'clearing, assart' (not, *pacè* Tengvik, OE *brēc* 'breeches')[60] — possibly an occupational name for a man in charge of burning away scrub, etc., from land newly cleared.

Godlef crepunder huitel, FDB 26 (Barton, ¾ acre).

Late OE *Godlē(o)f*;[61] *crepunder huitel* < OE *crēopan*, ME *crēpen* 'to creep' + OE *hwītel* 'blanket'[62] — of uncertain implication, but perhaps indicating a coward, a sly adulterer, or a layabout, the last suggestion chiming in with the smallness of the holding.

Goduine hachelard, FDB 30 (Hessett, 6 acres).

OE *Gōdwine; hachelard* < ME *hakken* (< OE **haccian*) 'to chop, mince up' + ME *lard* 'salt pork' — possibly an occupational name for a kitchenhand.[63]

Ædric hopeheuene, FDB 25 (Barton, 6 acres).

OE *Eadric; hopeheuene* < OE *hopian* 'to hope for, trust in' + OE *heofon* 'heaven' — possibly from a favourite saying of the bearer's.[64]

Uluric pichele cruste, FDB 37 (Great Livermere, ½ acre).

OE *Wulfrīc; pichele cruste* < ME *piken* 'to get, seek, steal' + OFr *crouste* 'crust' preceded by the definite article (a possible analogue *Pikecrumm*, with purely native elements, is recorded on Bury's territory *ante* 1206 — again perhaps an occupational

---

60 *Cf.* G. Tengvik, *Bynames*, p.385. For OE *brǽc, brēc* 'assart', see, e.g., A. H. Smith, *English Place-Name Elements*, 2 vols., English Place-Name Society, 25 and 26, Cambridge, 1956, pp.47–8. For further compounds in *burn-*, see J. Jönsjö, *MEN*, p.202.

61 See *'Willelmus'*, p.29.

62 'Coward' is Tengvik's suggestion at *Bynames*, p.389.

63 G. Tengvik, *Bynames*, p.385, notes the quasi-occupational meaning of this and other names of the type. B. Seltén, *SN*, p.20, also pp.22–3, notes equivalences with *-er* formations.

64 G. Tengvik, *Bynames*, p.385, also p.384.

name for a kitchenhand,[65] *cf.* the twelfth-century Canterbury form *Drinkedreste* 'drink the dregs' for a man alternatively specified as *scutellarius* 'scullion'.[66]

Ædric scaldehare, FDB 31 (Hessett, 2½ acres).

OE *Eadric; scaldehare* < ME *scalden* (perhaps < Med Lat *scaldāre* rather than OFr *escalder*) 'to scald, especially as prelude to skinning' + OE *hara* 'hare'[67] — another possible occupational name for a kitchenhand.

* Æilmer stachecoc, FDBN* 32 (Woolpit, 2½ acres).

OE *Æðelmǣr; stachecoc* < ME *staken* (*cf.* OE *staca* 'stake', *stacung* 'piercing', *stagan* 'to roast on a spit') + OE *cocc* 'male bird' — yet another possible occupational name for a kitchenhand.[68]

Godric stichehert, FDB 30 (Woolpit, 6½ acres).

OE *Gōdric; stichehert* < OE *stician*, ME *stiken* 'to stab (to death)' + OE *heorot* 'male deer' — perhaps an occupational name for a hunt servant responsible either for giving a beast the *coup de grâce* or for disembowelling it. The form parallels the *stichestac*, with OE *stagg(a)*, found in Domesday Book.[69]

As with the 'bahuvrihi' forms, all the bearers of these phrasal by-names have idionyms of pre-Conquest types, all but one indeed of classic Old English style. Again all have modest holdings, two little more than big gardens. As for the by-names themselves, their elements are predominantly native ones. Five of the eight instances look like informal occupational terms, and a further two like possible

---

65 G. Tengvik, *Bynames*, pp.386–7. For *Pikecrumm*, used independently of a holder of land in Bradfield at some time *ante* 1206, see *Kalendar*, p.102, also B. Seltén, *SN*, s.n.; *cf.* the mid-fourteenth-century Lincolnshire form *Pikelcromme* in J. Jönsjö, *MEN*, p.143 (where medial intrusion of an OFr definite article is too easily assumed). For other compounds in *pick-*, see B. Seltén, *SN*, pp.11–12, and J. Jönsjö, *MEN*, p.215; on meanings of this verb, see P. McClure, 'Nicknames', p.96, and *cf. MED*, s.v. *piken*, esp. senses, pp.6, 7, 8.

66 See C. Clark, 'People and languages in post-Conquest Canterbury', *Journal of Medieval History*, 2, 1976, pp.1–33, at p.20.

67 G. Tengvik, *Bynames*, p.387.

68 G. Tengvik, *Bynames*, p.387. For *stikestac*, see n.65 above; and, for further names in *stick-*, see B. Seltén, *SN*, p.17, and J. Jönsjö, *MEN*, p.218

69 G. Tengvik, *Bynames*, p.387.

parodic variants on that type: Wulfric, perhaps a kitchenhand, scrounges crusts from the (French-speaking) gentry; Godleof busies himself perhaps skiving, perhaps more reprehensibly still.

The formations in question — often called 'pickpocket' or 'Shakespeare' names — consist of a verbal stem followed usually by a direct object but sometimes by a complement of another kind.[70] That the verbal element is a stem form must be stressed, because there is a long (though not unbroken) tradition of calling such forms 'imperative-names', as though embodying command rather than characterization (in most languages verb-stem and imperative singular are, of course, formally identical).[71] How contemporaries understood such forms is implied, for instance, by Orderic Vitalis's glossing of the Old French *Meslebren* 'mix-bran' with the present-participal phrase *miscens furfurem*.[72]

---

70 G. Tengvik, *Bynames*, lists at pp.383–9 all then-recognized instances supposedly datable *ante* 1100, treating these as a unified corpus and disregarding the patent contrast between the tenants-in-chief and under-tenants with their purely French names and the freemen with their basically English ones: an unwise conflation that probably underlies his inclination towards ascribing the appearance of all such forms in England to French influence. P. H. Reaney, *The Origin of English Surnames*, London, 1967, p.280, allows for independent native genesis of the type. B. Seltén, *SN*, which omits the Bury names, is noncommittal as to aetiology (p.3), noting an apparent decrease with time in the proportion of French elements involved (pp.19–20). H. Marchand, *Word-Formation*, p.380–6, although acknowledging the colloquial character of English 'pickpocket' forms, nevertheless regards them as French-inspired — partly at least, it seems, because he dates their appearance no earlier than 'Late Middle English'. The colloquial character of these phrase-names is stressed by R. McKinley, *Sussex*, pp.362–4.

71 G. Tengvik, *Bynames*, pp.383–4, accepts uncritically the designation 'imperative names', as does H. Marchand, *Word-Formation*, pp.380–6. P. H. Reaney, *Origin*, p.279, retains the term only after some questioning '. . . an unsatisfactory term, as the verb may merely be the verbal stem and there is no clear indication in English that it was an imperative'; J. Jönsjö, *MEN*, p.30, accepts Reaney's stricture. B. Seltén, *SN*, p.3, describes the verbal element as 'formless'. H. Sauer offers the analysis 'verb (verb-stem) + noun (or adverb)' ('Compounds and compounding in Early Middle English: problems, patterns, productivity', in M. Markus, ed., *Historical English*, Innsbruck, 1988, pp.186–209, at p.200).

72 'Idem uir Rodbertus uocabatur, et Meslebren id est miscens furfurem cognominabatur': M. Chibnall, ed., *The Ecclesiastical History of Orderic Vitalis*, 6 vols., Cambridge, 1969–80, II, p.166 (similar participal renderings occur elsewhere). As a quasi-occupational term, the name might imply 'stablelad'; the bearer was a soldier of subordinate rank.

It is to the influence of such French nicknames that received wisdom has long ascribed the appearance in England of these forms.[73] Such explanation — tenable though it might seem to those working with corpora of miscellaneous forms divorced from context — begins to look less irresistable once the earliest forms are considered against their socio-economic backgrounds (a single source is always likely to yield greater truth than a miscellany). The present group of 'pickpocket' by-names, dating at least from no more than two generations after the Conquest and possibly from little more than one, was current among, and presumably created by, peasants still true to pre-Conquest traditions. For such men to have picked up (not necessarily with full understanding) ready-made nicknames imported by settlers might seem plausible. The sort of interlinguistic borrowing needed, on the other hand, for producing the forms found here would have required not only a grasp of the foreign syntax but internalization of it widespread and profound enough to impinge upon colloquial usage of the native language; for the vocabulary used is almost wholly English. Nor were French nick-names of this type impressively frequent among the recorded incomers: Tengvik listed only half a dozen of such alongside his nine purely native ones, and in the Suffolk Domesday the only 'pick-pocket' by-names found are (a) that of the well-known Tallboy, i.e., *taille-bois*, family of immigrants and (b) that of Ælfric *stikestac* 'stab stag', compounded from native elements and, like those in the present corpus, borne by a man with a classic Old English name.[74] The chief obstacle to accepting independent English generation of such forms has been a supposed lack of precedents. Two possible pre-Conquest cases were cited by Tengvik: (a) a Wulfwine *spillecorne* supposedly healed by the Confessor, but, apart from resembling (suspiciously, some have thought) the frequent Old French *gaste-blé*, this form is recorded only in William of Malmesbury's *Gesta Regum*:[75] (b) a form *Eylwine stikehare*, supposedly datable '1053' but betrayed by

---

73 *Cf.* above n.58.

74 *Iuonem tailebosc, Rad taillebosc; Aluric stikestac* (this last listed among freemen of Roger Bigot's, all with idionyms of pre-Conquest types): A. Rumble, ed., *Domesday Book: 34 — Suffolk*, 2 vols., Chichester, 1986, pp.1,122f.; 35,3; 7,77.

75 'Wulfwinus quidam, cognomento Spillecorn, filius Wulmari de Nutegareshale': W. Stubbs, ed., *Willelmi Malmesbiriensis Monachi de Gestis Regum Anglorum Libri Quinque*, London, 1887–89, pp.273–4. For further forms in *spille-*, see B. Seltén, *SN*, pp.16–17, and J. Jönsjö, *MEN*, p.218.

the Middle English orthography of the name *Æilwine* < OE *Æðelwine* and in fact taken from a grant purporting to be of the mid eleventh century but preserved only in thirteenth-century manuscripts.[76] Yet lateness of record, although weakening the evidential value of these forms, does not wholly discredit them. To these two, moreover, must now be added at least four well-authenticated 'pickpocket' forms, all composed from native elements, found in the 1066 stratum of the Winton Domesday.[77] Given that in early times such forms would seem to have been current mainly as nicknames and given too the paucity of nickname records antedating the mid eleventh century, the scarcity of pre-Conquest instances of the type remains inconclusive. Similar by-names were, it must be noted, current in medieval German dialects, where they excite controversy similar to that surrounding the English ones.[78] Little therefore hinders us from supposing 'pickpocket' names, *Satznamen*, to have been generated by various groups of Germanic-speakers independently of any Romance influences.

76 A. J. Robertson, ed. and trans., *Anglo-Saxon Charters*, 2nd edn., Cambridge, 1956, p.216, also n. on p.469 and P. H. Sawyer, *Anglo-Saxon Charters*, London, 1969, no. 1234; *cf.* G. Tengvik, *Bynames*, p.387. For names in *stick-*, see n.59 above.

77 O. von Feilitzen, 'Winton Domesday', p.218 (one or two forms listed there might perhaps be otherwise explained).

78 See R. Schützeichel, 'Shakespeare und Verwandtes', in E. S. Dick and K. R. Jankovsky, eds., *Festschrift für Karl Schneider*, Amsterdam, 1982, pp.137–52.

II

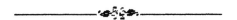

Addenda and Corrigenda to Tengvik[1]

† JOHN DODGSON

Gösta Tengvik's *Old English Bynames*, Nomina Germanica, IV, Uppsala, 1938 (hereafter *OEB*) remains a standard tool for work on Old English bynames. Recent work for the Phillimore edition of *Domesday Book* (Phill*DB*) has drawn attention to details which need correction, presented here in two lists. A — Addenda; B — Corrigenda.

Abbreviations

BCS   W. de G. Birch, *Cartularium Saxonicum*, 3 vols., London, 1855–93.

BT, BTSuppl. *An Anglo Saxon Dictionary* based on the collections of J. Bosworth, ed. T. N. Toller, Oxford, 1898; *Supplement to Bosworth-Toller*, ed. T. N. Toller, Oxford, 1921.

CGPN   T. Forssner, *Continental-Germanic Personal-Names in England in Old and Middle English Times*, Uppsala, 1916.

DB   *Domesday Book*: volume I, or 'Great Domesday Book', of the manuscript of the Exchequer Domesday in the

---

1 This article is based in part upon a paper delivered to the XVIth International Congress of Onomastic Sciences, Quebec, 1987.

	Public Record Office, London. Volume II of the manuscript, 'Little Domesday Book', is denoted by *LDB*. Both are included in A. Farley and H. Ellis, eds., *Domesday Book*, 4 vols., London, 1783–1816.
DBS	P. H. Reaney, *A Dictionary of British Surnames*, 2nd edn., revised by R. M. Wilson, Routledge and Kegan Paul, London, 1976.
Du Cange	Carolus Du Fresne, Sieur Du Cange, *Glossarium mediae et infimae Latinitatis*, Paris, 1840–50; ed. L. Favre, Niort, 1883–87.
EDD	J. Wright, ed., *The English Dialect Dictionary*, Oxford, 1898–1905
Ellis	H. Ellis, *A General Introduction to Domesday Book*, 2 vols., London, 1833; reprinted London, Muller, 1971.
EPNS	Volumes of *The Survey of English Place-Names* published by or for The English Place-Name Society.
ExonDB	*The Exon Domesday*; MS in the library of the Dean and Chapter of Exeter Cathedral; printed in vol. IV of the Farley and Ellis edition of *Domesday Book*.
Förstemann, *Personennamen*	E. Förstemann, *Altdeutsches Namenbuch, Band I, Personennamen*, 2nd ed., Bonn, 1900.
ICC	Inquisitio Comitatus Cantabridgensis, The Cambridge Inquiry, printed in N. E. S. A. Hamilton, *Inquisitio comitatus Cantabridgensis, subjicitur Inquisitio Eliensis*, London, 1876.
IE	Inquisitio Eliensis, the Ely Inquiry, printed with ICC.
LDB	*Little Domesday Book*, see under *Domesday Book*.
Nomina	*Nomina: A Journal of Name Studies relating to Great Britain and Ireland* published by the Council for Name Studies in Great Britain and Ireland, 1977 *et seq.*
OEB	Gösta Tengvik, *Old English Bynames*, Nomina Germanica, 4, Uppsala, 1938.
OED	*The Oxford English Dictionary, a corrected re-issue of a New English Dictionary on Historical Principles*, Oxford, 1933.

Phill*DB*	J. R. Morris, gen. ed., *Domesday Book*, 35 vols. in 40 parts, Phillimore, Chichester, 1975–86. Reference is to County volume, chapter and paragraph.
PNDB	Olof von Feilitzen, *The Pre-Conquest Personal-Names of Domesday Book*, Nomina Germanica, 3, Uppsala, 1937.
PNWD	Olof von Feilitzen, 'The Personal-Names and Bynames of the Winton Domeday', Martin Biddle, ed., *Winchester in the early Middle Ages*, Winchester Studies, I, Oxford, 1976, Part II, pp.143–239.
Redin	M. Redin, *Studies on Uncompounded Personal-Names in Old English*, Uppsala Universitets Arsskrift, 1919, Uppsala, 1919.
RMLWL	R. E. Latham, ed., *Revised Medieval Latin Word-List*, London, 1965.
Sawyer	*Anglo-Saxon Charters: An Annotated List and Bibliography*, London, 1968.
SPNLY	Gillian Fellows-Jensen, *Scandinavian Personal-Names in Lincolnshire and Yorkshire*, Copenhagen, 1968.
Weekley, *Surnames*	Ernest Weekley, *Surnames*, 2nd edn., London, 1917, reprinted 1927.

A — ADDENDA

A1 — Old English *bārbītere* 'boar-biter' (i.e. a boar-hound).

The name *Aluuinus Barbitre* is recorded in 1066 in the *Winton Domesday*; *OEB*, p.389 leaves it unexplained, but the interpretation was proposed by von Feilitzen at PNWD, p.207.

A2 — Old English *benc* 'a bench'.

In Phill*DB*, the surname of Osmund *Benz* a Derbyshire tenant 1066–86 (*DB*, fol. 278c; Phill*DB*, *DBS*, pp.17, 13) has been rendered 'Bent', after *OEB*, p.289 where it is related to the recorded Old English *bend* 'a ribbon' and a putative Old English **bent* 'a twisted thing'. But it seems to me there is more to be said than this.

First, the Norman French letter z could represent the Norman French sound [ts] substituted for the Old English sound [tʃ] and the spelling **BENZ** might well represent a Norman French treatment of Old English *Benc*, a byname from Old English *benc* 'a bench'. The Old English word can allude either to a structure or a piece of furniture or to a topographical feature, see Reaney, *DBS*, p.31, s.v. *Bench*[2].

Second, Tengvik might have referred to *CGPN*, p.44, s.vv. *Benza, Benzelin*, and to Förstemann, *Personennamen*, col. 246, s.vv. *Benzo, Benzlin*. On these, see *DBS*, p.31, s.v. *Bence*, where Reaney cites the English use of the patronymic *filius Bence* 1175 from Yorkshire, and *filius Benze* 1178 from Northumberland (these modifying the Old German personal-names *Ernisius* and *Ernulfus*, respectively), as well as our Osmund *Benz* from *Domesday Book* and one William *Bence* 1279 from Oxfordshire and a Roger *Bence* 1327 from Suffolk. See *Nomina*, 9, 1985, p.47, no. xxii.

A3 — ?Old English **ceafores-beard* 'cock-chafer's beard'; perhaps late OE **chevres beard*.

There is something odd about Tengvik's explanation, *OEB*, p.301, for the byname in the personal-name of the Berkshire tenant *Aluui ceuresbert* which appears in *DB*, fol. 63d (Phill*DB* BRK 65, 22). Tengvik acknowledged the difficulty in realizing the physiology and physiognomy implied by the byname 'Chafer's beard'; nevertheless that is how the name has to be construed if one is committed to a monoglot English derivation. However, if a French-English hybrid byname may be contemplated, we might then propose an allusion to that common domesticated animal which is better known for its beard than is the cockchafer, an insect which, though wild and untamed, is not hairy. The bearded animal is of course the goat, for which the Old French word is *Chievre*, Norman French *chevre*; which is the allusion of the *Domesday Book* bynames *Chevre, Capra* discussed at *OEB*, p.360. The *Domesday Book* byname *Ceuresbert* [tsevresbert] would seem an apt representation of an Anglo-Norman pronunciation, and spelling, of a byname formed in

---

2 The instance Robert *Benche* 1279 there cited could belong to the surname *Bence*.

English from Old English *beard* 'a beard' (not from Old French *barde*, one observes) and the Old Norman French *chevre* 'a goat', as if *Chevres berd* were either an incomplete translation of some unrecorded French byname **Barbe de chevre*, or, alternatively, were a deliberate original description. If one wanted to call a man 'goat's beard' in Old English one would coin a name with Old English *gāt* and *beard*, but if one wanted to coin, in English, a byname which meant 'man with the beard of a French goat' or 'French man with a goat's beard', one might well invent a hybrid such as *'chevre's* beard', as a mockery of the foreigner as much as a mockery of the beard.

This name and the Old English **nape-lēas* conjectured at A25 below, may be the result of interaction between the Anglophone and the Francophone name-forming process in early post-Conquest-England. At A37, below, Old English *wiccan-boded* appears to be an example of an uncomplementary, ominous, perhaps maledictory, byname in Old English, adopted and mispronounced by French speakers and recorded in a Norman French form. In the present name, *ceuresbert*, there may be evidence of the significant use of a French word by English speakers in the coining of an English byname. In the discussion of A11 below, Old French *Orescuilz*, we shall observe that there is no more than the conjectural possibility of a contemporary translation into Old English, *Gildenebeallucas*.

It is significant that there are very few occasions when *Domesday Book* bynames offer an illustration of interaction between the Anglo-Saxon and the Norman nomenclatures. *Domesday Book* is **the** document of the Norman domination of Anglo-Saxon England: its sympathies and intentions are those of a Norman aristocracy. All the more remarkable are the rare instances where English bynames are adopted into French usage, and French ones into English, for these are the signals of an interaction between two speech communities, the francophone ascendancy and the subject anglophone; and for such signals to get through the official, Norman, francophone, editing of the *Domesday Book* material requires a penetration of the French awareness by an English imagery.

The rarity must be a reflection of the near elimination of the Anglo-Saxon aristocracy between 1066 and 1086. By the time of *Domesday Book*, the giving and acceptance of bynames would have fallen almost exclusively to the Normans and would be couched almost entirely in their French and Latin medium.

A4 — *Cederli*, Godwinus, *OEB*, p.389.

The place-name Chitterley, Devon, see PNWD, p.193, EPNS, IX, p.555.

A5 — Old English *cielle*, adj., 'chill, cool'.

Got cill' is listed among the names of the burgesses of Colchester, Essex in 1086 (*LDB*, fol. 105a; Phill*DB* ESS B 3a). There were three burgesses there with the forename *Got* (Old Norse *Gautr*, Old Danish *Gøt*, see PNWD, p.160), that is, Got 'Chill', Got 'Hugh' and Got 'Fleet'. Got 'Hugh' bore a patronymic probably derived from the Old German personal-name *Hugo*; however, J. Insley, *Leeds Studies in English*, XVIII, 1987, pp.191, 198 n.74, draws attention to *DBS*, s.v. *Goodhew*, and proposes an Anglo-Scandinavian hybrid personal-name **Godhugi*. The byname of Got 'Fleet' is discussed at A9, below. Got 'Chill' was not included in *OEB* and the byname was reluctantly listed at *OEB*, pp.299–300 under the name of one *Chenuuichelle*, *Chenuicelle* (Old English *Cynewig cielle*) recorded at *DB*, fol. 164a, 169c; Phill*DB* GLS 1, 58; 66, 1 (see also *PNDB*, p.221).

A6 — *Clawecunte*, Godwinus, *OEB*, p.389.

The byname is explained by Old English *clawian* 'to scratch' and **cunte* 'vulva' at PNWD, p.210.

A7 — Old French *farcit*, adj., 'stuffed'.

OEB does not include the byname of Hugh *Farsi*, *Farsit*; he is named in ICC, p.93, and in IE, p.99 as a Domesday Survey juror in the Cambridgeshire hundred of Northstow, see Phill*DB* CAM Appendix N.

A8 — Medieval Latin *fatatus*, adj., 'haunted'.

> The surname of Radulfus *Fatatus, LDB*, fol. 79a, is left unexplained at *OEB*, p.389, but see *RMLWL*, s.v., recorded from *c*.1212; and note too Phill*DB* ESS 36, 8.

A9 — Old English *flēot*, Old Norse *fliotr*, adj., 'fleet, swift'.

> A byname not included in *OEB* appears in the personal-name *Gotflet* (*LDB*, fol. 106a, Phill*DB* ESS B 3a), for a burgess of Colchester, Essex. The byname *flet* probably represents the Old Norse adjective *fliotr*, whence Middle English *flete* 'swift', but there may have been an unrecorded Old English cognate **flēot*, which would have been the basis of the recorded Old English adjective *flēotig*. Reaney, *DBS*, s.n. *Fleet*, reported the bynames *le Fleet*, *le Fleot* from 1327, but did not include this instance from 1086 in *Domesday Book*. See also under A5, above.

A10 — Old German *Fram(m)in*, personal-name.

> *OEB* does not observe the *Domesday Book* instance of the surname function of this Old German personal-name (see Förstemann, *Personennamen*, col. 519), in the name of *Radulfus Framen*, 08, fol. 236d, Phill*DB* LEI 42, 9. See *Nomina*, 9, 1985, p.45, no. ii.

A11 — Middle English *Gildenballocks*, 'golden testicles'.

> The byname of the Essex tenant *Humfridus aurei testiculi* in *LDB*, fol. 100b (Phill*DB* ESS 90, 30) was probably Old French *Orescuilz*, which was in use in England as a surname until at least 1195. The Middle English equivalent *Gildynballokes* (the Old English would have been **gyldenbeallucas*) would seem to have been first recorded in the thirteenth century, in Yorkshire, and it is either an independent invention to describe a different case of the same Midas-like condition, or else it is a literal translation of the French surname. It seems mischievous of the editors of the Phill*DB* to use a Modern English version of the Middle English translation in reporting the name *aurei testiculi*, rather than the original Old French byname which the Latin represented. The editors of Phill*DB* have created in this

instance, an impression that there may have been already in progress in 1086, a translation or interchange between French and English bynames but it is less apparent in the case of the name *Gildenballocks* than it is in the case of *Chevresbeard*; see remarks under A3, above.

A12 — *Godeswale*, Edwin, *OEB*, p.389.

Mistake for *Godesawle*, Old English *gōdsāwol* 'good soul'. See *PNWD*, p.211.

A13 — Old French *Guisc(h)ard, -art*, Old Norman French *Wisc(h)ard*. A personal-name, see *DBS*, s.n. *Wishart*.

Byname of *Turstinus wiscart*, *LDB*, fol.106b (Phill*DB* ESS B3p) omitted from *OEB*, p.232.

A14 — *Gulee*, Lewinus, *OEB*, p.390.

Old French *goulee* 'big mouthful, words of abuse'. See PNWD, p.212.

A15 — *Gustate*, Lewold, *OEB*, p.390.

Unexplained by Tengvik, this is explained by Feilitzen, PNWD, p.212 (with the personal-name corrected to *Luwoldus*), as 'the imperative from Latin *gustare*, "to taste", a suitable nickname for a hospitable innkeeper'.

A16 — Old Norse *Hafri*, personal-name.

On the byname of *Uluuinus hapra* (*LDB*, fol. 94a, Phill*DB* ESS 62, 3), Tengvik, *OEB*, p.347, suggests a derivation from Old English *(ge)hæp* 'fit, suitable', with a Norman French suffix. This looks somewhat desperate, although an Old English name such as *Haepp, *Haeppa, is possible (it would be comparable with Old German *Heppo*, Förstemann, *Personennamen*, col.748; see *DBS*, s.v. *Happe*). Another way of solving the problem of the unlikely form *hapra*, neither more nor less desperate than Tengvik's, would be based upon the possibility of a confusion between the letters *f* and *p* in Insular Minuscule script. The spelling **hapra** written in the *Little Domesday Book* manuscript might well represent a miscopy of a spelling *hafra*, for an anglicized form of Old Norse *Hafri*, a byname based upon ON *hafr* 'a he-goat'. See S*PNLY*, s.vv. *Hafr, Hafri*; see also *Nomina*, 9, 1985, p.46, no. xv.

A17 — Old English *hwæt, hwet* 'bold, brisk'.

A palæographic analysis may help to solve the puzzle presented by the *Domesday Book* personal-name *Chemarhuec* (*DB*, fol. 61b, Phill*DB* BRK 35, 1), wrongly printed -HNEC in Ellis, vol. II, p.302. Phill*DB* BRK 35, 1 transforms this personal-name into *Kenmarchuc* without disclosing how the general editor, J. R. Morris, arrived at that form. The problem is whether (1) to suppose *Domesday Book's* form *Chemarhuec* represents the Old Breton personal-name *Kenmarhoc*, recorded 1062–70 by Loth (*Chrestomathie bretonne*, Paris, 1890; where also the forms *Kenmarcoc* 866, *Kenmaroc* 1240, *Kenvaroc* 1311), in which case the vowel of the final syllable *-huec* would be anomalous; or (2) to suppose *Domesday Book's Chemarhuec* a mistake for a form *Chemarhuet*, which, if we suppose a no more than orthodox assimilation of the nasal consonants, can be construed as a representation of Old English *Cynemær hwet*. *Cynemær* is a well-attested Old English masculine personal-name. The byname, here, would be the Old English adjective *hwaet, hwet* 'bold, brisk', and we can compare the name of *Edricus Chuet* in the *Winton Domesday*, 1066, noted *OEB*, p.125, PNWD, p.209. See *Nomina*, 1985, p.46, no. xviii.

A18 — Old English *idese, ides* 'a lady'.

The personal-name *Aluiladese* 1086, *DB*, fol. 61b, Phill*DB* BRK 31, 3, of a tenant in Berkshire, was adequately identified by von Feilitzen (*PNDB*, p.175) as a Latin first declension nominative form of the Old English feminine personal-name *Ælfhild* with a byname suffixed. The name is not included in Ellis, vol. II, p.26; the byname is not in Tengvik's *OEB*. Loss of phonetic post-consonantal voiced dental [d] in final position is a common feature in *Domesday Book* name-forms; it is reviewed by von Feilitzen in *PNDB*, Introduction §104. In the present compound the loss would be accelerated by the phonetic process of dissimilation from a closely adjacent [d], because the most obvious Old English word with the rare morpheme *dese* is the poetic word *idese*, the weak declension of Old English *ides* 'a lady' (see BTSuppl). The initial vowel of the byname *Idese* would elide after the inflexional *-a* of *Alfhilda*; the development indicated is *Alfhilda-idese* > *Alfilda-dese* > *Alfila-dese*. See *Nomina*, 9, 1985, p.48, no. xxxi.

A19 — Medieval Latin *investiatus*, adj., 'playful'.

Robertus inuesiatus (*LDB*, fol.15a; Phill*DB* ESS 6, 12) is the name of an undertenant in Essex in 1086. He is identified by *The Victoria County History of Essex*, vol. I, p.518, n.7, with *Robertus lascivus* (named in *LDB*, fol. 66b, Phill*DB* ESS 32, 28) another subordinate of Robert Gernon. Perhaps prompted by this identification and by the interpretations offered in *OEB*, p.348, the Phill*DB* editors have rendered Latin *invesiatus* as 'perverted' and *lascivus* as 'lascivious'. The word *lascivus* is well recorded. It means 'wanton, playful, (morally) relaxed'. The sense 'lascivious', however, might seem in Modern English to be too bold; being 'lascivious' is perhaps a more actively and deliberately sinful, less playful, state than being 'wanton'. The other Latin word *invesiatus*, is not elsewhere recorded. It is not in *RMLWL* nor in Du Cange. Tengvik rather desperately picked up the most resembling form he could find in Du Cange, Medieval Latin *invasatus* (compare Classical Latin *invasus*) 'possessed by a demon', and offered it in explanation of *invesiatus*. The editors of the Essex volume of Phill*DB* adopt the relation of this word to Classical Latin *invertere* 'to pervert' but this does not look like an authoritative and authentic derivation. The byname is already explained by P. H. Reaney, *DBS*, s.v. *Vaisey*, following E. Weekley, *Surnames*, p.186, n.1. as a Latinized form of Old French *enveisé, envoisié* 'playful'. Our Robert *invesiatus alias* Robert *lascivus* may not have been at all 'perverted' or 'lascivious' in the modern senses of those words; he may have been no more than 'gay' in any sense.

A20 — *Jeltfange*, Alwinus, *OEB*, p.390.

Perhaps Old English **gield-fenga* 'tax-gatherer', see PNWD, p.212.

A21 — Old Danish **kai* 'the left, left-handed'.

The personal-name *Dynechaie*, 1086, *LDB*, fol. 320a, Phill*DB* SFK 6, 191, of a Suffolk tenant in *Domesday Book*, is not explained by von Feilitzen at *PNDB*, p.229. As I have already demonstrated elsewhere, in the notes to Phill*DB* SFK, and in *Nomina*, 9, 1985, p.46, this unintelligible personal-name can be intelligently construed if certain palæographical and phonetic processes are invoked. Supposing a confusion of the letters *n* and *r* in an Insular Minuscule script; and supposing capital D to represent capital Ð, that is to say, taking letter *d* to represent an Anglo-Norman sound-substitution of [d] for the Old English or Old Danish sounds [ð] and [θ] and taking the Anglo-Norman digraph *ch* to represent the sound [k]; under all these conditions — which regularly obtain owing to the peculiar evolution of the *Domesday Book* texts — we can construe the name *Dynechaie* into *Thyrekaie*; and in that transformed state the name can be analysed as an obvious representation of the Old Danish personal-name Thyri with a byname *kaia*. That byname looks like either the Old English weak masculine nominative singular form, or the Latinized first declension inflexion, of that elusive putative adjective **kai* which must be supposed for the ancestor of the Middle English and Modern English dialect adjective *kay* 'left, left-handed', which is taken by *OED* and *EDD*, s.v. *kay* and by *DBS*, s.v. *Kay*, to be a Scandinavian loan-word in English (compare Danish dialect *kei* 'left-handed', Modern Danish *Keite* 'left-hand').

The proposed reconstruction of this *Domesday Book* personal-name would carry back to the eleventh century, the record of a word which has hitherto only emerged into literature in the fourteenth.

A22 — Old English *se langa* 'the tall one'.

Under *ðes Langa*, *OEB*, p.320 should be added *Rad' b'lang*, *LDB*, fol. 181b (Phill*DB* NFK 9, 100), perhaps *Radbod lang* rather than *Radulfus berlang*; see *Nomina*, 9, 1985, pp.43–4.

A23 — Old French *Malvoisin*, Middle English *Malveisin* 'bad neighbour'.

Malus Vicinus, LDB, fol. 447b is omitted from *OEB*, p.351. See note to Phill*DB* SFK 76, 1.

A24 — *Nalad*, Godwinus, *OEB*, p.390.

Old English *nā lāð*, adj. phrase, 'not harmful, not unpleasant', see PNWD, p.214.

A25 — Medieval Latin *sine napa*, adj. phrase, 'without a napkin', perhaps late Old English **nape-lēas*.

The name *Bernardus sine napa* is recorded in *ExonDB*, fol. 306b, for the plain *Bernardus* of *DB*, fol. 107d. The byname is left unexplained at *OEB*, p.390. It is probably a Latinization of the Old English byname function of an adjective formed upon the Old English suffix *-lēas*, '-less; lacking'. However, the proto-theme of that hypothetical formation eludes the present state of this art, for one does not know whether there existed in late Old English an equivalent, or a borrowing, of the words Old French *nape, nappe*, Medieval Latin *napa* 'cloth, tablecloth, linen, napery'. A late Old English or an early Middle English hybrid, **nape-lēas* might have to be supposed here, with the meaning 'lacking napery' perhaps 'without a nappy' (i.e. in need of a diaper). Otherwise, the Latin *sine napa* may show *napa* substituted for some similar but different Old English word, which opens up a range of alternative amusing candidates when one considers, for instance, Old English *hnaep* 'a cup', *cnapa* 'a boy', and *naep* 'a turnip'.

This name and **chevres-beard* could be early French/English hybrid surnames, see A3, above.

A26 — Old French *pancevolt* 'vaulted-belly; pot-bellied'.

G. Tengvik, *OEB*, pp.324–5, proposed 'paunch-face' from Old French *pance* 'paunch' and *volt* 'face'. *DBS*, s.n. *Pauncefoot*, and PNWD, p.216, read Old French *volt* 'vaulted, arched'.

A27 — *Porriz*, Godwinus, *OEB*, p.390.

Perhaps Old English *portic'* 'porch, portico, vestibule', see PNWD, p.215.

A28 — Old English *rætt* 'a rat'.

In *Nomina*, 9, 1985, p.48, no. xxx, I have drawn attention to the phonological and palæographical factors in the interpretation of the name of the Hampshire tenant *Aluuinus ret, DB*, fol. 50a, Phill*DB* HAM 69, 16. J. H. Round suggested in *Victoria County History of Hampshire*, vol. I, p.505, that the letters *ret*, which are interlined, may have been so inserted in order to emend the form *Aluuinus* to *Aluretus* (that is to say, to change the personal-name from Old English *Aelfwine* to *Aelfred*). But Dr Julian Munby, editor of Phill*DB* HAM, observed that the letters *uin* were not cancelled by the scribe, and the interlineation could represent the addition to the text of a byname not noted by Tengvik in *OEB*. Formally, *ret* is quite a feasible byname, being a variant of Old English *ræt* 'a rat' (exhibiting the late Old English or early Middle English phonetic development of [e] for Old English [æ] described in *PNDB*, §6, p.47). There is one Osbertus *Rate* named in the Darlington section, fol. 47v, in David Austen, ed., *Bolden Book* (Phill*DB*, vol. 35), whose byname appears to be a weak masculine variant, Old English **Rætta* 'the Rat'.

A29 — Old English *rōt*, adj., 'cheerful'.

This is noted by Tengvik as the basis of the byname of Aethelstan *Rota* named in the Anglo-Saxon charter, date 995, BCS 917, Sawyer 582. Tengvik does not observe the interlinear insertion at *DB*, fol. 13b of the byname of Azor *Rot* (Phill*DB* KEN 9, 19). P. H. Reaney, *DBS*, does not notice Azor *Rot* either. He associates the English surname *Roote* with those of the aforesaid Aethelstan *Rota*, and Walter and Ralph *Rota*, 1185, 1216.

A30 — *filius Saleuae*, Azur, 1086, *DB*, fol. 280c (Phill*DB* NTT S5).

Byname omitted from *OEB*, p.197; from Old English *Sǣlufu*, feminine personal-name (*PNDB*, p.353).

A31 — Old English *tēt* 'pet, darling'.

The personal-name form *Aluuatet* appears at *ExonDB*, fol. 109a
as a variant of the name of that *Aluuare* who is recorded in *DB*,
fol. 101c (Phill*DB* DEV 1, 63). The form *Aluuare* probably
represents the Old English feminine personal-name *Alwaru*
(see *PNDB*, p.154). The *ExonDB* form represents a name *Alware
tet* with elision of the inflexional vowel of the personal-name
and with loss of [r] as described in *PNDB*, §70, pp.83–4.

The suffixed byname *tēt* could represent the byname function,
not included in *OEB*, of an Old English putative noun *tēt*, *tǣt*,
which would be either a cognate of, or a loan word from, the
Old Danish and Old German byname *Tet* 'pet, darling', discussed
at *PNDB*, p.153, s.v. *Altet* and n.3; p.382, s.v. *Teitr*; Redin, p.70,
s.vv. *Taebba, Taetwa*.

A32 — Old English *thēof* 'a thief'.

The byname function is duly noted at *OEB*, p.375, but a further
observation is now possible. *DB*, fol. 112c, records the personal-
name *Aleuesdef*, of the tenant in 1066 of Iddlesleigh in Devon.
The corresponding entry in the *Exon Domeday* records her name
with a misspelling *Aleues clef* which suffices to show that *def* is
a byname. The forename is *Aleve* (Old English feminine *Aelgifu*,
PNDB, p.173) with an Anglo-Norman inorganic composition
suffix (see *PNDB*, p.106, §112). The byname *def*, representing
Old English *thēf, thēof* 'a thief', occurs again in the *Domesday
Book* account of Devon, at fol.112c (Phill*DB* DEV 25, 1) where
the pre-Conquest tenants of Villavin are named *Edlouedief* and
Eddeua, that is to say, in Old English, *Eadlufu thief* and *Eadgifu*.
The two Old English feminine personal-names alliterate and
have a common prototheme: their bearers may have been kin,
perhaps sisters, who were sharing the tenancy of an estate.
Moreover, their estate is listed in the *Exon Domesday* immediately
following the entry for the estate of *Aelgifu thef* at Iddesleigh.
Geographically, Iddesleigh is only some five miles away from
Villavin. The juxtaposition, the geography, and the byname in
common suggest the probability of a kinship between Eadlufu
and Aelgifu, perhaps members of a family sharing a byname
inherited from some felonious ancestor.

A33 — Old English *tilia* 'one who tills, a cultivator'.

The tenant of the manors of Manley and Nutcott, Devon, in 1066, is named *Alestan* at *Domesday Book*, fol. 117a (Phill*DB* DEV 46, 1–2): in the corresponding entries in *ExonDB* he is named *Alestantilia* and *Alestilla* — the latter spelling incorporates an abbreviation of the personal-name, such as **Alest'tilia*. The Phill*DB* editors render the byname by the modern English surname Tilley, and claim that this instance of the byname, in *DB*, antedates the first record in *DBS*, thirteenth century, of that tradition of the surname Tilley which is derived from Old English *tilia* 'one who tills' and the Old English verb *tilian* 'to till'. The byname is not explained in *PNDB*, pp.152–3, nor is it included in *OEB*, which at p.356 lists the byname *Til*, from Old English *til* 'good', which is obviously not our Alestan's byname.

A34 — Old English **topp(a)* 'a top-knot, a tuft'.

Domesday Book, fol. 105d records the name *Sauuinus* (Old English *Sǣwine*, *PNDB*, p.354) for one of the pre-Conquest tenants of an estate attached to the manor of Bridestowe, Devon (Phill*DB* DEV 16, 7). The corresponding *ExonDB* entry (at fol. 288b) names him *Sauuinus topa*. The byname may be the same as that of the Lincolnshire tenants Haldane *Tope* and his brother Ulf *Tope sune* (Phill*DB* LIN 7, 18 and CK 10), that is, a patronymic from the Old Danish personal-name *Topi* (see *OEB*, pp.164, 226, and *PNDB*, p.386, nn.8, 9). This is a comparatively rare, restricted Old Danish personal-name, according to *SPNLY*, p.291. Yet it appears as a personal-name in *Domesday Book* in the counties of Lincolnshire, Suffolk, Essex, and Hertfordshire, and also in Devon at *DB*, fol. 108a (Phill*DB* DEV 16, 146) in the form *Topic* (see *PNDB*, p.117 and §133). The form *topa* of Saewine's byname could represent the Old Danish personal-name; but it could equally well represent the byname function of the Old English word *toppa*, (rarely recorded, but likely to have been common in colloquial use), a weak declension of the strong noun *topp*, meaning 'a tuft, a forelock of hair' (see BT and BTSuppl; see also *OED*, s.v. *top* sb').

The editors of Phill*DB* DEV referred to *Saēwine Topa* as 'Saewine Tuft'.

A35 — Old Norse *úglíkr* 'unlike, different'.

The name of the Norfolk tenant *Ascolf unglicus* (*LDB*, fol. 117a) is explained in the note to Phill*DB* NFK 1, 61 as the Old German personal-name Ansculf (see *PNDB*, p.161), with a byname which was perceived but not explained in *OEB*. The byname *Unglicus* represents an anglicized form of the Old Norse adjective *úglíkr*. In *OEB*, p.130, Tengvik reported the byname with an exclamation mark, as an aberration for the Medieval Latin *anglicus*, 'English; the Englishman' as if it were an inaccurate parallel to the reference to *Willelmus unus anglicus* which appears a few lines farther down the same folio (117a) of *LDB*. See *Nomina*, 9, 1985, p.45, no. viii.

A36 — Old English **wambestrang*, adj., 'strong-bellied, strong in the belly'.

The byname of Godwinus *Wambestrang* (ICC, p.55; equivalent to the plain *Godwinus* of *DB*, fol. 195c; Phill*DB* CAM 27, 7) a Cambridgeshire tenant in *Domesday Book*, is not handled with assurance by Tengvik nor by the editors of Phill*DB*, who adhere to Tengvik's analysis. *OEB*, p.357, explains *Wambestrang* as representing an otherwise unrecorded Old English **wamb-streng*, a compound of Old English *wamb* 'belly' and *streng* 'string', meaning something like Middle English *womb-tie*, 'belly-band, waist-band'. However, we ought to consider that the form *Wambestrang* looks like an Old English compound of *wamb* with the adjective *strang* 'strong'. This would mean 'strong in the belly', signifying a person with a remarkable (good or bad) abdominal muscle-tone. This byname should suggest to us the possibility of an extension in the range and date of a type of compound adjective represented by the Middle English *headstrong* (from 1398), and the surname *Armstrong* (from 1250).

A37 — Old English **wiccan-boded*, adj., 'foretold by a witch'.

DB, fol. 167b, records the name of *Willelmus Goizenboded*, *Goizinboded*, (Phill*DB* GLS 34) whose byname is reported but left unexplained at *OEB*, p.390. This byname appears in records contemporary with, or derived from, *Domesday Book*, as *Guezenboeth* (Hemming's Cartulary, see Phill*DB* WOR, Appendix V) and *Guiz in bod'* (Evesham Cartulary, see Phill*DB* WOR EvK 116). The byname also appears in the Evesham Cartulary (Phill*DB* WOR EvN 14), in a severely altered form, *Cunteboiz*, of which the anotomical or physiological literal significance need not be investigated here, for the spelling could represent either a completely altered form, the result of a complicated phonological and scribal disintegration and reconstruction of the byname *Guizenboded*, or a different byname unintelligible as regards the deuterotheme.

However, the curious byname *Goizenboded, Goizinboded*, can be immediately recognized as a compound upon *-boded* the past participle of the Old English verb *bodian* 'to announce, to foretell'. But the prototheme does not become intelligible unless we take the Anglo-Norman spelling *goi* to represent the Old French sound [gwi] or [gi] substituted for Old English [wi]; and the Anglo-Norman spelling *z* to represent the Old French sound [ts] for the Old English sound [tʃ] usually spelled *c* or *cc*. We may then transform the spellings *Goizen-, Goizin-* into the pronunciation [witʃən], a fair representation of the Old English *wiccan* the oblique case inflexion of Old English *wicce* 'a witch'. The records of this byname show us a Norman-French garbling of an Anglo-Saxon name for one of the Norman landowners, an ominous name in the language of the subject, English, which the speakers of French seem to have accepted into their own use, leaving us to wonder whether they understood what it meant, and if they did, why they did not coin a French equivalent. See *Nomina*, 9, 1985, p.47, no. xxvii, and remarks under A3, above.

A38 — Old English *wudu-henn 'a wood-hen'.

The byname of *Goduuinus cudhen, -gudhen* (*LDB*, fol. 17b and 99a respectively; Phill*DB* ESS 9, 5 and 90, 1) is left unexplained in *OEB*, p.390. The initial consonant would represent the Norman-French sound substitution of [gw], [g] for Old English [w] in an otherwise unrecorded Old English word *wudu-henn. The English word *woodhen* for the female of the woodcock, is first recorded in 1281, *OED*. But here it is, this wood hen, camouflaged in Norman-French feathers, lurking undetected in a *Domesday Book* thicket in 1086. See *Nomina*, 9, 1985, p.47, no. xxviii.

B — CORRIGENDA

p.39, line 7 — For '*Charborough* . . . 90)' read 'Cherbourg, Normandy'. See Phill*DB* DOR 54, 8 note.

p.40, line 27 — For 'Colintuna' read 'Colintona'. For 'Collington . . . 111)' read 'Colyton, Devon'. See EPNS, IX, p.621, Phill*DB* DEV 1, 13.

p.44 — s.v. *de Medehalle*. For '(unidentified)' read 'perhaps Maidenhall, Gloucs.'. See Phill*DB* GLS 70.

p.89, line 3 — For 'PNNbDu 10' read 'PNNbDu 90'.

p.94 — s.n. *de Jorz*. Add 'Robertus de Iorz, written Lorz in Farley's edition'. See Phill*DB* LEI 42, 5 and *Nomina*, 9, 1985, p.46, no. xx.

p.201 — s.v. *filius Torulf*. The reference at 113 (D) is to Ricardus *filius Turoldi*.

p.202 — s.n. *filius Ungemar*. For 'Radulfus' read 'Oger'. See note on Phill*DB* RUT R14.

p.218 — s.n. *Friedai*. Cf. *Friendai* Phill*DB* LEI 2, 7, from the Old Frisian variant. See *Nomina*, 9, 1985, p.48, no. xxxii.

p.240 — s.n. *Camerarius*, Line 4 from foot, before '81(Do)' insert 'Odo'; line 5 from foot, for 'Odo' read 'Odinus'.

p.312 — s.v. *Grossus*. Line 4 from foot, for '(Sf)' read '(Nf)'. The form *Fæto* is nominative singular.

p.325, line 12 — Add ' "Arched foot" '. See PNWD, p.214, s.v. *Pancheuot*'. Cf. A26, *pancevolt*, above.

p.327, line 6 from foot — For 'pike' read 'pile'.

p.344 — s.v. *Diues*. Add 'see also *Faira*, p.312'. Cf. PNWD, p.210.

p.364, line 2 from foot — Add ' "Goat-bleat" might indicate the corncrake's call'.

III

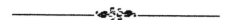

In quest of lost Danes:
The Scandinavian element in English surnames

GILLIAN FELLOWS-JENSEN

A FEW YEARS AGO there was a brief report in a London newspaper to the effect that a man by the name of Attack, with an extensive record of criminal conduct, had been brought before a Magistrates' Court charged with assault. Since the accused's name was spelt and pronounced in exactly the same way as the common noun which could be used to describe his misdemeanour, it would not have been unnatural for counsel to plead that his criminal career was bound up with the negative expectations attached by society to his surname. An anthroponymist, on the other hand, would have realized that the modern form of the surname must belie its true origin. The stress on the second syllable shows that the name cannot be the natural development of a name of Germanic origin or of an exotic name adopted by the English at the period when hereditary surnames were coming into use in England. The modern English word *attack*, which functions both as noun and verb, was apparently not adopted from French *attaque(r)* until the beginning of the seventeenth century and is extremely unlikely to have given rise to an English name. The standard explanation of the surname *Attack* was until recently that it originated as a northern Middle English topographical surname **atte āc*, 'at the oak-tree', as in the forms *Atte Ak'* 1301 and *atte Ake* 1332 recorded in the Lay Subsidy Rolls for the North Riding of Yorkshire.[1] The normal development of this surname would have

---

1 *Cf.*G. Kristensson, *A Survey of Middle English Dialects 1290–1350. The Six Northern Counties and Lincolnshire*, Lund Studies in English, 35, 1967, p.17.

41

been either to *Attack* or *Attock*, with stress on the first syllable, or, with loss of the preposition, to *Oak*.[2] The irregular development of *Attack* with stress on the second syllable would then have been the result of remodelling by shift of stress at some time after 1600, on analogy with the French loanword. That the name *Attack* can in some cases have developed from the topographical by-name is possible but no evidence has yet been forthcoming to prove that such a development has taken place. George Redmonds' painstaking and scholarly work on Yorkshire documents, on the other hand, has revealed that the Yorkshire surname *At(t)ack*, which has a focal point of distribution in the Dewsbury/Wakefield area and can be traced back to the middle of the seventeenth century, has in fact developed from a now-lost place-name across the county border in the parish of Altham, Lancashire (1280 *Ayothalgh*, 1445 *Aythalgh*). The conflicting recorded forms of the place-name do not provide a firm enough base on which to base a definite interpretation but the generic is clearly *halh*, 'nook'.[3]

The surname *Attack*, with its dramatically negative connotations and a development that has obscured its innocuous origin even from anthroponymists awake to the dangers of basing interpretations on modern forms of names, is perhaps an extreme case but it is not unusual for bearers of names to have completely erroneous ideas about the origins of these. That the surname *Fellows* originated as a nickname with the sense 'comrade, companion' borne by the homonymous common noun was suggested over a century ago by Charles Wareing Bardsley.[4] Henry Harrison elaborated on this interpretation by pointing out that the common noun *fellow* is a borrowing from Scandinavian *félagi*, meaning 'partner',

---

2 *Cf.* M. T. Löfvenberg, *Studies on Middle English Local Surnames*, Lund Studies in English, 11, 1942, pp.140–1; P.H. Reaney, *A Dictionary of British Surnames*, London, second edition 1976, s.n. *Attack* and *Oak*; R. A. McKinley, *A History of British Surnames*, London and New York, 1990, pp.87–8.

3 George Redmonds mentioned this surname in passing in a paper read at the Society for Name Studies conference at Alston Hall on 3rd April, 1993, and he has generously supplied me with information about early records of the Lancashire place-name and of the surname in Lancashire and Yorkshire.

4 C. W. Bardsley, *English Surnames: Their Sources and Significations*, first edition 1873, p.506, and *A Dictionary of English and Welsh Surnames*, London, first edition 1901, p.284.

suggesting that the final -*es* or -*s* is a genitival inflexion indicating 'son of', and noting that the disappearance of the form *Fellow* from the nomenclature was probably to be attributed to 'the partial disrepute into which the term has fallen'.[5] The derivation from the Scandinavian by-name or common noun *félagi* is quoted as the primary explanation of the surname in the dictionaries of P. H. Reaney,[6] Basil Cottle,[7] and Patrick Hanks and Flavia Hodges.[8]

It may be that some of the present bearers of the name can trace their name back through the records to an ancestor bearing Scandinavian *félagi* as a forename or by-name of status. That the forename *Félagi* was in use in England in the Viking period is suggested by its occurrence in *Domesday Book*, where a pre-Conquest tenant in Essex was named *Félaga*.[9] The common noun *félagi* had been adopted into Old English as *fe(o)laga* and used in the modified sense of 'comrade' in the *Anglo-Saxon Chronicle* for the year 1016 of the two kings Edmund and Knut, and in its original sense of 'partner' in two eleventh-century East Anglian wills.[10] Since the term was current in the English spoken in East Anglia, the possibility must be taken into account that the use of the word as a forename or by-name may have arisen in England. The *Bele le Felawe* and *Robert le Felawe* whose appearance in the late thirteenth-century Hundred Rolls was noted by Bardsley[11] and the *Robert le Felagh* and the *Rob. le Felawe* who are recorded in the Subsidy Rolls for Sussex and Warwickshire respectively under the

---

5 In *Surnames of the United Kingdom: A Concise Etymological Dictionary*, 1–2, London, 1912–18, at 1, p.145.

6 P. H. Reaney, *Dictionary of British Surnames*, p.126.

7 B. Cottle, *The Penguin Dictionary of Surnames*, London, second edition 1978, p.136.

8 P. Hanks and F. Hodges, *A Dictionary of Surnames*, Oxford, 1988, p.179.

9 P.R.O., *Little Domesday Book*, ff.95a, 102b (2x).

10 *Cf.* D. Hofmann, *Nordisch-Englische Lehnbeziehungen der Wikingerzeit*, Bibliotheca Arnamagnæana, 14, Copenhagen, 1955, §§ 324, 331; D. Whitelock, *Anglo-Saxon Wills*, Cambridge, 1930, nos. 31, 34; P. H. Sawyer, *Anglo-Saxon Charters. An Annotated List and Bibliography*, Royal Historical Society Guides and Handbooks, 8, London, 1968, nos. 1519, 1531.

11 C. W. Bardsley, *Dictionary of English and Welsh Surnames*, p.548.

year 1327[12] clearly bear by-names of status. In the case of Richard *Felawe* twelfth century (Lichfield, Staffordshire) and Walter *Felagh* 1256 (Northumberland), both noted by Reaney,[13] John *Felagh* 1276 (Somerset), noted by Bardsley,[14] John, Stephen and William *Felawe* 1327 (Essex),[15] and William *Felawe*, 1379 (Rugby, Warwickshire), noted by Ingrid Hjertstedt,[16] the surname may also have originated as a status by-name. Alternatively, however, these may be instances of the forename *Félagi* functioning as a surname or the common noun functioning as a by-name in a sense such as 'good, loyal friend' or 'associate in crime', both of which are evidenced in English sources.[17]

In England both the name and the common noun acquired a secondary genitive in *-es*. The Yorkshire place-name Felliscliffe, for example, is recorded in *Domesday Book* of 1086 as *Felgesclif* and it seems most likely that the specific of this place-name is the Scandinavian personal name *Félagi*,[18] while the same name in its Middle English development *Felawe* forms the specific of Fellowsfield Common in Hertfordshire (*Felawysfeld* 1351).[19] This secondary genitive might account for the forms taken by the modern surnames *Fellowes* and *Fellows*. Richard McKinley has noted two medieval instances in Oxfordshire, where the Hundred Rolls contain references to *Agnes Felawes* and *Elena Felawes* 1278–79.[20] It seems

---

12 P. H. Reaney *Dictionary of British Surnames*, p.126, and I. Hjertstedt, *Middle English Nicknames in the Lay Subsidy Rolls for Warwickshire*, Studia Anglistica Upsaliensis, 63, 1987, p.106.

13 P. H. Reaney, *Dictionary of British Surnames*, p.126.

14 C. W. Bardsley, *Dictionary of English and Welsh Surnames*, p.284.

15 In J. C. Ward, ed., *The Medieval Essex Community. The Lay Subsidy of 1327*, Essex Historical Documents, 1, 1983, pp.46, 55, 105.

16 I. Hjertstedt, *Middle English Nicknames*, p.106.

17 *Middle English Dictionary*, Ann Arbor, s.v.

18 A. H. Smith, *The Place-Names of the West Riding of Yorkshire*, 5, EPNS, vol. 34, Cambridge, 1961, p.132.

19 J. E. B. Gover, A. Mawer and F. M. Stenton, *The Place-Names of Hertfordshire*, EPNS, vol. 15, Cambridge, 1938, p.134.

20 R. McKinley, *The Surnames of Oxfordshire*, English Surnames Series, 3, London, 1977, p.217.

more likely that *Felawes* in these names is an andronymic (indicating relationship to a husband) and that Agnes and Elena were the wives or widows of men known for some reason as *Felawe* than that the genitive *-es* had been used to turn the personal name into a patronymic. Among small free tenants, bond tenants and poorer townspeople, such patronymic surnames would in fact seem to have come into use in the late thirteenth century and the fourteenth century, particularly in the south-west Midlands.[21] In most of the recorded cases, however, the personal name in the *-es* patronymics is a forename of Norman introduction such as *Richard* or *William* or a diminutive or pet-form of such a name, e.g. *Dickin* or *Will*. It is very rare for a name of Scandinavian origin to have acquired such an *-(e)s* patronymic ending in England, although *Grimes* from *Grímr* is a striking exception. It seems unlikely that a patronymic *Felawes* would have developed from the rare forename *Félagi*. All the records of *Felagh/Felawe* as a surname can be most satisfactorily explained as status names that arose in England after the Scandinavian common noun had been borrowed into English, while the form *Felawes* seems likely to be an andronymic.

The surname *Fellow(e)s* is not particularly common but there is a marked concentration in Staffordshire. It does not seem likely that all the *Fellow*s in this county can trace their names back to an andronymic *Felawes*. It would therefore seem advisable to take into account the secondary explanation of the surname in the standard dictionaries, namely that it might be a development from an older topographic **feld(es)hūs*, 'field-house'. The 1327 Subsidy Roll for Staffordshire lists *Will'o de felthous* (Waterfall), *Ph'o del Felthouses* (Grindon), *Thoma Atte feldeshous* (Trysull and Seisdon) and *Joh'e Attefeldeshous* (Himley), while the 1332 Roll lists *Henr' de Felhouse* (Grindon), *Joh'ne de Feldushous* (Himley) and *Thom' de Feldeshous* (Trysull and Seisdon).[22] These references may be to one of the surviving places with this name, for example Field House in

---

21 R. McKinley, *History of British Surnames*, pp.118–19.

22 *Cf.* G. Wrottesley, ed., 'The Subsidy Roll of A.D. 1327' and 'The Subsidy Roll of A.D. 1332–1333', in *Collections for a History of Staffordshire*, William Salt Archaeological Society, Old Series VII, 1886, 197–255 at pp.217, 221, 252, 254, and X, 1889, 77–132 at pp.114, 129–30.

Waterfall (SK 0850) or Felthouse in Grindon (SK 0753) but they may alternatively be to now-lost houses in fields.[23] Surnames deriving from compounds in *-hūs* are fairly common. They developed in many different ways, with weakening of the second element demonstrated, for example, in *Windows* from **windhūs*, 'winding-house', and *Widdows* from **widuhūs*, 'wood-house'.[24] It is significant that the three compounds in *-hūs* which developed forms in *-ows* are those in which the resulting form is homonymous with a modern genitive singular or nominative plural form of a common noun — *fellow, widow, window* — and the surnames can be assumed to be remodellings under the influence of these appellatives. It is much more likely that the surname *Fellow(e)s* in Staffordshire originated as a topographic term than that it derived from the rare Scandinavian personal name or by-name, first and foremost because of the general rarity of occurrence of surnames derived from Scandinavian personal names or by-names of status.

Scandinavian forenames have left little impression on the surnames of even those areas of England such as Yorkshire where they had retained their popularity right up to the Norman Conquest, and there are two main reasons for this. The first is that in the wake of William the Conqueror followed a comparatively limited number of personal names, mainly of Continental Germanic or biblical origin, which swiftly attained an immense and lasting popularity in England. The only men bearing Scandinavian forenames listed in the Register of the Freemen of the City of York between 1272 and 1759, for example, are: *Gamellus de Topclyf* 1370, *Ingare Johnson* 1461, *Godmondr Johnson, Iselandman* 1474, *Thurstanus Romesbothom* 1477 and *Thurstanus Lodge* 1522.[25] *Godmondr Johnson* is expressly stated to be an Icelander and his nationality is further betrayed by the faithful reproduction by the scribe of the nominative *-r* in his name, an *-r* for which there is no reliable evidence of survival in names brought to

---

23 Two relevant names are noted by J. P. Oakden, *The Place-Names of Staffordshire*, 1, EPNS, vol. 55, 1984: Field House in Penkridge, p.94, and Field House Farm in Haughton, p.165.

24 *Cf.* P. H. Reaney, *The Origin of English Surnames*, London, 1967, p.44, and *Dictionary of British Surnames*, s.n. Windus and Widdowes.

25 F. Collins, ed., *Register of the Freemen of the City of York*, 1–2, Publications of the Surtees Society, 96 and 102, 1897, 1900, at 1, pp.68, 181, 195, 199, 244.

Yorkshire in the Viking period,[26] and it is possible that *Ingare Johnson* was also a recent arrival from Iceland or Scandinavia, while *Gamel* and the two *Thurstans* are more likely to be Yorkshiremen born. George Redmonds has drawn my attention to the way in which names of Scandinavian origin such as *Harold, Thurston* and *Augrim* < *Auðgrímr* cling on in parts of England long after the thirteenth century.[27]

The second reason for the comparative rarity of occurrence in Yorkshire of surnames derived from Scandinavian forenames applies equally to all kinds of surname of Scandinavian origin. In the Viking period neither the Vikings nor the English among whom they settled were accustomed to use surnames. They normally referred to each other by their forenames alone. Even though the list of Yorkshire festermen for a man called *Ælfric* that is recorded in a document from about the year 1050[28] must be assumed to have had legal significance, for example, most of the festermen are only recorded by their forenames, in spite of the fact that names such as *Ulf, Ulfcetel, Alfcetel, Grimcetel* and *Godwine/Godwina* are borne by more than one festerman. The list does include, however, men who are registered with descriptions that correspond to the main types of surnames classified by Richard McKinley:[29] surnames derived from personal names (generally patronymics), e.g. *Þorcetel Unbainasuna*, occupational surnames, e.g. *Farðein greua*, nicknames, e.g. perhaps *Asmund ros'*, and locative surnames, e.g. *Ailaf in Braiþatun*. The only one of McKinley's surname-types without parallel in the list of festermen is the topographical surname such as **atte ac, *feldhus*.

I shall devote the rest of this paper to examining the significance of the surname-like descriptions which do occur in eleventh-century sources and in the Register of Freemen and to identifying English surnames which may have developed from these. In the list of festermen *Þorcetel* is described as *Unbaina suna*. The name *Þorcetel*, from *Þorketill*, was of common occurrence in Yorkshire and the

---

26 *Cf.* G. Fellows-Jensen, *Scandinavian Personal Names in Lincolnshire and Yorkshire*, Navnestudier, 7, Copenhagen, 1968, § 144.

27 In a letter in April 1993. It would be interesting to make a special study of the survival of forenames of Scandinavian origin in England.

28 Library of Dean and Chapter of York Minster, York Gospels MS, f.153d; printed in W. Farrer, ed., *Early Yorkshire Charters*, 1, Edinburgh, 1914, no. 9.

29 R. McKinley, *History of British Surnames*, pp.10–11.

patronymic may have been included to distinguish this man from other *Porcetels*. He is, however, the only bearer of this name in the list. For the correct explaination of the employment of the patronymic here we should perhaps look to the homeland of the Vikings. It has been convincingly demonstrated that in Denmark in the Viking period patronymics were primarily employed as a means of boasting of the bearer's family connections.[30] More or less contemporary with *Porcetel Unbaina suna* is another Yorkshireman, who refers to himself as *Orm Gamalsuna* on a carved stone sundial which he had set up on the church at Kirkdale to commemorate his own generosity.[31] It seems likely that this *Orm* was the son of the Northumbrian thane *Gamel filius Orm* who is reported by Symeon of Durham to have been treacherously slain by order of Earl Tosti in 1064.[32] *Orm* would thus have been boasting not only of his generosity but also of his relationship with the renowned *Gamel*.

It must not, of course, be assumed that every record in a post-Conquest source of, for example, a *Gamel filius Chetelli* involves a boast on the part of the man in question about his parentage. Often the patronymic merely serves to make an identification precise and the majority of the patronymics are to be looked upon as descriptions and not as surnames. As the use of hereditary surnames gradually became more widespread in England, surnames derived from personal names did come into use but the form taken by such names in the early years was the forename standing alone in nominative case without the addition of a genitival inflexion or -*son*, for example *Robertus Unbayn* 1274 and *Stephanus Gamel* 1296, both freemen of York.[33] This fact had been noted by Charles Bardsley in 1873, when he pointed out that such pre-Conquest forenames as have survived in surnames 'are found in their simple unaltered dress'.[34] In spite of this, there has been a tendency to assume that the development of

---

30 J. Kousgård Sørensen, *Patronymer i Danmark 1. Runetid og Middelalder*, Navnestudier, 23, Copenhagen, 1984, pp.191–200.

31 E. Okasha, *Hand-List of Anglo-Saxon Non-Runic Inscriptions*, Cambridge, 1971, no. 64.

32 *Cf.* T. Arnold, ed., *Symeonis Monachi Opera Omnia 2. Historia Regum*, London, 1885, p.178.

33 F. Collins, *Register*, 1, pp.2, 6.

34 C. W. Bardsley, *English Surnames*, p.20.

the forename + *son* type of surname is a reflex of Scandinavian influence, probably simply because it was commoner in northern England than in the south, where other kinds of hereditary surnames had established themselves at an earlier date. As pointed out by John Kousgård Sørensen, however, the formation of a patronymic designation by the addition of *-son* to the father's forename was an old Germanic system familiar to the English and the Scandinavians alike.[35] William Camden had dismissed the theory of a Scandinavian origin for the *-son* surnames as early as 1605, writing, 'Neither is it true, which some say, Omnia nomina in son sunt Borealis generis, whereas it was usual in every part of the Realm',[36] but although his conclusion is correct, his reasoning is not so, for there was a distributional variation between the two types of surnames in the medieval period, with names in *-son* occurring most frequently in the north Midlands, the north of England and southern Scotland.[37] A more soundly based rejection of the theory of a Scandinavian origin for the names in *-son* was provided by Camden's contemporary Richard Uerstegan in the very same year.[38] Uerstegan argued that surnames such as *Johnson, Tomson, Nicolson, Davison, Saunderson* and the like cannot be 'descended of Danish race' because the Danes did not use such names as *John, Thomas, Nicholas, David* or *Alexander* in the Viking period and that had surnames of Danish origin survived in England, 'they would have been more markable, because we should then have heard of *Canutson, Ericson, Gormoson, Hadingson, Haraldson, Rolfoson*, and such like'. The only names in *-son* which Uerstegan is willing to allow may have come from the Danes are 'such as have the termination son composed with some such name as hath among us been long time out of use, as *Swanson*, rightly *Sweynson*, and such like'. This is a very pertinent observation. The Register of Freemen contains hardly any instances of surnames in *-son* in the early years. Several men are distinguished as being the son of their father, e.g.

35 J. Kousgård Sørensen, *Patronymics in Denmark and England*, 1983, p.3.

36 W. Camden, *Remains concerning Britain*, London, 1605. p.142 in the reprint from 1870.

37 R. McKinley, *History of British Surnames*, p.119.

38 R. Uerstegan, *Restitution of Decayed Intelligence in Antiquities Concerning the most noble, and renowned English Nation*, Antwerp, 1605, reprinted London, 1653, pp.237–8 in the edition of 1653.

Joh. filius Nicholai, but there is no way of knowing whether or not the Latin description is a reflex of a patronymic surname. A close examination of the Register of Freemen from the years 1272–1387 reveals only the following instances of names in *-son*: *Thomas Hulleson, piscator*, 1308, *Thomas, fil. Thomae Hullson junior, piscarius*, 1333, *Ricardus Hulleson, piscator*, 1334 (these three men are probably related to each other; the patronymic is formed from *Hulle*, a diminutive of *Hugh*); *Johannes Saunderson, mason*, 1346 (*Alexander*); *Willelmus Mondson, de Friton, walker*, 1351 (? a pet-form of *Edmund*); *Joh. Dykson, de Novo Castro, chapman*, 1352 (*Dick < Richard*); *Johannes Mabson, de Castelforth, walker*, 1353 (*Mab < Mabel*); *Robertus Hamsone, de Tollerton, bocher*, 1354 (*Hamo*); *Johannes Davydsone, de Kyrkby, maltster*, 1354 (*David*); *Johannes Nallson, de Cawod, bocher*, 1355 (? *Nall < Ann*); *Robertus Hanson, de Housum, pestour*, 1357 (*Hann < John*); *Willelmus fil. Adæ Densone, de Aldeburgh, pouchemaker*, 1362 ('dean'); *Johannes Dandsone, maryner*, 1363 (*Dand < Andrew*); *Henricus Hwetsone, schipman*, 1363, (*Huwet < Hugh*); *Johannes Dandsone, junior, maryner*, 1366; *Joh. Richardson, de Stokton*, 1373; *Joh. Robynsone, de Barneby, hoseer*, 1374 (*Robin < Robert*); *Thomas Dandesone, teighler*, 1375; *Thomas Adamsone, porter*, 1376; *Willelmus Clerksson, milner*, 1381 ('clerk'); *Robertus Doggeson, pistor*, 1385 (*Dogge < Roger*); *Joh. Dykonesson, junr., maryner*, 1387 (*Dickon < Richard*); *Robertus Pieresson, Smyth*, 1387 (*Piers*); *Johannes Dyesson, plasterer*, 1387 (*Dye < Dionysius*). It will be noted that with the exception of the two patronymics formed from the occupational terms 'dean' and 'clerk', not only were all these patronymics formed from names introduced into England by the Normans but most of them are formed from pet-forms of these names. It is also clear that it is not until the middle of the fourteenth century that *-son* surnames begin to occur at all frequently. From the whole period 1272 to 1759 there are only three instances of *-son* surnames formed on a Scandinavian base: *Johannes Gunson, tailliour*, 1438; *Petrus Ingarson, taillour*, 1545 and *Tho. Swainson, linningweaver*, 1623. The surnames *Gunson, Ingerson* and *Swainson* were borne in 1984 by subscribers listed in the York and District Telephone Directory (YDTD).

Of more frequent occurrence in the Register of Freemen are the surnames consisting simply of a Scandinavian forename in nominative case. Occasionally the origin of the surname would seem already to have been forgotten at the time when the surname was entered in the list, for some of the Scandinavian forenames have been mistaken for place-names and preceded by *de*, for example *Thomas de Thurkhill, tannour*, 1276; *Johannes de Thurkill, fischer*, 1343; *Thomas de Thorkyll*, 1365; *Willelmus de Ketill, cordwaner* 1326; *Willelmus de Ketyll, draper*, 1372; *Nicholaus de Thurstan, wright*, 1386. The prefixing of *de* to personal name to form a surname is not unprecedented. I have noted elsewhere that an *Edwardus de Charles* 1300, was descended from a *Karolus de Wayderoba*, and a mid-thirteenth-century *Radulphus de Trehamton'* from a Breton called *Treantune*[39] and Bo Seltén has noted that the French method of expressing relationship by means of the preposition *de* occurs in sources from Norfolk.[40] In some cases confusion may have arisen with place-names because of the similarity between the endings of the personal names and place-name elements such as *hyll, stān* and *tūn*.

I include here a list of the first occurrences of the Scandinavian forenames which function as surnames in the Register of Freemen. Where the surname is listed among the subscribers in the YDTD in 1984, the modern form is added in brackets: *Unbayn*, 1276; *Thurkhill*, 1276 (Thirkill); *Gamel*, 1296 (Gamble); *Touk < Tóki*, 1297 (Tooke); *Grime*, 1301 (Grimes); *Arkill*, 1310 (Arkle/Arkell); *Ketelbarn*, 1324; *Ketill*, 1326 (Kettle); *Thurstan*, 1330 (Thurstan); *?Scartholf*, 1333; *Tubbe*, 1334 (Tubb); *Turpyn < Þorfinnr*, 1335 (Turpin); *Ally*, 1352; *Astyne < Ásketill*, 1363 (Astin); *Sturgys < Þorgísl*, 1363 (Sturgess); *Owgryme < Auðgrímr*, 1368; *Hemyng*, 1373 (Hemming); *Snell*, 1388 (Snell); *Ingolf*, 1391; *Thorbrand*, 1397; *Lyolf*, 1401; *Colstan*, 1408 (?Colston); *Brand*, 1411 (Brand); *Hake*, 1415 (Hake); *Thoralde*, 1438; *Dolfyn*, 1438; *Swayne*, 1445 (?Swan); *Olyff < Óleifr*, 1449 (Olive); *Skeldyng*, 1470 (Skelding); *Gudrede < Guðrøðr*, 1517; *Haveloke < Óláfr*, 1536; *Magnus*, 1549 (Magnus); *Harrold*, 1561; *Colgram*, 1561; *Salmund*, 1618 and *Oddy*, 1657 (Odd). It should be noted that three of these names, *Turpyn, Astyne* and *Sturgys*, appear in forms betraying Norman influence.

In the Register of Freemen there are only twelve occupational or status surnames which can most satisfactorily be explained as

---

39 G. Fellows-Jensen, 'The surnames of the tenants of the Bishop of Lincoln in nine English counties *c.*1225', *NORNA-rapporter*, 8, 1975, 39–60, at p.57.

40 B. Seltén, *The Anglo-Saxon Heritage in Middle English Personal Names. East Anglia 1100–1399*, vol. 1, Lund Studies in Engish, 43, 1972, p.51.

of wholly or partially Scandinavian origin. Three of these names must have denoted the status of the original bearer: *Willelmus Lousyng, carpenter,* 1326 (**lausing,* 'freedman'); *Johannes Dryng, mercer,* 1451 (*drengr,* 'young warrior') and *Radulphus Husbond, yoman,* 1577 (*húsbóndi,* 'householder'). Only the last of these men bore a surname at all appropriate to his occupation. The names Dring and Husband were borne by subscribers in the YDTD in 1984. Four of the surnames, none of which survives in York and district, are occupational terms proper: *Nicholaus le noutehird,* 1296 (**nautahirðir,* 'cowherd'); *Ricardus Gayterd, lynwever,* 1500 (**geitahirðir,* 'goatherd'); *Johannes Copper, sledman,* 1445 (?*koppari,* 'cup-maker', as in the first element of the York street-name Coppergate), and *Leonardus Skepper, inkeeper,* 1562 (**skeppari,* 'basket-maker'). All four names may have been coined in England from Scandinavian linguistic material. The first two names are perhaps compounds in English *hirde* rather than Scandinavian *hirðir.* The last four names to be discussed in this class are all compounds in *-man*: *Petrus Laxman, chaloner,* 1374 (*lax,* 'salmon'); *Robertus Waytheman, fissher,* 1437 (*veiði,* 'hunting'); *Ricardus Gadman, hosteller,* 1440 (*gaddr,* 'goad') and *Alanus Botheman, marryner,* 1542 (Danish *bōth,* 'booth'). Two of these names occur in 1984 as Wademan and Boothman. It might be argued that surnames in *-man* are English formations involving a Scandinavian first element but it should be noted that *Bodeman, Laxman* and *Wetheman* are recorded as by-names in Denmark[41] and that surnames in *-man* of Scandinavian origin occur frequently in Normandy.[42]

Slightly more common in the Register of Freemen than the surnames derived from Scandinavian occupational terms are those derived from Scandinavian nicknames or by-names. In some cases there original by-names may already have been in use among the Vikings as forenames, as was the case with names such as *Gamall* and *Grímr* that have been treated here as forenames. One group of by-names represented among the English surnames is

41 G. Knudsen, M. Kristensen and R. Hornby, *Danmarks gamle Personnavne. II. Tilnavne,* Copenhagen, 1949–64, pp.95, 663, 1188. *Laxmand,* however, is explained here as a reflex of *lagsman* 'companion'.

42 L. Musset, 'L'anthroponymie au service de l'histoire: Les surnoms normands en *-man*', *Études Germaniques,* 2, 1947, pp.133–43.

that consisting of words from the animal world. The Register of Freemen contains the following examples: *Hugo Skarf, piscator,* 1305 (*skarfr,* 'cormorant'); *Willelmus Pa, zonarius,* 1320 (*pái,* 'peacock'); *Thomas Gayte, molendinarius,* 1330 (*geit,* 'she-goat'); *Simon Gouke,* 1350 (*gaukr,* 'cuckoo'); *Thomas Lax,* 1351 (*lax,* 'salmon'); *Robertus Orr, cordewaner,* 1353 (*orri,* 'black grouse'); *Thomas Graa, cordewaner,* 1377 (*grár,* 'grey one' or 'wolf'); *Willelmus Crake, carnifex,* 1386 (*kráka* or *krákr,* 'crow, raven'); *Johannes Galt, raper,* 1413 (Danish *galt,* 'hog'); *Ricardus Grice, wryght,* 1413 (*gríss,* 'young pig') and *Ricardus Kaa, taillour,* 1433 (Danish *kā,* 'jackdaw'). Eight of these names survive to be borne in 1984 by subscribers in the YDTD: Scarfe, Po(cock), Gaite, Lax, Orr, Crake, Grice and Kay. In the case of *Hugo Skarf,* who was a fisherman, the by-name 'cormorant' may have been indicative of his occupation. The other by-names were almost certainly all hereditary surnames.

Another group of by-names of Scandinavian origin represented among surnames in the Register of Freemen is made up of adjectives or nature: *Johannes le slegh,* 1333 (*slœgr,* 'cunning'); *Ricardus Trigg, draper,* 1355 (*tryggr,* 'trusty'); *Johannes Meke, tyeller,* 1442 (*mjúkr,* 'meek'); *Karolus Sparke, loksmyth,* 1464 (*sparkr,* 'lively'); *Willelmus Bayne, wolman,* 1467 (*beinn,* 'ready, hospitable'); *Johannes Scayff, merchaunt,* 1525 (*skeifr,* 'awry'); *Johannes Snar, fishemonger,* 1529 (*snarr,* 'swift'); *Robertus Blayk, surgyeon,* 1573 (*bleikr,* 'pale'). Several of these names survive as surnames in the 1984 YDTD: Slee, Trigg, Tate, Meek, Spark(e), Bayne, Scaife/Skaife, Snarr and Blake, and it seems likely that most of the names were borne as hereditary surnames by the freemen, although the employment of the French definite article in the first instance may indicate that it was looked upon as a characterizing term rather than as a name.

Other surnames derived from by-names of Scandinavian origin are: *Willelmus Ragg,* 1283 (*rag,* 'rag'); *Johannes Gest, taverner,* 1322 (*gestr,* 'guest, stranger'); *Johannes Baune, barker,* 1455 (*baun,* 'bean'); *Robertus Broddes, tayllour,* 1515 (*broddr,* 'spike'); *John Legg, taylor,* 1629 (*leggr,* 'leg-bone'). Of these, Ragg, Guest and Legg(e) survive in YDTD for 1984.

The groups of surnames of Scandinavian origin discussed so far have not accounted for very many of the present-day surnames in the York district. It is the two groups of names which remain to be discussed that have made the most substantial contribution to the surnames of Yorkshire. These are the topographical and locative surnames.[43] Topographical surnames are derived from terms for features of the landscape, whether natural or man-made, whereas locative surnames from the names of specific places. In practice it can sometimes be difficult to distinguish between a topographical surname and a locative one. Among the names borne by the freemen, for example, surnames whose modern reflexes are Lund, Dale, Holmes, Crook and Aske, are probably topographical surnames, as suggested by records such as *Johannes del Lunde*, 1306 and *Rog. del Dale, de Luda*, 1366, although the possibility of derivation from specific place-names such as Lund, Dale (Town), Crook, Holme and Eske[44] cannot be excluded. For the purpose of the present study, names such as *Lund* have been treated as topographical surnames.

The Scandinavian topographical surnames borne by freemen are quite numerous and some of them became extremely popular. Practically all of them have survived to the present day. The names occurring in the Register of Freemen will be listed here in tabular form, first terms for natural features and then those for cultural artifacts. (See Table 1)

A sub-group of topographical names is formed by the 22 by-names of location derived from the four points of the compass and the Scandinavian prepositional phrase *í bý*, 'in the village'. Kenneth Cameron has noted that names of this type are common in the parts of Lincolnshire north of a line drawn from Lincoln to Cleethorpes and suggested that the name-type is likely to have spread into Lincolnshire from the East Riding of Yorkshire.[45] The popularity of the type in Yorkshire is confirmed by the number of instances recorded in the Register of Freemen. Here there are eight Northebys, four Sothebys or Sudebys, six Estibys, Estebys or Esterbys, one Ousteby and one Owstaby, one Westeby and one Westiby.

The only group of surnames that remains to be discussed is that containing locative names. Some of the surnames derive from place-names borne by more than one locality, while place-names

43 R. McKinley, *History of British Surnames*, p.10.

44 G. Fellows-Jensen, *Scandinavian Settlement Names in Yorkshire*, Navnestudier, 11, Copenhagen, 1972, pp.92, 93, 94, 97, 100.

45 K. Cameron, 'Bynames of Location in Lincolnshire Subsidy Rolls', *Nottingham Medieval Studies*, 32, 1988, pp.156–64.

Table 1

Register	1st occ.	Element	YDTD
Sleght	1302	*slétta*, 'plain'	Sleight
Rayne	1305	*rein*, 'strip'	Raine
del Lunde	1306	*lundr*, 'grove'	Lund
Skowgh	1355	*skógr*, 'wood'	
del Bekke	1356	*bekkr*, 'stream'	Beck
del Karre	1362	*kjarr*, 'undergrowth'	Carr
del Dale	1366	*dalr*, 'valley'	Dale
del Banke	1370	*banki*, 'slope'	Banks
del Gyl	1384	*gil*, 'ravine'	Gill
in ye Wra	1395	*vrá*, 'nook'	Wray, Wroe
Croke	1397	*krókr*, 'bend'	Crook
del Fell	1422	*fell*, 'hill'	Fell
Hulme	1420	*holmr*, 'island'	Hulme
Holme	1435	*holmr*, 'island'	Holmes
Hagge	1470	*hogg*, 'clearing'	
del Rigge	1495	*ryggr*, 'ridge'	Rigg
Greyn	1506	*grein*, 'fork'	
Skarre	1512	*sker*, 'rock'	Scarr
Myars	1515	*mýrr*, 'mire'	Myers
Keld	1521	*kelda*, 'spring'	Keld
Ingg	1563	*eng*, 'meadow'	Ing
Thwaite	1576	*þveit*, 'clearing'	Thwaites
Aske	1577	*askr*, 'ash-tree'	Aske
Slack	1634	*slakki*, 'hollow'	Slack
del Lathes	1296	*hlaða*, 'barn'	
del Garth	1363	*garðr*, 'enclosure'	Garth
del Kyrk	1385	*kyrkja*, 'church'	Kirk
Bothe	1387	*bóth*, 'booth'	Booth
Brigg	1472	*bryggja*, 'causeway'	Brigg(s)
Loft	1480	*loft*, 'upper floor'	Loft

such as Thornton and Newby are borne by many localities. Although it is only 'unique' names that can be employed for studies of demographical movement in the medieval period,[46] it does not seem unreasonable to assume that the surnames borne by the

46 P. McClure, 'Patterns of Migration in the late Middle Ages: The Evidence of English Place-Name Surnames', *The Economic History Review*, 32, 1979, pp.167–82.

freemen of York which are identical in form with place-names in Yorkshire are likely to derive from these.

The best way to give an indication of the geographical and linguistic origin of the place-names which function as surnames in the Register of Freemen is in tabular form. Table 2 shows the probable geographical location of the place-names reflected in the surnames recorded for single years at intervals of a century.

Table 2

Year	Total	Yorks	Britain	France	% from Yorks
1272	28	26	2		93
1372	21	12	8	1	57
1472	33	17	13	3	57
1572	26	16	9	1	61
1672	72	49	21	2	68

Table 3 shows the probable linguistic origin of the place-names involved (excluding French localities).

Table 3

Table	Total	Celtic	English	Scand	Hybrid	French	% Scand
1272	28		20	3	5		29
1372	20	1	13	3	2	1	25
1472	30		26	3	1		13
1572	25		17	2	6		32
1672	70	3	44	18	4	1	31

The locative surname was extremely common in Yorkshire in the medieval period. In the Register of Freemen it accounts for 28 out of 36 descriptive terms in 1272 (78 per cent); 21 out of 33 in 1372 (64 per cent); 33 out of 82 in 1472 (40 per cent); 26 out of 63 in 1572 (41 per cent) and 71 out of 281 in 1672 (25 per cent). The very high percentages of locative surnames among freemen in 1272 and 1372 probably reflect the fact that many of the men were distinguished by reference to their place of origin or residence rather than by the employment of a surname. A survey of the surnames borne by the population of Yorkshire in 1379 based on taxation returns and similar sources has shown that only about 29 per cent were locative names.[47] The decrease in the percentage of locative designations among the freemen is balanced by a dramatic increase in the number of surnames derived from personal names, from 1 out of 36 in 1272 to 92 out of 281 or 33 per cent in 1672. In spite of the inroads made in the course of time by surnames derived from personal names, locative surnames have remained common in Yorkshire. It has recently been calculated by Kay H. Rogers that about 30 per cent of the subscribers listed in the telephone directory of York and district in 1979 bear locative surnames.[48] Allowing for the degree of uncertainty involved in discussing the origin of modern surnames, it is striking that of these approximately 20,000 locative surnames, about 6,500 seem to derive from place-names of wholly or partly Scandinavian origin. This means that about 32 per cent of the locative surnames in twentieth-century Yorkshire betray Scandinavian influence and it is interesting that this percentage would not seem to have varied greatly through the centuries. My samples taken at intervals of a century from 1272 to 1672 revealed the following percentages of locative surnames betraying Scandinavian influence: 29 per cent in 1292; 25 per cent in 1392; 13 per cent in 1492; 32 per cent in 1592 and 31 per cent in 1692.

Looking for traces of the Danes in Yorkshire surnames, then, is mostly likely to meet with success if the search concentrates on the topographical and locative names. These, of course, reflect first and foremost the distribution in the county of major and minor place-names of Scandinavian origin. Even though the evidence of the surnames does not alter the picture provided by the place-names, however, it does throw interesting sidelights on society in Yorkshire both in the Viking period and in the succeeding centuries. The Danes have not been lost without trace. There are many left behind, even after imposters such as the Fellowses have bowed themselves out of the arena.

47 R. McKinley, *History of British Surnames*, p.22.

48 I am greatly indebted to Kay H. Rogers for allowing me to quote from the results of her painstaking work on the names of the subscribers in the York and District Telephone Directory, 1979. Reference can now be made to K. H. Rogers, *Vikings and Surnames*, York, 1991.

IV

Habitation Surnames:
Some notes on *A Dictionary of Surnames*
by Patrick Hanks and Flavia Hodges[1]

MARGARET GELLING

A PARTICULARLY USEFUL feature of the *Dictionary of Surnames* by
P. Hanks and F. Hodges is the provision of information about
regional distributions. When a surname derives, as many do, from a
very small settlement, the chances of locating the place are greatly
increased if the searcher knows where to look for it. I was able to do
some work of this kind for the *Dictionary* before publication. Now
that the book is in print, it has been possible to make a more leisurely
search, and I find myself able to offer suggestions for some habitation
surnames which were not pinned down in 1988. In particular, I
have searched for Lancashire and West Midland names in the five
volumes of the E.P.N.S. survey of Cheshire, a work for which there
is as yet no index.

Suggestions[2] are offered for 18 surnames, and more tentative
comments are made on a few others. The identification put forward
for CRUTCHLEY/CRITCHLEY was arrived at independently by
M. Pafford, and is included in an excellent paper on north
Staffordshire names cited below under BEARDMORE. Some of my

---

1 Oxford, 1988.

2 Counties cited here are pre-1974; abbreviations for counties are those usual in
English Place-Name Society volumes; and references such as PN Db are to the
Society's county surveys.

other proposals may be known to surname students. The only claim made here is that they were not easily available at the date of publication of the Hanks and Hodges *Dictionary*.

The 18 surnames of which locations are proffered are listed first, followed by a list of names which are located to regions but for which I have been unable to find a wholly convincing place of origin. Tentative comments are offered about some of these, and also for some items in the third list: habitation surnames which appear in the *Dictionary* without mention of any regional bias.

I hope that the provision of these lists will stimulate a search for origins by other place-name scholars. A number of explanations should come to light when we have detailed place-name surveys for such counties as Durham, Northumberland, Staffordshire, Norfolk, Suffolk, Lincolnshire and Hampshire. It will be noted that Nottinghamshire and Yorkshire have a relatively high number of unlocated names in spite of being covered by E.P.N.S. surveys; but the E.P.N.S. volumes up to 1943 were less detailed than later ones, and not so likely to include every lost or very small settlement.

It seems absurd not to be able to locate places such as Ayckbourn and Fairclough, which are limited by their vocabulary to definite parts of the country. Michael Pafford, in his paper on north Staffordshire names, says 'It is frustrating to be unable to locate the place from which a name as common as Beardmore derives and that is only one example'. We can only go on trying.

I am very well aware of the heavy criticism to which the Hanks and Hodges *Dictionary* has been subjected by surname specialists. It is, nevertheless, the largest collection of organized material available for study, and it would be good to feel that it can be used constructively, especially as there seems to be no prospect of a comprehensive surname dictionary which will satisfy more rigorous scholarly requirements.

1. Surnames whose place of origin is certainly or probably located.

ADSHEAD, Lancs. Adshead Green, SJ 868767, in Over Alderley township, Cheshire. PN Ch I, 100, gives early spelling *Addeshed* 1337 *et freq*.

ASBURY, West Midlands. Astbury, a parish, SJ 846616, Cheshire. PN Ch II, 268, gives early spellings. These are mostly *Astbury*, but also *Asbury* 1544, *Asbery* 1585, and this is the modern pronunciation.

BICKERDIKE, Yorks.   Perhaps a drainage channel near Bicker, Lincolnshire, or Byker, Northumberland.

BODLEY, West Midlands.   *Buddeley*, a lost settlement in Tabley Superior, Cheshire, is *Bodelegh* 1320 (PN Ch II, 60).

BRACKPOOL, Sussex.   This is very likely to be from Brapool Barn in Patcham. despite the doubts expressed in the *Dictionary* (PN Sx II, 294).

BRADY.   One source may be the district of Stafford anciently called *Broadeye*, on the western edge of the medieval town. This was *Brode Eye* in 1597 (A. J. Kettle, 'The early street-names of Stafford', *Essays presented to J. Sidney Horne*, ed. D. Johnson, *Transactions of the Staffordshire Historical and Civic Society*, 1974–76, 52).

BROOKFIELD, Lancs.   Brookfield is an extremely common minor name in Cheshire. Available forms are mostly nineteenth-century or modern, but Brookfield House in Nether Peover is *le Brocfeld* 13th (PN Ch II, 90).

CHALKLEY, S. England.   Perhaps Chalkley Farm in Hawkesbury, Gloucestershire, ST 767859, which is well-recorded from the twelfth century (PN Gl III, 29–30).

COCKCROFT, Yorks. and Lancs.   Cockcroft, SE 024179, in Rishworth township, West Riding. Early forms, from 1297, are all from surnames, but (as with BRACKPOOL *supra*) this does not invalidate the identification (PN WRY III, 73).

CRUTCHLEY, CRITCHLEY, West Midlands.   Croichlow Fold, SD 773145, near Holcombe Brook, S.W. of Ramsbottom, Lancashire. Forms given in E. Ekwall, *The Place-Names of Lancashire*, Manchester, 1922, 63, include *Cruchelowe* 1324, *Crychelow* 1525, *Croichelay* 1563. The name is *Crochley* on the nineteenth-century Ordnance Survey map.

FALKINGHAM, West Yorks.   Possibly a variant form of Folkingham, Lincolnshire.

GLAZEBROOK, Lancs. and Devon.   There is a Glaze Brook in Devon, a small tributary of the River Avon. Early forms given in PN D I, 6, are *Glas* 13th, *Glase, Glass* 1287, 1297. The full name, *Glazebrook*, is not noted until 1827, but may well have been current earlier. Glazebrook House is at SX 690591, but this is not shown on the nineteenth-century map, and may not be ancient.

HALSEY, near London.   The origin could be Alsa in Stanstead Mountfichet, Essex. Early forms in PN Ess 533 include *Alsieshey* 1268, *Alsesheye* 1284, *Alseywode* 1547. Alsa Lodge is at TL 517264. The name is *Assey* on the nineteenth-century map.

HUCKFIELD, Somerset.   Uckfield in Sussex would suit. It is *Huckefeld* 1308 (PN Sx II, 396).

KEENLYSIDE,   N. England.   Keenleyside Hill, NY 786550, is in County Durham, in West Allendale. The name is that of a house, and early spellings (*Kenleya* 1230, *Kynley* 1343, *Keneley* 1547, *Kinleyside* 1608) are given in A. Mawer, *The Place-Names of Northumberland and Durham*, Cambridge, 1920, 125.

LINDOP, Yorks.   Lindup Wood, SK255675, in Edensor, Derbyshire. Early spellings in PN Db 91 include Lindop *c.*1250, *Lindhop* 1306. The 1306 reference is to a wood, but earlier ones are from surnames, which indicates that there was a habitation.

ORMSHAW, Lancs.   Homeshaw Lane, SJ 755553, in Haslington, Cheshire. Early forms in PN Ch III, 13, include *Ormeshalgh* 1299, *Ormeshaae* 1521, from surnames.

PALETHORPE, Notts.   Perlethorpe SK 645710, PN Nt 91. There is a series of *Palethorp(e)*, *Palthorpe*, *Pailthorpe* forms from 1619–1775.

2.   Surnames which have a regional bias, but whose place of origin has not been located.

a.   North England

General to *North England* are AYCKBOURN, BLAMIRE, BRIGDEN, PADDON.

More precisely located are:

Lancashire: AINSCOUGH, ASHALL, BLACKHURST, CHARNLEY, CHESTWORTH, CORNALL, COULTHURST, FAIRCLOUGH, HEYWORTH, KERFOOT, MARSLAND, REDDINGTON, ROWBOTTOM, SEDDON, WINROW. For CHARNLEY, Charley in Leicestershire is formally suitable, but is probably too distant.

Northumberland: DRYDEN (also *Cumberland*), HAWDON, HESLOP, HINDMARSH, KIRKUP, SOULSBY. ROUTLEDGE is located to the Scottish border.

Yorkshire: AUDSLEY, AVEYARD, BEANLAND, BRETHERICK, CROSSFIELD, FEARNSIDE, GOSNEY, HEMINGWAY, LEAROYD, PALEY, THREAPLETON.

b. The Midlands

General to the *Midlands* is INSLEY. General to the *East Midlands* is HOPCROFT. There is a longer list for the *West Midlands*, and this is given at the end of this section.

More closely located surnames are:

Lincolnshire: CHESELDINE, PULVERTOFT.

Northamptonshire: DUNKLEY.

Nottinghamshire: BEARDSLEY, BOWLEY, BRENTNALL, CALLADINE, HEMSTOCK, HUFFTON, REDGATE, SMEDLEY, SULLEY. For HUFFTON, Uftonfields in South Wingfield, Derbyshire, might be worth considering. This is *Ufton(e)* from the late twelfth century on (PN Db 336), and there could have been a form with inorganic *H-*. As regards REDGATE, Nottinghamshire has Redgate Wood in Kirklington, but the name has not been noted earlier than 1826, so may not be ancient (PN Nt 170).

Staffordshire: BEARDMORE, BILLINGHAM. M. Pafford, 'North Staffordshire names', *Staffordshire Studies*, 2, 1989–90, 67, instances BEARDMORE as a place-name which he has tried in vain to locate.

West Midlands: BADHAM, BARNFIELD, BASTABLE, BLACKHAM, BREAKWELL, CHATTAWAY, DUGMORE, EDGINGTON, HARTLAND, HAWKESFORD, LITTLEFORD, LONGMORE, MARKLEW, MASEFIELD, MAYBURY, NORTHALL, PITTAWAY. Two of these, BARNFIELD and LONGMORE, are common minor names. There does not appear to be a West Midland Barnfield for which early documentation has been found. Longmore Farm in Solihull, however, is recorded *c.*1240 (PN Wa 74). There is a Littleford in Newent, Gloucestershire, but no early references have been noted.

c.   East Anglia

General to *East Anglia* are CUDMORE/CUTMORE, GREENACRE, RODWELL. GARNHAM is found in *Suffolk* and north *Essex*, GOREHAM in *Norfolk*.

d.   South England

HOCKEY, HOLTHAM/HOLTUM, OUSLEY, REDWOOD, SUMMERHILL are general.

More closely located are:

> *Hampshire:* HOLDRUP.
>
> *Surrey:* SPAUGHTON.
>
> *Wiltshire:* TITFORD.
>
> SILVERTON occurs in *Kent* and *Sussex*, WORSFOLD in *Kent*, *Surrey* and *Sussex*.

e.   South-west England

General to the area are HONEYFIELD, NORGROVE, SCANTLEBURY, SCUDAMORE.

More closely located are:

> *Bristol:* BRESSINGTON, HEADFORD, SILVERTHORN.
>
> *Devon:* BALKWELL, BUNNEY, CHISWELL, GREET (also *Cornwall*), LUXMORE, RADMORE. There are several places called Greet, the Gloucestershire example being the nearest to Devon. Bunny (Nottinghamshire) seems too far away for BUNNEY, and the same objection applies to Radmore, Staffordshire.

3.   Unlocated surnames which do not have a regional distribution.

BOLTWOOD, BONHAM, BRAMWELL, BRAXTON, BUNCOMBE, BURCHFIELD, CANTWELL, CARSLAKE, CHATFIELD, CROXFORD, FLEETWOOD, FOXWELL, GARFIELD, GARWOOD, HAYHOE, HURFORD, LETHABY, LOVEGROVE, LUXFORD, OSCROFT, OSWELL, RACKLEY, SELFRIDGE, SLADEN, SNELLGROVE,

SWANSBOROUGH, TAPPENDEN, TILDEN, TISDALL, WADHAM, WEBSDALE, WEDGEWOOD, WELLESLEY, WHEATON. For LUXFORD, Lostford in Shropshire might be worth considering; *Loskesford* is a frequent early spelling, with occasional *Luskesford*. For OSWELL, Hanks and Hodges quote an early form Wyswall, which could be from Wirswall in Cheshire. Wirswall has a spelling *Wyswall(e)* t.Hy 3 (PN Ch III, 112). The *Wyswall* family were in Shropshire in the fifteenth century, and Wirswall is on the Shropshire/Cheshire border. More information is needed about the overall distribution of the surname. For WHEATON, M. Pafford, *loc. cit.*, 75, suggests derivation from the affix to Wheaton Aston, Staffordshire. Aston Eyre in Shropshire was also *Wheaton Aston* until 1695 (PN Sa I, 24), but it is perhaps unlikely that either place would give rise to the surname, since there is no sign of the affix replacing the place-name (as sometimes happens with manorial affixes).

Plate 1 — 'an oak, whose boughs were moss'd with age'
(Shakespeare, As You Like It, *Act IV, Scene II)*
an old Arden oak-tree; Crowley's Oak, Ullenhall.

V

—————— •◄⠬⠯⠳►• ——————

Names and Settlement in the Warwickshire Arden

DELLA HOOKE

Introduction

ARDEN IS THE NAME traditionally given to the higher part of the old
county of Warwickshire which lies to the north-west of the river
Avon. The name is derived from Celtic *ardu*, 'high, steep' land,[1] and
refers to the two upland massifs which lie to the west and east of the
Tame-Blythe valley.

The western upland is largely composed of Mercia Mudstone
which produces heavy, red-coloured clay soils, but which is
interbedded with Triassic sandstones which frequently give rise to a
more broken terrain. Large areas are also overlain with glacial sands
and gravels. This area is at its highest along the north-western
boundary of the old county, where the land rises towards the
Birmingham Plateau, reaching 165m. near the western corner of
Tanworth-in-Arden and 174m. in Sutton Coldfield. To the east of
the Tame-Blythe valley, the uplifted horst of the East Warwickshire
Plateau brings Upper Coal Measure and Permian beds to the surface
which again reach 177m. in Bentley and 181m. in Meriden. It is
place-name evidence which helps to identify the region which was
already referred to as *Eardene* by 1088, reaching at least from
Tanworth-in-Arden on the west to Weston-in-Arden in Bulkington
on the east, and from Yardley on the north to Henley-in-Arden on
the south.[2]

---

1 A. Mawer and F. M. Stenton, *The Place-Names of Warwickshire*, English Place-Name
  Society, vol. XIII, Cambridge, 1936, pp.11–12.

2 *Ibid.*, p.12.

By 1148, the region was being referred to as the 'Forest of Arden' and there are slight indications that there may indeed have been a legal forest here in the eleventh and early thirteenth century (see below). Although medieval forests were not necessarily heavily wooded, all the traditions of Arden seem to suggest ample woodland interspersed with more open areas of heathland, pasture and arable. Shakespeare conjures up pictures of an ancient wooded landscape frequented by huntsmen in his *As You Like It* (*c*.1596–1600) with his oak 'whose boughs were moss'd with age', or

> 'whose antique root peeps out
> Upon the brook that brawls along this wood.'

But like the 'shady groves' and 'rough woodlands' of Michael Drayton's *Poly-Olbion* (1612), which gave shelter to the hart and hind, much of this was by then largely literary exaggeration. Woodland was not absent but it was more the tree growth of a *bocage* type countryside which appears in the writings of Leland and Camden in the sixteenth century,[3] with trees deliberately grown in the hedgerows of the small irregular fields of the region.

Place-names

It is probably the incidence of the *lēah* place-name, indicative of a wooded countryside, which gives the earliest secure evidence of the nature of Arden. In time, environmental evidence may cast more light upon the type and intensity of land use in the region in the prehistoric period but at present such investigations have been limited to a number of unrepresentative valley locations. Archaeological evidence is dominated by the presence of tile and pottery kilns which are likely to have been located in a managed woodland environment. *Lēah* was, however, widely used in the eighth and following centuries for settlements in a wooded landscape, the word having originally meant 'wood'. It may be suspected that it carried some intimation of the economic usage of land and a meaning of 'wood-pasture' frequently seems to be suggested (Appendix 1). This may also have been the major use of the woodland recorded in quantity in Arden in *Domesday Book*, which should probably be thought of as wood-pasture rather than uninterrupted woodland, much of it open woodland

---

3 L. Toulmin Smith, ed., *The Itinerary of John Leland in or about the years 1535–1543*, London, 1906–10; W. Camden, *Britannia*, 1586 (1607).

heavily interspersed with fields given over to pastoral activity (Figure 1).

In the early years of the Anglo-Saxon kingdoms, western Arden, which is to be the subject of this paper, had been a frontier zone, for the boundary of the kingdom of the Hwicce passed through the heart of the area, the diocesan boundary preserving its course. Indeed, it may have been a much more ancient frontier.[4] Woodland was present along much of the Hwiccan boundary and may have been deliberately preserved in such a locality, as on the bounds of many early German kingdoms. The soils of the Mercia Mudstone are more acidic than the clays found in the south of the county and although large areas are overlain by glacial drift this is of a variable but often infertile nature. Soil-type, then, was a contributory factor in the different development of Arden and Feldon.

The region appears to have served as a zone of seasonal pasture and woodland resources, and holdings here were to remain linked to manors in the more intensively developed arable regions of the county: the Avon valley and the Feldon to the south. These links were perpetuated in manorial and ecclesiastical dependencies: Nuthurst was granted in the late seventh or early eighth century as a wooded estate with Shottery near Stratford, Tanworth was a dependent manor of Brailes in the south of the county in 1086, and Bushwood in Lapworth remained part of the manor of Old Stratford. Other estates remained chapelries of mother churches established in the south of the county or formed detached parts of southern hundreds. The date of origin of such links between Arden and Feldon remains unknown but it is not inconceivable that such an arrangement had developed by the late Iron Age, a period when woodland is now known to have been in scarce supply.

The links between the Arden and the Feldon were also perpetuated in a north-west–south-east orientation of routeways which has survived, in part, to the present day. At some stage, some of these may even have functioned as droveways, as in the Weald.[5] Parish

4 W. J. Ford, 'Settlement patterns in the central region of the Warwickshire Avon', in P. H. Sawyer, ed., *Medieval Settlement, Continuity and Change*, London, 1976, pp.274–94; D. Hooke, *The Anglo-Saxon Landscape, The Kingdom of the Hwicce*, Manchester, 1985.

5 A. Everitt, *Continuity and Colonization: The Evolution of Kentish Settlement*, Leicester, 1986.

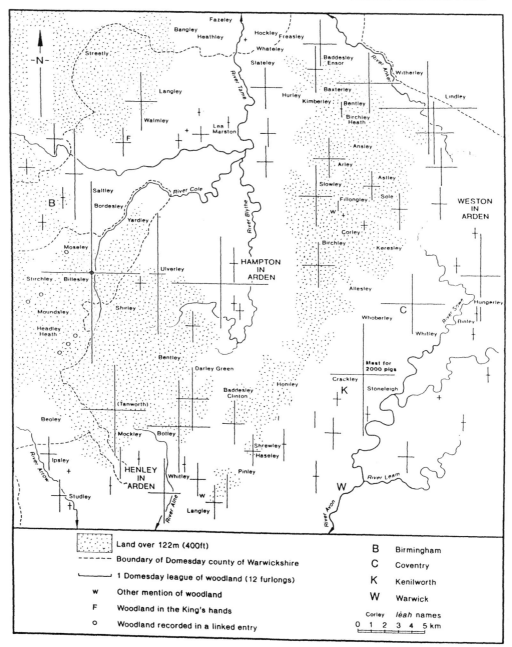

Figure 1 — Domesday woodland in Arden.

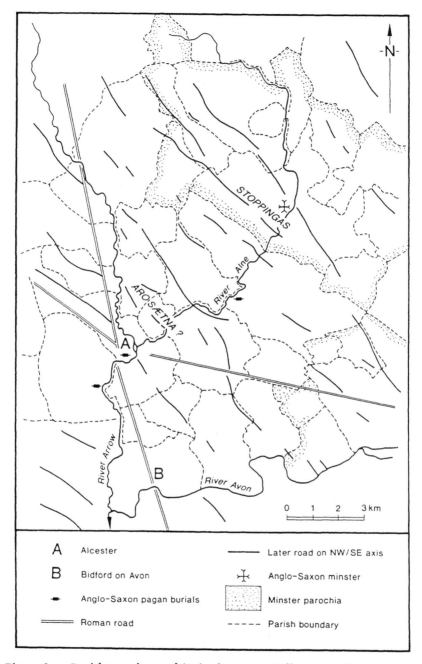

Figure 2 — Parishes and parochia in the Arrow Valley in Anglo-Saxon times.

boundaries follow a similar orientation. However, the focus obviously altered according to the needs of the age. At an early stage of the Anglo-Saxon take-over, the Roman town of Alcester seems to have remained a focal point. Place-name chronology has been rightly questioned in recent years but here an *-ingas* place-name is found in a position secondary to a primary area of pagan burial (Figure 2), a hierarchy suggested by several recent studies.[6] Thus, in the early eighth century a minster was established at Wootton Wawen which was said to lie in the *regio* of 'the territory which from ancient times is called the Stoppingas'[7] and the *parochia* of that minster, according to later ecclesiastical evidence, extended across the headwaters of the river Alne (Figure 2). It seems that at an early stage this territory may have been allotted to a group of incoming Anglo-Saxons. The folk, of whatever race, who occupied Arrow-Alne heartland may have been known as the *Arosætna*.[8]

Saints' names

In Kent, Alan Everitt has examined church dedications to investigate settlement chronology.[9] It is well known that dedications can be changed, but, in Warwickshire, as elsewhere, they can also be used to suggest settlement hierarchy (rather than stages of colonization). Again, they confirm the secondary nature of the Arden area. In Hwiccan territory 'primary' dedications are often to St Peter, as in the cathedral church at the seat of the bishopric in Worcester, a church of seventh-century foundation. This is the dedication at Wootton Wawen (Figure 3). Also within this group are what may be thought of as secondary dedications to St Mary, for the church established alongside St Peter's at Worcester soon after AD 960 was dedicated to St Mary. These dedications are, for instance, found on

6 J. McN. Dodgson, 'The significance of the distribution of the English place-name in *-ingas, -inga-* in south-east England', *Medieval Archaeology*, 10, 1966, pp.1–29.

7 P. H. Sawyer, *Anglo-Saxon Charters, an Annotated List and Bibliography*, London, 1968, S.94; W. de Gray Birch, *Cartularium Saxonicum*, 1885–99, B.157.

8 W. de G. Birch, *ibid.*, B.297, B.297A, B.297B; W. Davies, 'I. Tribal hidage: the text', in W. Davies and H. Vierck, 'The contexts of Tribal Hidage: social aggregates and settlement patterns', *Fruhmittelalterliche Studien*, 8, 1974, pp.224–36.

9 A. Everitt, *op. cit.*, pp.225–58.

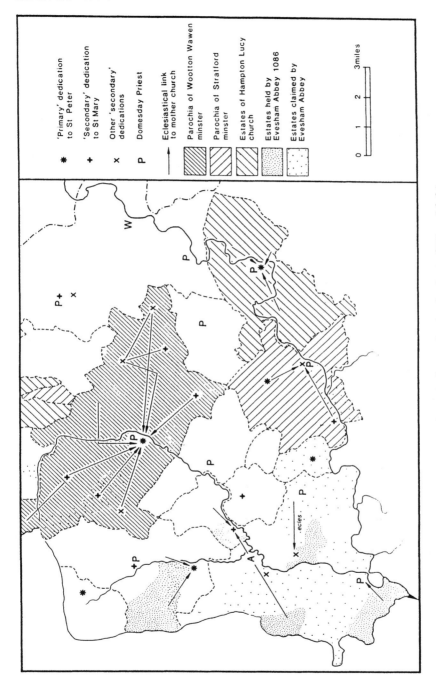

Figure 3 — Ecclesiastical organization in Central Warwickshire.

the margins of the Wootton Wawen *parochia* where daughter churches might first be established. Another band of similar dedications penetrates the area from the Blythe valley. Within Arden, however, are found the dedications of 'wilderness parishes', including, for instance, those of St John the Baptist (at Honiley, Knowle, Henley, Berkswell, Beausale and Aston Cantlow), or to the various hermit saints like St Leonard and St Giles (Appendix 2). Both the latter are particularly appropriate in Arden, for St Giles is said to have offered sanctuary to a stag wounded by a hunting party while St Leonard (a French saint) is said to have cured a queen taken ill while on a hunting foray in the forest[10] At Spernall, in the Arrow valley, both saints are honoured, for a daughter church of Coughton was established by the twelfth century and dedicated to St Leonard, while another chapel dedicated to St Giles was associated with a small nunnery granted land near the northern parish boundary before 1198.

There are obvious anomolies in the pattern. At the focal point of Alcester, where one would expect every indication of an early minster and an early dedication, there is a notable gap. There is nearby, however, an *ecles* name indicative of a surviving Romano-British Christian community and a dedication to St Milburga, a Mercian princess, while Alcester appears to have been 'the celebrated place called Alne' at which an ecclesiastical council was held in AD 709.[11] There are primary dedications just beyond the royal estates of Alcester and Bidford but none within and the explanation for this must lie in the success of Evesham Abbey, beside the Avon some miles to the south-west, to draw to itself estates in this territory. The reason for Alcester's apparent denegation is unknown but there are legends of the townspeople's refusal to listen to the preachings of Ecgwine, the bishop of Worcester who founded the abbey at Evesham in the eighth century. Interestingly, the area which seems to have been immediately dependent upon Alcester can be shown from Domesday assessments to have been very close to one hundred hides while the Wotton Wawen *parochia* is only just short of being a 50-hide unit (49 hides and 12 acres in 1086, the 12 acres being part of the manor of Oldberrow, in Arden).

10 F. Arnold Forster, *Studies in Church Dedications or England's Patron Saints*, 1899, vol. 2, pp.46–51, 110–13.

11 A. W. Haddan and W. Stubbs, *Councils and Ecclesiastical Documents relating to Great Britain and Ireland*, 3, Oxford, 1871, pp.281, 283.

Settlement names in charters

The claims of the church of Evesham extended to Oldberrow, an estate within the *parochia* of Wootton Wawen, which Evesham was to hold at the time of the Domesday survey. At that time the estate consisted of only 12 acres of arable land but with two pigmen and a league of woodland.[12] The spurious charter of Evesham claims that the abbey acquired the estate in AD 709 and is accompanied by a boundary clause of probable ninth-century date.[13] The charter bounds suggest that the abbey was claiming not only the estate of Oldberrow but the demesne land of Tanworth and an area of ancient woodland called 'the old wood' at Mockley in Wootton Wawen itself (Figure 4). A 'broad road' followed the previously mentioned north-west–south-east orientation on the southern boundary of the estate, a routeway which can be traced from the Roman Ryknield Street to the river Avon and beyond.[14] There is also mention of a *scirhylt* which may refer to a wood near the boundary of the kingdom.[15]

The charter bounds also refer to a probable settlement, *wynes wyrðe*, which may have been a farmstead. The whole of this region can be shown to have been an area of scattered farmsteads or hamlets in the later Anglo-Saxon period,[16] but near Tanworth there seems to have been a cluster of 'worth' settlements, although only this one was actually recorded in documents by 1086 (Figure 5). There was also a *cot* settlement, *Bickerscote*, in the same cluster. Of these, only Tanworth, the manorial nucleus established at the end of a prominent ridge, was to survive as a hamlet, for Bickerscote is a single farm and

---

12 *Domesday Book*, 23, J. Plaister, ed., 'Warwickshire', 1976, EW, 6.

13 P. H. Sawyer, *op. cit.*, B.124; H. P. R. Finberg, *The Early Charters of the West Midlands*, Leicester, 1961, no. 204, p.88.

14 D. Hooke, 'The Oldberrow charter and boundary clause', *West Midlands Archaeological News Sheet*, 1978, pp.81–3; D. Hooke, 'The reconstruction of ancient routeways', *The Local Historian*, 12, 1977, pp.212–20.

15 Old English scīr, 'district, division'; the same names occur in Leigh near the western boundary of the kingdom (P. H. Sawyer, *op. cit.*, S.1437).

16 D. Hooke, 'Village development in the West Midlands', D. Hooke, ed., *Medieval Villages, a Review of Current Work*, Oxford University Committee of Archaeology, Monograph no. 5, Oxford, 1985, pp.125–54.

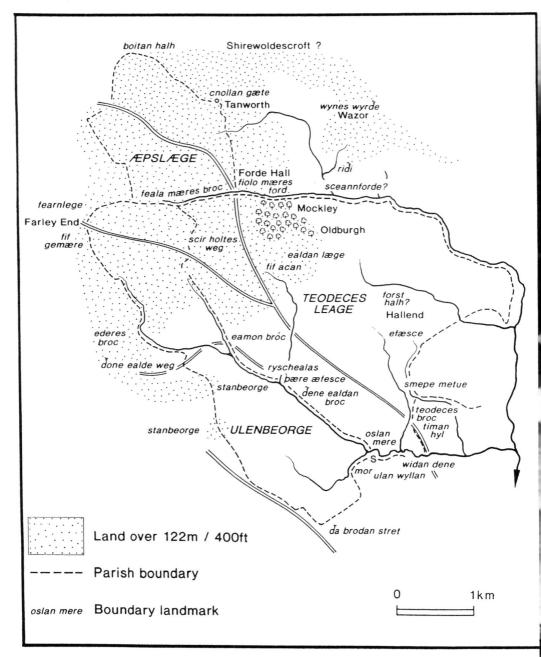

Figure 4 — Anglo-Saxon charter evidence in Oldberrow and Ullenhall, Warwickshire.

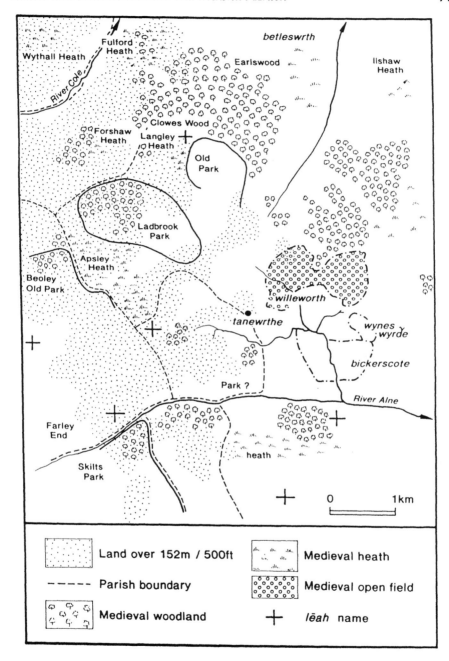

Figure 5 — Early settlement centres in Tanworth-in-Arden, Warwickshire.

willeworth and *wynes wyrðe* now mere field-names.[17] Only Tanworth was to have a small open-field system by the twelfth century, one which had extended over the area of *willeworth*. Beyond this nucleus seems to have been the wood-pasture of the Domesday survey, for the nearest Old English settlement names known are Betlesworth and Cheswick in the north of the parish. There are few surviving pre-Conquest charters for this area so that this one casts valuable light upon the earliest stages of medieval settlement evolution in western Arden. *Worð* names are not uncommon in Arden and show an increased frequency in the more wooded regions of the West Midlands generally.[18]

Name survival

The ability to use early-recorded names to study the evolution of land use and settlement patterns inevitably depends upon name survival. A surprising number of landmarks used in the boundary clauses of pre-Conquest charters can be accurately located today because they have given rise to minor place-names or field-names. A comprehensive study of the Worcestershire charters has enabled such name survival to be tabulated and analysed. A frustrating situation often exists, however, when a name can be traced through into the medieval period but is then lost before subsequent cartographic evidence can clarify its precise location. The *cisburne* of a possible eleventh-century boundary clause of Hallow in Worcestershire, for instance, was still recorded as the *chiseburn* in 1240,[19] but it is no longer certain which stream bore this name.[20] Similarly, two *stanbeorge* features in the pre-Conquest Oldberrow boundary clause noted earlier gave rise to two distinct field-names 'Bradbarwe' and 'Stanbarwe'

---

17 B. K. Roberts, 'The Forest of Arden, Warwickshire, 1086–1350', unpublished University of Birmingham Ph.D. thesis, 1965; Tanworth-in-Arden Tithe Award and Plan, 1839, Warwickshire County Record Office.

18 D. Hooke, *Anglo-Saxon Landscape of the West Midlands: The Charter Evidence*, British Archaeological Reports, 95, Oxford, 1981, pp.294–6.

19 A. Mawer and F. M. Stenton, *The Place-Names of Worcestershire*, English Place-Name Society, 4, Cambridge, 1927, p.129, n.1.

20 D. Hooke, *Worcestershire Anglo-Saxon Charter-Bounds*, Woodbridge, 1990, p.109.

recorded in 1365,[21] but only one such name, 'Great Stanberries', can be located on nineteenth-century plans,[22] although both locations can be identified with reasonable certainty.

There are three surviving boundary clauses of pre-Conquest origin for the core area of Arden under discussion here. The Oldberrow clause noted above covers an area somewhat more extensive than the present parish while the estates of Aspley and *Teodeces læge* remained recognizable divisions within the large minster parish of Wootton Wawen. The boundary clauses name some 52 different landmarks. Of these, however, only four survived as identifiable names into the nineteenth century. In addition to the Stone barrow noted above, *ulan bearhe*, 'Ula's barrow', may even then have been a reference to the settlement core of Oldberrow itself and *wynes wyrðe*, also noted above, was probably also a settlement. *Fearnlege*, 'the ferny wood or clearing', noted on the boundaries of both Oldberrow and Aspley, gave rise to the name Farley's End, recorded on Henry Beighton's map of Warwickshire published in 1725, and a field-name 'Farley Field' is recorded in the Beoley Tithe Award for 1843. The wood was probably an extensive one which lay near the north-western corner of Oldberrow but within Beoley parish.

Although a full study of the Warwickshire charters is not yet complete,[23] it seems that name survival was probably greater in open-field regions where furlong names were passed down in the manorial courts for hundreds of years. The names of the small enclosed fields which covered most of Arden were readily altered upon change of ownership, and, on the south-western fringes of Arden, in the Arrow valley, much enclosure had occurred piecemeal by the sixteenth and seventeenth centuries, leaving few detailed records of early furlong names. Indeed, in Coughton, where the open fields survived into the late seventeenth century, even the names of the open fields themselves changed in the middle of that century.[24]

21 Archer Deeds, Shakespeare Birthplace Trust Record Office, Stratford-upon-Avon.

22 'Plans and areas of estates of Francis Holyoake Esq.', 1820, 1821, Warwickshire County Record Office, CR 1094.

23 D. Hooke, *Warwickshire Anglo-Saxon Charter-Bounds*, (in preparation).

24 Coughton, Manorial Court Rolls, Warwickshire County Record Office.

Settlement names and surnames

The presence of much early manorial waste and wood in the Arden region helped to produce many of the features still found in its present landscape, among them the predominantly dispersed pattern of settlement.

The evolution of medieval settlement patterns can be traced rather more fully in the parish of Tanworth because numerous medieval land charters survive. Grants of land were being made by the Earl of Warwick, who held the manor, to colonists throughout the twelfth and thirteenth centuries. From footholds in the open-field core they were able to enclose land on the margins of the woodland and waste, specifically as 'new land', heath (*brueria*, especially before 1240) and waste (*vasta*, especially after 1250), and 'new assart', and eventually to consolidate their holdings.[25] Roberts has been able to trace the holdings of the Cherlecote and Wistanscroft/Wystanescroft families whose names suggest that they had been attracted to the parish from the Avon valley, from Charlecote and Bishopton, both near Stratford.[26] This pattern is common in other Arden parishes, found, for instance, in Hampton-in-Arden and Little Packington. Such holdings displayed, until recently, a pattern of small irregular fields, although woodland survived on the plateau to the north-west until much later times (Figure 6). Initially suggestive of assarting, such small fields continued to serve the requirements of a predominantly pastoral economy throughout the later Middle Ages and, in part, survived later agricultural change.

Much of the rest of the Tanworth parish-area seems to have been occupied by degraded woodland, although it is not clear whether any of this land could have fallen into disuse after cultivation in an earlier period. The place-name 'shaw', usually taken to refer to 'a small or narrow wood', seems to indicate a mixture of rough grassland and woodland over the drift-based soils of the plateau, giving rise to the names recorded in the twelfth–fourteenth centuries: Forshaw, Aldershaw, Fenshaw, Ilshaw, and Hawkshaw. These may have been belts of woodland left separating major enclaves of

25 B. K. Roberts, *op. cit.*

26 B. K. Roberts, *ibid.*; D. Hooke, 'Village development', p.143.

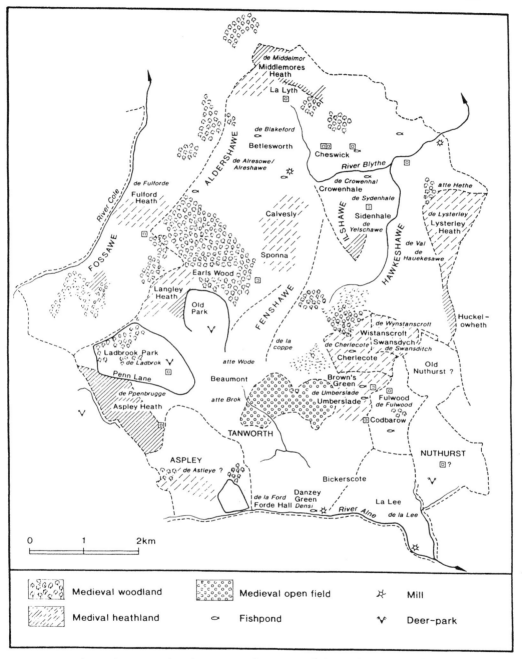

Figure 6 — Locational surnames in Tanworth-in-Arden, Warwickshire.

clearance similar to those found in the Weald. Heathland was also recorded and Aspley, Langley, Listerly, Fulford, Hockley and Middlemore Heaths lay near the boundaries of the parish and may have represented the climax vegetation of particularly gravelly areas. Eventually all this land was to be enclosed and it was probably the featureless nature of the drift-covered plateau, together with the relatively late date of much of its enclosure, that produced the pattern of small but more regular fields still characteristic today. The north-west–south-east road pattern is clearly visible, but the apparent orientation of much of the fieldscape is likely to have developed in relation to this pre-existing road pattern rather than any underlying one of ancient enclosure.

Another feature characteristic of Arden which reflects the availability of waste is the manorial deer-park. Arden may indeed have been a royal forest for a time after the Norman Conquest, for two areas of manorial woodland had been 'taken into the hands of the king' by 1086 and one of them, at least, is likely to have lain within Arden.[27] The Forest of Feckenham, mostly within Worcestershire, also reached eastwards as far as the river Arrow in 1300.[28] Although the 'Forest of Arden' of Drayton and Shakespeare may have been little more than a folk-memory by the seventeenth century, there is an earlier reference to it in a thirteenth-century saint's life.[29]

Royal forest was not to be maintained and manorial lords were enclosing private parks upon their demesnes in the twelfth, thirteenth and fourteenth centuries. They were constrained from enclosing so much waste that it would be detrimental to their tenants' requirements for common pasture, but the traditional 'law of Arden' enabled them to enclose that which was superfluous to these needs.[30] Deer-parks were particularly frequent in this region and on the manors further to the south. In Tanworth, Ladbrook Park had

---

27 D. Hooke, 'The Warwickshire Arden: the evolution and future of an historic landscape', *Landscape History*, 10, 1988, pp.51–9; *Domesday Book*, pp.6, 8, 27.3.

28 J. West, 'The forest offenders of medieval Worcestershire', *Folk Life*, vol. 2, 1964, pp.80–115.

29 F. Arnold-Forster, *op. cit.*, p.158.

30 D. M. Stenton, ed., *Rolls of the Justices in Eyre for Lincolnshire (1218–19) and Worcestershire (1221)*, Selden Society, vol. 53, 1934, pp.lxvi–ii, 448–9.

been enclosed by *c*.1350 and the demesne 'Old Park' by 1372.[31] Within these parks, woodland was often conserved and many such woods have managed to survive. The duties of caring for a park gave rise to a byname indicating such an occupation and in 1327[32] William *le parcare* was probably employed on the lord's park in Alcester which had been enclosed from Alcester Heath once the area had been released from the king's forest of Feckenham. 'Parker' surnames are recorded at the same date in Upton Haselor nearby and in Weddington, Ryton in Bulkington and in Coventry, in the north-east of the county, while the Henry Parker at Kenilworth was no doubt associated with the royal parks which surrounded Kenilworth Castle.

Within Arden, many tenants were able to attain a high level of prosperity in the climate of manorial encouragement of colonization of the waste, low labour dues and a thriving land economy. Their farmsteads were frequently moated, the moat undoubtedly an expression of status as much as a functional feature. In some parishes grants of arable and waste were made to small monastic communities, such as the nunnery of Pinley founded in Rowington *c*.1125. Such settlements formed the chief components of the dispersed settlement pattern. But additional settlement throughout these parishes is attested by thirteenth-century bynames. Obviously people could move within manors and from manor to manor, like the Ladbrokes (a village-name in the Feldon) and the Cherlecotes of Tanworth, but sources such as land charters and tax assessments record the names of many other inhabitants whose earliest holdings can be accurately located (Figure 6).[33] Many of the families took their names from local features (Appendices 3 and 4). In the medieval period new settlement served to intensify the typically dispersed nature of the settlement pattern. The road pattern is also often irregular as it links these scattered holdings.

It is clear that minor settlement sites were often much less stable than the more established holdings and the less wealthy members of the population, too, were apt to move around, especially in the

---

31 L. Cantor, *The Medieval Parks of England. A Gazetteer*, Loughborough, 1983, p.78.

32 Lay Subsidy Roll for 1327, *Midland Record Society, Supplement to Vol. V*, ed. E. A. Fry, 1899–1902.

33 See p.81.

rather freer society which characterized woodland regions.[34] Nevertheless, there seems to be a reality in locational bynames which renders them useful to settlement analysis.

Many medieval bynames indicate people who lived near woodland. Such names recorded in Studley, for instance, in 1327,[35] include Roger *atte Hurste* and Alexander *de la Holte*. Others indicative of employment associated with the exploitation of woodland resources include William *de Collehurste* recorded in Spernall and Walter *de Colehurste* in the adjacent parish of Great Alne, suggesting woods used by colliers for charcoal. This particular block of woodland lay in the north of Great Alne parish near the Spernall boundary and in part survives today. In the same parish, Robert *le Wodeward* was distinguished by his occupation from Robert *atte Wod* and Robert *atte Heth*. Of 44 names related to vegetation type entered in the 1327 lay subsidy (Appendix 3), 30 incorporated woodland terms, with *hurst* the most commonly occurring, and *lēah*, wood and *sceaga* also each used in at least four different names. Heath occurred in seven names.

Locational names also helped to distinguish the inhabitants of a parish and among these hill-names occur most frequently in 1327, with 17 such names recorded in the study area, indicated by the terms *hyll, copp, cnoll* and *hōh*, but with marsh-names a close second (15), using the terms *mōr, mersc* and *fenn*. Such features would have been prominent and well known within the individual parish. Other features referred to in 1327 include valleys (five times), springs (three times), nooks (*halh*) (five times), brooks (six times), fords (four times) and sundry features such as dykes, gates, parks and lanes. In general, buildings are seldom referred to in such a context, although one barn is noted and three mills.

Another feature typical of the Arden settlement pattern is the cluster of cottages which is often found alongside a patch of former common waste. Bynames denoting people living beside greens are found already in the 1327 and 1332 lay subsidy rolls, with William *atte Grene* in Bearley, John *atte Grene* in Wilmcote Parva and Margery *atte Grene* in Aston Cantlow.[36] By the fifteenth century small tenant

---

34 C. Dyer, *Hanbury: Settlement and Society in a Woodland Landscape*, Leicester, 1991, pp.52–8.

35 Lay Subsidy Roll for 1327, *op. cit.*

36 *The Lay Subsidy Roll for Warwickshire of 6 Edward III (1332)*, trans. and ed., W. F. Carter, Dugdale Society, vol. VI, London, 1926.

farmers and others had built their houses beside the waste, although in later times many such dwellings were occupied by the landless labourers and the village poor. Patches of waste often lingered at crossroads or alongside the wide trackways which were common before the nineteenth century. Although many such cottages were deserted after the final enclosure of the waste, many survive and are again characteristic of the region, bearing such names as . . . End or . . . Green. Often such settlements adopted the name of the family who lived there and such a name might change several times over the centuries. Mere Green in Morton Bagot, for instance, so-called in 1714, was to become known as Woodwards Green in 1807 and Chester's Green a little later, a T. Chester having been the occupant of one of the houses in 1807.[37]

Frequently the labourers and small farmers who lived on the greens carried out ancillary trades such as shoe-making or participated in cottage industries. Needle-making was, for instance, common in such communities throughout the seventeenth and eighteenth centuries, especially in areas near Redditch where the trade may have been introduced by the monks of Bordesley Abbey. It is not clear, however, whether it was this trade which gave rise to the name 'Needlers End' in Balsall. Tainters Green in Solihull, *teynto(u)rs grene* in 1332, is likely to have obtained its name from the practice of stretching cloth to dry after it had been fulled and Tilehouse Green in Solihull, *tylhous ovene* in 1375,[38] may refer to the making of tiles there, a trade again carried out locally in many parishes using local clays and the readily available wood to fuel the ovens or kilns.

Many green names reflect vegetation type, but as they frequently bear the township or parish name this is not always indicative of immediate land use. Nevertheless, an overwhelming number of the vegetation names are related to woodland and suggest that the patches of waste left at parish margins, for instance, may not always have been open heathland. Such names include those derived from OE *lēah*, 'wood', later 'clearing in a wood', such as Lee Green in Solihull or Lye Green in Claverdon, *sceaga*, 'shaw, a small, narrow wood', such as Forshaw Heath in Solihull, as well as direct references

37 D. Hooke, *The Arrow Valley Project I. Morton Bagot, a Parish Survey*, 'Part 1: The landscape, a topographical study', University of Birmingham School of Geography Occasional Paper No. 24, Birmingham, 1987, pp.60–2.

38 A. Mawer and F. M. Stenton, *op. cit.*, pp.74–5.

to tree species such as limes and hazels (Appendix 4). Indeed, a number of nineteenth-century commons, then open grassland, bore wood-names, such as Chessett's Wood in Knowle or Earls Wood in Tanworth, and early maps and records confirm that they had once been wooded. In 1628 the common in Shrewley parish was described as having 'many hundred trees therein, whereof the inhabitants take great benefit in time of mast'.[39] Others on lighter drift soils may well have been open heathland. Of the 32 vegetation names given to greens which are listed within the study area in *The Place-Names of Warwickshire*, 17 indicate the presence of woodland, using the terms *lēah, sceaga, wudu* and *holt* most frequently, while nine are heath names.

Increased settlement around the greens and consequent grazing pressure undoubtedly led to the destruction of scrub and woodland in the later historical period and few greens were anything more than rough pasture by the nineteenth century. Towards the end of the period of Parliamentary Enclosure there was increased pressure for their enclosure, some of it based on the desire to regulate settlement by the 'undesirable poor'. Few commons escaped destruction, many of them simply absorbed into adjacent land holdings. A few of the crossroad greens were not so easily taken in and Lye Green in Claverdon remains an example of this kind of green while Yarningale Common in the same parish is a larger unenclosed area, now reverting to a brushwood cover.

The visible landscape of Arden still displays many of the features which have been shaped by centuries of changing land use, particularly by the adaption of a well-wooded environment to a primarily farmed landscape, albeit one in which pastoral farming has usually predominated. Inevitably, much of the landscape today is overlain by the effects of twentieth-century urban pressures — by long-distance roads, commuter settlement and 'urban-fringe' type of developments — but the atmosphere of 'old Arden' has by no means been destroyed. Beyond the visible landscape, however, the minor names of the region also provide a reliable record of the evolution of settlement and land use, captured, for all able to interpret them, on the modern map.

---

39 S. C. Ratcliff and H. C. Johnson, eds., *Warwick County Records I: Quarter Sessions Order Book – Easter 1625 to Trinity 1637*, Warwick, 1935, p.57.

APPENDIX 1

Lēah-names in western Arden and the Arrow valley

Lēah-name	*Earliest spelling*	*Parish-name*	*Meaning*
Vegetation names			
Bentley	*bentley heth* C.15	Solihull	*bēonet*, 'bent-grass'
Haseley	*haseleia* 1086	Haseley	*hæsel*, 'hazel'
Hytall Lane	*haiteley* C.13	Solihull	*hæðiht*, 'heathy'
Kixley	*kyckesleye* C.14	Knowle	?ME *kyx*, 'hollow-stalked' plant (e.g. cow parsley)
Ragley	*rageleia* 1086	Arrow	?**ragge*, 'moss, lichen
Ulverley	*ulverlei* 1086	Solihull	ME *holvyr*, 'holly'
Weethley	*withelega* 1086	Weethley	*wiðig*, 'withy'
Animal and bird names			
Buckley	*buckelye* C.13	Beaudesert	*bucca*, 'bucks' (gen. pl.) (or Bucca?)
Darley	*derley* C.13	Knowle	*dēor*, 'deer, wild animal'
Hullies (FN)	*ulelega* C.13	Lapworth	*ūle*, 'owl'
Honiley	*hunilege* C.13	Honiley	*hunig*, 'honey' (or Hūna?)
Rookley (FN)	*rokeley* C.15	Tanworth	?*hrōc*, 'rook' (or Hrōc?)
Studley	*stodlei* 1086	Studley	*stōd*, 'stud (of horses)'
Shape, location or physical characteristic			
Brownley	*brunele* C.13	Beausale	?*brūn*, 'brown'
Bearley	*burlei* 1086	Bearley	?*burh*, 'fortification'
Crowley	*creule* C.13	Wootton Wawen	**creowel*, 'fork (of a road)'
Henley	*henle* C.12	Wootton Wawen	*hēah*, 'high'

Langley	*longgele* C.14	Solihull	*lang*, 'long'
Langley	*longelei* 1086	Langley	*lang*, 'long'
Oversley	*oveslei* 1086	Oversley	?*ofer*, 'bank' (or Ofe)
Shelly	*shelley* C.14	Solihull	*scylf*, 'shelf'
Shirley	*syrley* C.13	Solihull	*scir*, 'bright
			or boundary'
Shirley Wood	*sherley feild*	Berkswell	*scîr*
Shrewley	*seruelei* 1086	Shrewley	*scrǽf*, 'cave, pit'
Whitley	*witeleia* 1086	Wootton	
		Wawen	*hwît*, 'white'
Witley	*whytele* ED IV	Solihull	*hwît*, 'white'

Personal names or occupation

Baddesley	*badesleia* C.12	Baddesley	
		Clinton	'Bæd(d)i'
Billesley	*billes læh* 704	Billesley	'Bill'
Botley	*butteleia* C.12	Wootton	
		Wawen	'Botta'
Ipsley	*epeslei* 1086	Ipsley	'Ippe'
Kingley	*kyngleyam* C.12	Arrow	'king'
Listelow	*listerleia* C.13	Packwood	ME *li(te)stere*, 'dyer'
Nunley	*nuneleia* C.12	Wroxall	'nuns'
Pinley	*pileneie* C.12	Rowington	'Pinna'

Other associations

Lee Green	*le lee* C.14	Solihull	
Ley Fields (FN)	*la lee* C.13	Wootton	
		Wawen	
Lye Green	*la legh* C.13	Claverdon	
Mockley	*molkeleia* C.13	Wootton	
		Wawen	
Wallace (FN)	*whaveleye* C.14	Lapworth	

APPENDIX 2

Church dedications

Primary dedications

St Peter	Bickenhill
	Coughton
	Ipsley
	Wootton Wawen
	Bishopton (late dedication)
	Binton
	Hampton Lucy
	Wootton Wawen
St Mary	Balsall
	Hampton-in-Arden (with St Bartholomew)
	Bearley
	Studley
	Kinwarton
	?Luddington
	Ullenhall (the Virgin)
	Oldberrow
	Haseley
	Haselor (and All Saints)
	Wolverton
	Lapworth
Holy Trinity	Arrow
	Hatton
	Morton Bagot
	Norton Lindsey
	Stratford-upon-Avon
St Milburga	Wixford

?St Andrew   Temple Grafton

?St Swithin   Barston

'Wilderness' dedications

St John the Baptist   Berkswell
                        Beausale
                        Aston Cantlow
                        Honiley
                        Wasperton
                        Henley-in-Arden
                        Knowle (with St Lawrence and St Anne)

St Giles   Exhall
                        Spernall priory
                        Packwood

St Leonard   Spernall
                        Wroxall
                        Charlecote

Other ?late dedications

St James   Baddesley Clinton
                        Great Packington
                        Snitterfield
                        Weethley
                        Alveston

St Ann   Knowle

St Lawrence   Meriden
                        Bidford
                        Rowington

St Thomas   Nuthurst

St Bartholomew   Little Packington

St Alphege   Solihull

St Nicholas   Alcester
                        Beaudesert

St Mary Magdalene	Great Alne
	Tanworth
All Saints	Billesley
	Preston Bagot
	Sherborne
St Michael	Budbrooke
	Claverdon
St Matthew	Salford Priors

APPENDIX 3

A list of the topographical-type bynames recorded in the 1327 lay subsidy roll for Warwickshire for western Arden and the Arrow Valley

Walter de Caludene, Packwood
Johne atte Coppe, Lapworth
Geffr' atte Heth, Lapworth
Johne de Broksawe, Lapworth
?Hugh Pebbemor', Lapworth
Alice atte Well, Lapworth
Johne in the Lone, Lapworth
Rond de Hantssawe, Tanworth
Richard de Alresowe,
    William de Alr'ssawe, Tanworth
Thomas de Val, Tanworth
Richard de Middelmor,
    Roger de Middelmore, Tanworth
Simon atte Hethe, Tanworth
Walter de Swanesdych, Tanworth
?John de astleye, Tanworth
Robert atte Bathe,
    William atte Bathe, Tanworth
Ffulcon de Ppenbrugge, Tanworth
Robert de Crowenhal, Tanworth
Robert de Sydenhal,
    Henry de Sydenhale, Tanworth
John atte Berne, Tanworth
John de la Lee, Tanworth
William de Ffolewode, Tanworth

Roger atte Hurste, Studley
Alexander de la Holte, Studley
John de Waldeg'ue, Studley
John de Weshull, Studley
Roger Onderhull, Spernall
William Roubarwe, Spernall
William de Collehurste, Spernall
Henry de Grenhull, Morton Bagot
William atte Hul,
    Richard atte Hul, Morton Bagot
John ad Portam, Rowe'Alne
Richard de Roweleye,
    John de Roweleye, Rowe'Alne
Walter de Colehurste, Rowe'Alne
Robert atte Wode, Rowe'Alne
Robert atte Heth, Rowe'Alne
Thomas Brochole, Aston Cantlow
John Pathelowe, Wilmecote
Richard Underwode, Billesley
John atte Assche, Snitterfield
William atte Grene, Bearley
John atte Mor',
    Thomas atte Mor',
    Richard atte Mor', Wolverton
William atte Grene, Fulbrook

Richard atte Mers, Sherbourne
?Richard de Colehull,
   Norton Lindsey
William de Hull, Langley
Reginald atte Mor', Claverdon
Richard de Deredene, Claverdon
Richard de Littleford,
   Preston Whitley
John de Bissebrok, Preston Whitley
Alan de la Knolle, Rowington
Robert de Brochole, Rowington
Margery de Inwode, Rowington
John atte Hull, Rowington
Nicholas atte Leye, Rowington
Thomas de Inwode, Pinley
John Wedegate, Pinley
Roger de Hennebroke, Offord
William atte Hule, Offord
William atte Pirie, Beausale
Emma atte Grene, Haseley
John de Wodeford, Budbrooke
?Robert de Luntecombe, Budbrooke
Richard atte Mulne, Budbrooke
?William de Milethorn, Budbrooke
Henry de la Heth, Budbrooke
John atte Coppelinde, Wroxall
Henry de Kyckesleye,
   John de Kyckeslegh,
   Wroxall (Knowle?)
Adam atte Linde,
   Thomas atte Linde, Wroxall
Alice in the Hurne, Hatton
William in the Lone, Wootton Wawen
Richard le Ffreyth, Henley
Gilbert infra barram, Henley
John atte Hethe, Berkswell
Clement de Colehurste,
   John de Colehuste, Berkswell
Richard de Nuttebroke, Berkswell

Galfred atte Berne, Balsall
Adam de Ffarnehale, Balsall
Galfred de Ffarnehale, Balsall
Alice atte Ffenne, Balsall
Alice de Bradenoke, Balsall
John de Thotenhull, Balsall
Walter atte Mor, Barston
Roger in le Hurne, Barston
Gilbert de Westhull,
   John de Westhull, Barston
Alan de Ruydon,
   William de Ruydon, Barston
John atte Birches,
   William atte Birches (2),
   Adam atte Birches,
   Thomas atte Birches, Solihull
Richard de Brochurste, Solihull
Roger de Smalbroke,
   Richard de Smalbroke, Solihull
Richard atte Heth, Solihull
Richard de Ffelford, Solihull
Henry de Colemore, Solihull
Lawrence de Ffynchale, Solihull
Richard atte Slou, Solihull
William de Bockemor, Solihull
William de Caldeford, Solihull
Robert de Bockemor,
   Richard de Bockemor, Solihull
Bernard atte Shawe, Solihull
Thomas atte Orchard, Solihull
John de Middelmor, Solihull
Robert Blythe, Solihull
Thomas atte Walle, Solihull
Richard de la Lee, Sheldon
John de Brochurste, Sheldon
John de Blakenhale, Sheldon
Thomas on the Hull, Sheldon
William atte Halle, Bickenhill
John atte Well, Bickenhill

Prioress de Hinewode, Bickenhill
William in la Hoo, Bickenhill
William de Brochurste,
     Kynton Lynden, Bickenhill
William atte Welle,
     Kynton Lynden, Bickenhill
Adam atte Parke,
     Hampton-in-Arden
John de Westhull, Hampton
Thomas atte Mulne, Hampton
Adem de Coppethorn,
     William de Coppethorn, Hampton
Thomas atte Yate, Hampton

William de Nonneleye, Baddesley Clinton
Reginald atte Mulne,
     Great Packington
Hugh de pco, Little Packington
William atte Brok, Sambourne
John atte Mor', Sambourne
Thomas atte Hurste, Ipsley
John othe Hethe, Coughton
Matthew de Hull, Coughton
William othe Hull, Coughton
Nicholas atte Wode, Alcester
Petronilla de Haselholte, Alcester
Robert de Rudinge, Alcester

Analysis of topographical-type bynames

Vegetation names 32 including	woodland 29
	heath 7
	tree-type 12
Animals and birds 0	
Location 80 including	hills, tumuli 19
	valleys 5
	marsh 15
	brooks 6
	nooks 5

APPENDIX 4

Names of commons, heaths and greens

Vegetation names (including *lēah*)

Bentley Heath, Solihull, *Bentley heth* C.15.

Buckley Green, Beaudesert, from *Buckelye* C.13.

Brownley Green, Beausale, from *Brunele* C.13.

Darley Green, Knowle, *Derley* C.13, *dēor, leah*.

Forshaw Heath, Solihull, *Fossawe* C.14, *sceaga*, 'shaw'.

Corsty Green, Morton Bagot, C.18, (earlier *le longrene*).

Hazelwood Green, Preston Bagot, from *Haselholt* C.13.

Heath End, Snitterfield, *Hethe* C.14, *Heathen End* C.19.

Henwood Hall, Solihull, *Hinewudesheth* C.12, *higna*, 'community' with *wudu*.

Hitall Lanes End, Solihull, C.17, from *Haiteley* C.13, *lēah*.

Ilshaw Heath, Tanworth, *Ilshawe heath* C.15; John de *Yelschawe* 1377, *sceaga*.

Lee Green, Solihull, from *le lee* C.14, *le green* C.16, *lēah*.

Littlewood Green, Studley, *Lyttelwode* C.16.

Lode Heath, Solihull, *la lewode* C.14.

Lye Green, Claverdon, *la legh* C.13; John de *la legh*.

Lyndon Green, Sheldon, *lind*, 'lime-tree'.

Lyndon End, Solihull, from *Linde* C.13, *lind*, 'lime-tree'.

Netherwood Heath, Balsall, C.19.

Pinley Green, Rowington, *Pindley greene* C.17 from *Pileneie* C.12, *lēah*.

Ryton End, Barston, *de Ruydon* C.14, *ryge*, 'rye', but a family name.

Shirley Green, Berkswell, C.19, *lēah*.

Shirley Heath, Solihull, from Shirley, *lēah*.

Wootton Green, Balsall, C.19, *wudu-tūn* but a family name C.16.

Yew Green, Hatton, *Ewe Green c.*1830; Hugh *atte Grene* C.14.
Coughton: John *othe Hethe*, 1327.
Great Alne: Robert de *la hethe*, 1327.
Alne: Robert *atte heth*, 1327.
Budbrooke: Henry *de la heth*, 1327.
Lapworth: Geoffrey *atte Heth*, 1327.
Solihull: Richard *atte heth*, 1327.
Tanworth: Simon *atte Hethe*, 1327.

Animal and bird names

Cornet End, Berkswell, *Cronesend* C.16, *cran*, 'heron'.
Darley Green, Knowle, *Derley*, C.13, *deor, lēah* (see above).
?Kite Green, Preston Bagot.
Tadpole Green, Rowington.

Shape, location, or physical characteristic

Barnmoor Green, Claverdon, from *Bernemore*, C.15, *mōr*, 'marsh'.
Carol Green, Berkswell, *le Carnewilleheth*, C.13, *Carwell grene*, C.16, *wielle*, 'spring'.
Chadwick End, Balsall, *Chaddyche*, C.16, *dic*, 'dyke'.
Church Green, Morton Bagot, C.18.
Copt Green, Lapworth, *le coppe grene*, C.14; John de *la Coppe*, 1323, *copp*, 'summit'.
Copt Heath, Solihull, *le coppe*, C.14, *cophethe*, C.15, *copp*, 'summit'.
Eastern Green, Berkswell, C.19.
Fen End, Balsall, C.14, *fenn*, 'fen'.
Fulford Heath, Solihull, *fulford heythe*, C.16; Richard de *Fulforde*, 1332.
Greenhill Green, Morton Bagot, from *grenehull*, C.14; Henry de *Grenehulle*, 1327.
Hall End, Wooton Wawen, *cf. Hallemede*, C.15.
Hockley Heath, Tanworth, *Hucleloweheth*, C.13, 'Hucca's hill or barrow'.
Hollyberry End, Meriden, *holiberyend*, C.16, ?*burh, beorh*.
la longrene, Morton Bagot, C.14 (later Gorsty Green).
Mars Hill, Studley, *Merce Green*, C.19.
Mere Green, Morton Bagot, C.18, *gemǣre*, 'boundary' (later Woodwards/Chester's).
Meer End, Balsall, C.16, *gemǣre*, 'boundary'.
Poundley End, Rowington, *Ponday End*, C.16, *ēg*, 'island'.
Walsal End, Balsall, *Westhull End*, C.16, 'west hill'.

Personal names and occupations

Blunts Green, Wootton Wawen; William *Blund*, 1247.

Brown's Green, Tanworth; John *Brun*, 1327.

?Burton Green, Berkswell, C.19.

Butler's End, Great Packington, family name *Butler*, C.17.

Catherine de Barnes Heath, *Katherine barnes heath*, 1602, ?Keteleshed, C.14, Solihull.

Chester's Green, Morton Bagot (earlier Mere Green).

Cheswick Green, Tanworth, from *Chesewych*, C.13, cheese, *'wic'*.

Church End, Studley, C.19.

Clarke's Green, Studley; Thomas *Clericus*, 1327.

Cowpers Green, Oldberrow, C.18.

Danzey Green, Tanworth; John *Denesy*, 1313.

?Denns Green, Wootton Wawen, 1830.

Dickens Heath, Solihull, *Dickens*, C.17.

Dickens' Heath, Tanworth, *Dickins heathe*, C.16; Thomas *Dykens*, 1524.

?Eave's Green, Meriden.

?Flint's Green, Berkswell, C.19.

Freeman's Green, Oldberrow, C.19; William Freeman, 1716.

Garratts Green, Solihull.

Garrett's Green, Sheldon.

Geary's Heath, Great Packington, family name *Gerey*, C.16.

Gilbert's Green, Tanworth, *Gylbert grene*, C.16; Robert *Gilbert*, 1367.

Hardwick Green, Studley, C.18.

Haslucks Green, Solihull, *Haselucks greene*, C.17, Solihull; Richard *Haselocke*, 1580.

Kemps Green, Tanworth; Thomas *Kempe*, *c.*1220.

Kims Green, Wootton Wawen.

Majors Green, Solihull; Thomas *Mager*, 1469.

Mousley End, Rowington, *Molsowe end*, C.16; Alan de *Moulesho*, 1288.

?Needlers End, Balsall, *Nelders*.

?Norton's Green, Knowle, C.19, family name *Norton*, C.17.

Tainters Green, Solihull, *teynto(u)rs grene*, C.14, 'place where cloth was stretched'.

Terry's Green, Tanworth; Nicholas *Tyrrye*, C.16.

Tilehouse Green, Solihull, *tylhous ovene*, C.14; *Tilehouse grene*, C.16.

Traps Green, Wootton Wawen; Nicholas *Trappe*, 1441.

Truemans Heath, Solihull, *trewmans heythe*, C.16.

Turners Green, Rowington; John *le Turner*, 1288.

Waring's Green, Tanworth; Thomas *Waryng*, 1332.

?Well's Green, Sheldon.

Whitlocks End, Solihull, *Whitloxend*, C.16, 'Wihtlāc's end'.

Woodwards Green, Morton Bagot, C.19, (earlier Mere Green, later Chester's).

Parish and township names

Aspley Heath, Tanworth, from *Æspleage*, C.10.

Balsall Heath Common from Balsall.

Bickenhill Heath.

Dunnington Heath, Salford Priors.

Elmdon Heath, Solihull.

Escote Green, Barston, C.19.

Exhall Heath, Exhall, C.18.

Haseley Green, Haseley, from the parish name; William *atte Grene*, Ed.III, *?Edrichesgrene*, Ed.I, Emma *atte grene*, 1327.

Kineton Green, Solihull, *Cinctun* with green (added).

Knowle Common from Knowle.

Mappleborough Green, Studley, from *Mapelberge*, 1086, 'maple-tree hill'.

Marston Green, Bickenhill, *Marston Green*, C.19, from Marston.

Morton Common from Morton Bagot.

Oversley Green, Oversley, from the parish name; *oversleygrene*, C.16, *lēah*.

Preston Green, Preston Bagot; John *atte Grene*, 1332.

Reeves Green, Berkswell, C.19.

Rowington Green, Rowington; William *atte Grene*, 1297.

Sambourne Common from Sambourne.

Sheldon Heath, Sheldon.

Shelfield Green, Aston Cantlow.

Shrewley Common from Shrewley *lēah*.

Studley Common, Studley, *Studley heath*, C.17.

Ulverley Green, Solihull, from Ulverlei, 1086, holly, *'lēah'*.

Wavers Marston Common.

Wootton Heath, Wootton Wawen, *le hethe*, C.16.

Wroxall Common from Wroxall.

Other associations

Aston Cantlow; Margery *atte grene*, 1327.

Bearley; William *atte grene*, 1327.

Dials Green, Great Packington, C.19.

Elver's Green, Knowle, C.19; *Elvordis*, C.15.

Fulbrook; William *atte grene*, 1327.

The Green, Snitterfield; Thomas *atte grene*, 1315.

Hampton Lucy; John *atte grene*; Robert *atte grene*, 1327.

Kites Green, Preston Bagot, C.18.

Tidbury Green, Solihull.

Wilmecote (Parva); John *atte grene*; John *othe grene*, 1327.

Worlds End, Solihull, 1830.

Yarningale Common, Claverdon, *Yarningale*, C.17.

Analysis of green, heath names

Vegetation 32 including woodland 17; heath 9; tree-type ?4.

Animals and birds 4.

Location, shape and physical characteristics 19 including hills, tumuli 6; marsh, fen 2; ford 2; boundary 3; orientation 1; spring 1.

Personal names and occupations 39.

Parish and township names 28.

VI

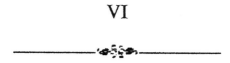

The Place-name as Surname in Wales

PRYS MORGAN

LOCATIVE SURNAMES are not usually associated with Wales, a country famous for patronymics and surnames based on them, yet in the earlier stages of taking fixed surnames, mainly in the later Middle Ages and sixteenth century, over 260 families took surnames based on Welsh place-names. This is, of course, a tiny proportion when compared with locative surnames in England. Fuller details of early examples of these surnames have been given by the author elsewhere,[1] and the opportunity can be taken in this essay to list the names very briefly in groups based on the pre-1974 counties, to give wherever possible the place-name on which the surname is based, together with a discussion of the irregular distribution pattern of such names across Wales.[2]

---

1 Prys Morgan 'Locative surnames in Wales — a preliminary list', *Nomina*, 13, 1990–91, pp.7–24, for a list with early examples and evidences of present-day distribution, and full bibliographical references. Only abbreviated references are given in this chapter, which should be read in conjunction with the article mentioned.

2 A good general treatment of locative surnames is R. A. McKinley, *A History of British Surnames*, London, 1990, pp.51–7; and for Wales, see T. J. Morgan and P. Morgan, *Welsh Surnames*, Cardiff, 1985, pp.27–31, and various locative surnames treated separately in the list of surnames. For Welsh place-names, see Melville Richards, *Welsh Administrative and Territorial Units, Medieval and Modern*, Cardiff, 1969, but the location of parishes is set out clearly in C. J. Williams and J. Watts-Williams, *Parish Registers in Wales*, Aberystwyth, 1986. An invaluable help also is William Rees, *An Historical Map of South Wales and the Border in the Fourteenth Century*, Cardiff, 1933. Authorities differ over the precise total of parishes in each county.

It should be mentioned at the start that certain names have been excluded from the study. There seemed to be insufficient evidence to connect *Rawbone* with the village of Ruabon; *Lanfear* cannot be connected with certainty to any of the many places called Llanfair. Although *Scourfield* is common in west Wales, and there is a place-name Scourfield in south Pembrokeshire, the evidence also suggests that the family is descended from a settler from Cumbria during the late Middle Ages. Names such as *Blodwell* and *Hargest* have been excluded since Llanyblodwell and Hergest lie a few yards over the border in England. Excluded also from our calculations are purely Welsh families who took, in the later Middle Ages, their locative surnames from places over the border. This meant excluding Rhirid ap Dafydd who married, in about 1393–4, the daughter of Sir Alexander Myddelton of Myddelton, Shropshire, taking from her the surname *Myddelton*; excluding likewise Rhirid's contemporary Dafydd ab Ieuan Goch, *floruit* 1370s–1421, who married Gwenhwyfar, daughter of Ieuan ap John ab Eynon of Swyney, and from whose lands at Swyney near Oswestry he appears to have adopted the surname of *Holbache*. The surname survives in North Wales to this day, but the location lies just outside Wales.[3]

Anglesey

Alaw (river Alaw); *Anglesey, Anglesea* (isle or county of Anglesey); *Bodveurig* (estate of Bodfeurig near Aberffraw); *Bodychen* (estate of Bodychen near Gwalchmai); *Brwynog* (Brwynog near Llanfflewin); *Holyhead* (Holyhead); *Llyvon, Llyvone* (probably commote of Llifon).[4]

A total of seven names in an island containing 79 parishes shows the locative surname conspicuous by its near-absence. There is no early evidence for the surnames *Anglesey* and *Holyhead* but their incidence today in the Chester area points to their being the names of early emigrants from Anglesey. *Llyvon* appears among townsmen at Conwy in the sixteenth century. *Bodychen* and *Bodveurig* are rare Anglesey examples of a type of gentry name found more commonly in Caernarfonshire and Denbighshire.

3 For Holbache, see *Dictionary of Welsh Biography*, London, 1959, s.n., and Hon. Mrs Bulkeley Owen, *The Founder and First Trustees of Oswestry Grammar School*, Oswestry, n.d. but *c*.1900.

4 For the ramifications of gentry families over north Wales, see J. E. Griffith, ed., *Pedigrees of Anglesey and Caernarvonshire families*, Horncastle, 1914.

Breconshire

Bealth (Builth); *Breckon, Brecknock, Breckonshire* (town and county of Breconshire); *Clanvow* (tentatively identified with Glynfach, formerly Clynfwch or Clanhogh, near Hay); *Delahay* (possibly from Hay); *Erwood* (Erwood); *Garth* (Garth); *Honthie* (river Honddu); *Lywel* (Llywel).[5]

A total of eight names in a county of 78 parishes is a very low number, especially considering that the county is on the English border, conquered at the end of the eleventh century by the Normans. Several of these surnames are clearly those of emigrants from the county, *Lywel* found in Monmouthshire, *Bealth* found mostly in Pembrokeshire, *Breckon* and its variants, even *Brokenshire*, found often in neighbouring English counties. Hay-on-Wye is here suggested as one possible source for the name *Delahaye*, since it is found in the locality. Philip de Clanvow died in 1350, and was descended from a well-attested Welsh family, connected with the area of Hay. *Clanvow* may be an attempt to anglicize Llanfocha, the Welsh for St Maughan's in Monmouthshire, but Theophilus Jones in his *History of Brecknockshire* says that Glynfach (spelt in various ways) was the Welsh section of the lordship of Hay, and it is tempting to connect *Clanvow* to it, but without any certainty. Another possible source is the place-name Cilonw.

Caernarfonshire

Bangor (Bangor); *Bodurda* (estate of Bodwrdda in Lleyn); *Bodvel* (Bodfel); *Bodyan* (estate of Boduan in Lleyn); *Brumor, Brymore* (estate of Brynmor near Penmaenmawr); *Brynker, Brunker* (estate of Bryncir); *Cadlan* (Cadlan, Pwllheli); *Carnarvon* (Caernarfon); *Carreg* (estate of Carreg in Lleyn); *Conway* (Conway, Conwy); *Coytmore* (estate of Coedmor); *Daron* (river Daron or Aberdaron); *De Ganou* (possibly Degannwy); *Glyn, Glynne* (estate of Glynllifon); *Gunnis* (estate of Gwynnus in Lleyn); *Lleyn* (the Lleyn peninsula); *Madryn* (estate of Madrun in Lleyn); *Nevyn* (Nefyn); *Quellyn* (estate of Plas

---

5 Extensive genealogies of Breconshire families are to be found in the second volume of Theophilus Jones, *History of Brecknockshire*, Brecon, 2 vols., 1805, 1809, second edition, Brecon, 1898; but for this and most other counties, the fullest account of Welsh families is P. C. Bartrum, *Welsh Genealogies, A.D. 1415–1500*, 12 vols, Aberystwyth, 1983, especially vol. 12, in the index of surnames.

Quellyn on Llyn Cwellyn, Snowdonia); *Saython* (estate of Saethon in Lleyn); *Trygar, Trygarn* (estate of Trygarn in Lleyn).[6]

A total of 21 names in a county of 73 parishes is by Welsh standards fairly high, but it is striking that many of them are the names of gentry houses. *Carreg* appears as early as 1396, but the majority appear in the sixteenth century. *Bangor* (to be distinguished from another *Bangor* family from Bangor on Dee) appears in 1406, *Daron* in 1395. McKinley[7] says that *Carnarvon* appears as a surname already in fourteenth-century Liverpool.

Caernarfon was the centre of English administration in North Wales, and Conwy a flourishing borough and garrison town, open to outside influences. *Conway* is a remarkably common name in many parts in Britain, and it should be noted that the family of Conwy of Botryddan in Flintshire claimed to be descended from the family of 'Coniers', not 'Conway'.[8] *Conway* was also used in Ireland as an anglicized version of an Irish surname. Presumably it was the English influence from the town of Caernarfon which gave rise to so many locative surnames based on gentry houses.

Cardiganshire

Cardigan (town or county of Cardigan); *Glais* (possibly from Penglais near Aberystwyth); *Pencoed* (unidentified).[9]

This county was one of the most thinly populated in Wales, and locative surnames are conspicuous by their almost total absence. John Pencoed appeared as early as 1312, the Glais family in the early fifteenth century, and *Cardigan* has been found in Pembrokeshire, Swansea, Llandaff and elsewhere down the centuries. This then is a good example of a remote area, free from the Anglo-Norman naming patterns.

Carmarthenshire

Conwil (Caeo, in full Conwil Gaeo or Cynwyl Gaeo); *Elvett* (possibly from Conwil Elvet or Cynwyl Elfed); *Emlyn* (lordship of Emlyn, or

---

6 Besides the sources mentioned in previous footnotes, see A. Hadley, ed., *The Parish Registers of Conway*, 1541–1793, London, 1900.

7 R. McKinley, *op. cit.*, p.42.

8 J. E. Griffith, *Pedigrees*, p.260.

9 A rich source of late medieval names and surnames is R. A. Griffiths, *The Principality of Wales in the Later Middle Ages — I: South Wales*, Cardiff, 1972.

Newcastle Emlyn); *Kidwelley, Kidwalley* (Kidwelly); *Kynin* (river Cynin); *Llandubia* (Llandybie); Laugharne (Laugharne); *Pembrey* (Pembrey or Pen-bre); *Ungoed* (possibly Hengoed near Llanelli); *Whitland* (Whitland).[10]

The total of 10 locative names in a county of some 83 parishes is proportionately low, comparable to the counties of Brecon, Radnor and Monmouth, but far lower than the neighbouring counties of Pembroke and Glamorgan. The surname *Kidwell* has been excluded from consideration here, because the evidence for connecting it with Kidwelly is uncertain, though families bearing the surname claim that they do originate there. *Emlyn* appears in the area as early as 1357, but of course there must be English families bearing the surname who take it from the medieval female name Emlyn. *Ungoed* has the superficial appearance of being derived from two Welsh words meaning 'Ashwood', but since the earliest examples appear in the early seventeenth century so close to Hengoed, this seems a more likely place of origin. *Conwil* is unusual in that it comes from remote inland hill-country, appearing in the parish registers from the eighteenth century to around 1900, and survives today probably in female lines. The south-western corner of the county may be considered the easternmost extension of the 'Little England' of south Pembrokeshire; even so, it produced no locative surnames except the fairly common one of *Laugharne*.

Denbighshire

Allett, Allott (river Aled); *Allington* (estate of Allington or Trefalun); *Almor* (estate of Almer); *Berwen* (probably Berwyn hills); *Bromfield* (lordship of Bromfield); *Caledfrine* (Caledfryn, possibly near Llannefydd); *Cluett, Cludd* (river Clwyd); *Dee* (probably river Dee); *Denbeigh, Denby* (Denbigh); *Dutton* (villages of Dutton near Wrexham); *Erles* (estate of Erlas near Wrexham); *Erthig, Eyrthigg* (estate of Erddig near Wrexham); *Eyton* (Eyton); *Holt* (Holt); *Keelan, Keelon* (Cilan, near Llanfair Dyffryn Clwyd); *Kyffin* (various places called 'Cyffin' meaning 'borderland'); *Maysmor, Mashmoore* (estate of Maesmor near Wrexham); *Moss* (Moss valley near Wrexham);

---

10 T. J. and P. Morgan, *Surnames*, p.201 s.n. 'Ungoed'; I am grateful to Mr Emrys Williams of the National Library of Wales, Aberystwyth, for helping me identify Ungoed with Hengoed, and for much information on the Conwil family.

Rixham (probably Wrexham); *Sontley* (estate of Sontley near Wrexham)'; *Trevallyn* (estate of Trefalun, Allington); *Trevenant* (Trefnant); *Trevor* (Trefor); *Wrexham* (Wrexham); *Yale* (lordship of Iâl, or estate of Plas-yn-Yale near Wrexham).[11]

Counting *Rixham* and *Wrexham* as one, the total of 24 locatives in a county of only 66 parishes is a fairly high proportion, the great majority being along the English border around Wrexham, with a small handful such as *Cluett* in the Vale of Clwyd. *Trevor* appears as early as 1343 and is derived from an estate near Llangollen, and there is still a Lord Trevor at Brynkinallt in the same district.[12] *Dee* appears occasionally as a surname in north-eastern Wales and Chester, and may possibly derive from the river-name, although sometimes (as in the case of the Elizabethan magus Dr John Dee) it transliterates *Du* 'black'. There are many places called Dutton, but there are several villages called Dutton near Wrexham, and *Dutton* being a very common name in the same area, it has been thought right to include the surname in this list. Some of these locative surnames were taken by Welshmen into Shropshire, *Keelan* being found in Oswestry by 1563, and *Allett* in the same period in Oswestry as descendants of the poet Tudur Aled; other names were taken much further afield to America: Elihu Yale, benefactor of Yale University, deriving his name from Plas-yn-Yale, and Sanford L. Cluett, the inventor of the 'sanforized' shirts, deriving his from Clwyd.

Flintshire

Bangor (Bangor-on-Dee, Bangor Iscoed); *Broughton* (estate of Broughton near Worthenbury); *Buckley* (Buckley); *Callcott* (Calcot near Brynford, Holywell); *Cayrus, Carus* (Caerwys); *Ffacnalt* (estate of Fagnallt near Nannerch); *Flint* (Flint); *Hanmer* (estate of Hanmer);

---

11 For Wrexham names, see A. N. Palmer, *A History of the Country Townships of the Old Parish of Wrexham*, Wrexham, 1903, and for much information on north-eastern Wales, see D. R. Thomas, *History of the Diocese of St Asaph*, 3 vols., Oswestry, 1903–13; but for the vast numbers of Welsh emigrants to Shropshire, the invaluable source is *Shropshire Parish Registers*, published by the Shropshire Parish Record Society, Shrewsbury, 1898–1943. I am grateful to Dr Hywel Wyn Owen for identifying Moss with the Moss valley for me.

12 For Elihu Yale, see *D.N.B.*, and for Matthew de Trevor in 1343 see D. R. Thomas, *Diocese of St Asaph*, 1, p.327.

Hawarden, Harden (Hawarden); *Holywell* (Holywell); *Hope* (Hope); *Mealer, Mealor* (lordship or districts of Maelor); *Mold, Mould* (Mold); *Mostyn* (Mostyn, or estate of Mostyn); *Moulsdale* (lordship of Moldsdale); *Overton* (Overton); *Panton* (estate of Plas Panton, Bagillt); *Pennant* (topographical, literally 'top of the dingle' near Whitford); *Skeyvioke* (Ysgeifiog); *Soughton* (Soughton); *Whitford* (Whitford).[13]

Flintshire had only 29 parishes, and so the total of 21 locative names is high by Welsh standards, the names being all in the eastern section of the county or in the detached section in Maelor, showing openness to English influence. *Pennant* had already appeared as a surname in the fifteenth century, but it was said that *Mostyn* was forced upon Richard ap Hywel of Mostyn in order that he might set an example to the rest of the Welsh gentry by taking a fixed surname. *Mostyn, Broughton, Ffacnallt, Panton, Pennant* and *Hanmer* are estate names of a kind to be found also in the counties of Caernarfon and Denbigh. *Carus* is still to be found at Caerwys, and *Hanmer* in and around Hanmer. Certain names such as *Holywell, Hope* and *Overton* present difficulty because there are other places in England with the same names. They have been included here because *Holywell* appears in Conwy in the eighteenth century, *Overton* not far from Overton in the records of the Flintshire Quarter Sessions in the same century, and the painter Thomas Jones of Pencerrig, also in the same century, claimed that his Hope ancestors came from *Hope* in Flintshire.

Glamorgan

Avan, D'avene (river Afan, lordship of Avan); *Barry* (Barry); *Blaene* (topographical 'blaenau', meaning 'hill-country'); *Britton* (possibly from Britton Ferry, or Britton near Aberthaw, which is now Burton, or, thirdly, Britton Thorpe, which is now the Drope, near Cardiff); *Caagh* (river Caiach); *Canton* (Canton in Cardiff); *Cardiff* (Cardiff); *Clin, Clyn* (probably Clyne near Neath); *Cogan* (Cogan); *Cornely* (Cornelly); *Coita* (possibly Coity); *Corndune* (Corntown); *Corrog, Correck* (river Corrwg or abbreviated from Glyncorrwg); *Cowbridge* (Cowbridge), *Coyd, Coyde* (topographical, 'coed' meaning 'wood').

---

13 Several Flintshire families are discussed by Thomas Pennant, *A History of the Parishes of Whiteford and Holywell*, London, 1796.

Coydmore (not identified, 'coedmor' meaning 'great wood'); *Fagan* (possibly from St Fagan's); *Fairwode* (Fairwood near Swansea); *Ffeirwater* (Fairwater); *Gannocke* (unidentified, possibly abbreviated from Morgannocke, a form of 'Morgannwg', the Welsh for Glamorgan); *Gower* (lordship or peninsula of Gower); *Hengott* (Hengoed); *Horton* (Horton); *Kenifick* (Kenfig); *Kery* (possibly abbreviated from Porthkerry); *Kibor* (lordship of Kibbor, Ceibwr); *Knapp* (Cold Knap near Barry); *Landaf* (Llandaff); *Landogh* (Llandough); *Landymore* (Landimore in Gower); *Lanmaes* (Llanmaes); *Lanririt* (Llantrithyd); *Lantrissen* (Llantrisant); *Lauleston* (Laleston); *Lestalbont* (Llystalybont); *Lougher* (Loughor); *Marychurch* (St Marychurch); *Neath, Neth* (Neath); *Nottage* (Nottage); *Penhard* (Pennard); *Penmark* (Penmark); *Pennarth* (Penarth); *Penrice* (Penrice); *Penthlyne* (Penllyn, Penlline); *Pill* (possibly topographical 'pill' meaning 'tidal creek'); *Raath, Roth, Roath* (Roath in Cardiff); *Rudyng* (possibly Rhydding near Neath); *Sylly, Sully* (Sully); *Swansey, Swansea* (Swansea); *Taaffe, Taffe* (possibly river Taff); *Wallas*, near Ewenny.[14]

The Glamorgan total of 51 locative surnames seems fairly high, but the county had 137 parishes, and so the proportion of names to parishes is about the same as that for Denbighshire, and lower than those for Pembrokeshire or Flintshire. *Horton, Landymore, Penhard* and *Penrice*, and obviously *Gower* itself, come from the highly Anglicized peninsula of Gower, a disappointingly small total, while the great majority come from the Vale of Glamorgan. *Caagh* is a great rarity from upland Glamorgan, as is the short-lived *Blaene*, which should be distinguished from the better-known *Blayneys* arising in Heyop in Radnorshire or the best-known *Blayneys* of Tregynon in Montgomeryshire. The Norman *advenae* in some cases already had surnames such as *De Turberville*, in other cases took surnames from their conquests, such as *De Barry* or *De Cogan* (though it should be remembered that common folk at a later date also adopted *Barry* and *Cogan* as surnames in the locality), and these conquerors took their

14 An invaluable discussion of surnames, especially locatives, is D. Elwyn Williams, 'A short inquiry into surnames in Glamorgan from the thirteenth to the eighteenth centuries', *Transactions of the Honourable Society of Cymmrodorion*, 1961, 2, London, 1962, pp.45–87; but this and other treatments of Glamorgan names depend on the genealogies of G. T. Clark, *Limbus Patrum Morganiae*, London, 1886, and the immense collection of medieval charters in G. T. Clark, *Cartae et alia Munimenta . . . de Glamorgan*, 5 vols., Talygarn and Cardiff, 1909.

Glamorgan surnames such as *Barry, Cogan, Rothe, Kenifick* and maybe *Fagan* and *Taaffe* also, to medieval Ireland. *Fagan* does not appear as a surname in Glamorgan, but others do, and it is likely that there is no lineal connection between those families and the families of the twelfth-century conquerors of Ireland.[15] The native lords of Afan had taken the surname *Avan* or *D'Avene* in the late Middle Ages, and the families of *Horton, Cornely* and *Penrice* were also gentry, but in the main the Glamorgan gentry took patronymic surnames in the later Middle Ages, such as *Mathew* of Llandaff or *Herbert* of Swansea, and so on. *Marychurch* was established as a gentry name not in Glamorgan but at Norchard, near Tenby in Pembrokeshire. It should be pointed out here, too, that *Canton* and *Wallas* also arise separately from other place-names in Pembrokeshire. *Pill* appears in sixteenth-century Glamorgan, and it also appears in seventeeth-century Pembrokeshire, and in other places, so that one must consider that it could either derive from the coastal feature, a pill or creek, or it could derive from Pill (a part of Newport in Monmouthshire) or from Pill (the village on Milford Haven, Pembrokeshire). *Gannock* cannot easily be explained, but it appears more than once in the Pembrokeshire Hearth Tax in 1670,[16] and might possibly be an abbreviated form of Llangynog; but since Gannocke and Morgannok exist in the medieval charters of Glamorgan as forms of Morgannwg (Glamorgan), this is suggested as the source of the surname.

Merioneth

Corewenne (Corwen); *Dolgelley* (Dolgellau); *Dovye* (probably river Dovey); *Mawddwy* (lordship of Mawddwy); *Merioneth* (Merioneth); *Maysmore* (estate of Maesmor, Tywyn); *Nanney* (estate of Nannau, Dolgellau); *Penllyn* (Penllyn); *Trausfynydd* (Trawsfynydd).

The county of Merioneth was small and thinly populated, with

---

15 The most useful guides to Welsh locative surnames in Ireland are E. McLysaght, *Irish Families, their Names, Arms and Origins*, Dublin, 1953, and his *A Guide to Irish Surnames*, Dublin, 1964.

16 F. Green, ed., 'Pembrokeshire hearths in 1670', *West Wales Historical Records*, vols. 9, 10, 11, Carmarthen, 1920–26, prints the Hearth Tax *in extenso*, and contains references to William Gannocke of Dale, and Owen Gannocke of Carew. These references were omitted from the article on surnames by P. Morgan, *Nomina*, 13, 1990–91.

only about 34 parishes, so that proportionately the total of nine locative names is not so tiny. *Dovye* and *Trausfynydd* are found in the Shropshire parish records, the surnames of emigrants from Merioneth, while *Dolgelley* is the name of a mercer of Ruthin in the sixteenth century. *Maysmore* (which should be distinguished from Maysmore near Wrexham) and *Nanney* are examples of gentry estate names, of a type more common in the counties of Caernarfon, Denbigh and Flint.

Monmouthshire

Baslak (Bassaleg); *Brangwyn* (probably Bryngwyn); *Carlyon* (Caerleon); *Carne* (abbreviated from Pencarn near Newport); *Gwent, Whent* (region of Gwent); *Kemeys, Kemmis* (Kemeys Inferior); *Macken, Machan* (possibly Machen); *Magor* (Magor); *Monmouth* (Monmouth); *Oldcastle* (Oldcastle); *Parquin* (unidentified, possibly somewhere called 'Parc Gwyn' near Abergavenny); *Penalth* (Penalt); *Raglan* (Raglan); *Risca* (Risca); *Tintern* (Tintern); *Undy* (Undy); *Wenlloug* (district of Wentloog); *Whitson* (Whitson); *Wildcrek* (Wilcrick); *Winston, Winstone* translated from Tre-wyn (Pandy).[17]

Monmouth had about 117 parishes, but has only 20 locative surnames, a surprisingly low total for a county on the English border, with a coastline no more than six miles from Avonmouth and Bristol. *Brangwyn* appears near Abergavenny in 1292, and although there are other villages with the name Bryngwyn, the Monmouthshire Bryngwyn is so close to Abergavenny that it seems the likeliest source of the name. It is not suggested here that all *Carlyon* families arise from Caerleon, but that those in Newport or neighbouring English counties probably do. Several surnames are found early on in other Welsh counties, *Carne* and *Raglan* among the Glamorgan gentry, *Undy* and *Macken* or *Machan* in Pembrokeshire, though the identification with Machen is only tentative. Arthur Machen's surname was a *nom de plume*, although the author came from Caerleon. *Whitson* can, of course, be derived from other places of that name, or from a patronymic, but the many *Whitson* families

---

17 In addition to sources mentioned above, see J. A. Bradney, *A History of Monmouthshire*, 4 vols., London, 1904–33, and also, for the locative names mentioned here, his *Parish Registers of Llantilio Crossenny*, London, 1916, and *Parish Registers of Llanddewi Rhydderch*, London, 1919.

in the Cardiff, Monmouthshire, and Bristol areas, suggest the coastal village of Whitson as the origin of the families there. The same observation may well be true of *Winston*, but it is fairly common in areas of South Wales such as Merthyr, and it has always been accepted that it first appears in the late medieval period in the family living at Tre-wyn, Pandy, near Abergavenny. It is possible that the house was then known as Winston. A branch of the Winstons moved to Standish in Gloucestershire, married into the Churchills, taking Winston with them as a baptismal name.

Montgomeryshire

Blayney, Blaney (topographical, 'blaenau' meaning 'hill-country'); *Brethin, Breathing* (Breidden hills); *Cain, Caine* (river Cain); *Carreckova* (Carreg Hova); *Coyd* (topographical, 'coed' meaning 'wood'); *Cyveliok* (district of Cyfeiliog); *Deythur* (district or lordship of Deuddwr); *Forden* (Forden); *Glyn* (abbreviated from Clynclywedog, near Llanidloes); *Karenion* (Caereinion); *Kedewyn* (lordship of Cedewain); *Kemais* (Cemais, Cemmaes); *Kerry* (Kerry); *Kyffin* (Cyffin near Llangadfan); *Montgomery, Mungomeri* (Montgomery); *Myvod* (Meifod); *Penryn* (Penthryn, earlier Penrhyn); *Pool, Delapole* (Welshpool); *Tannatt* (river Tanat); *Trouscoit* (Trawsgoed).[18]

Montgomeryshire was a small county of no more than about 55 parishes, so the 20 locative surnames are a respectably large total. *Carreckova* and *Karenion* appear in the Shropshire parish registers, obviously the names of emigrants. *Kedewyn, Keri, Mungomeri* are names of Welsh soldiers at Agincourt 1415,[19] again far away from a Welsh context. Most of the locative surnames come from the Severn valley, but *Glyn* and *Kyffin* are from the fairly remote hill-country, and *Blayney* appears first with Ieuan or Evan Blayney of Gregynog near Tregynon as early as 1406. The *Blayneys* were a separate family from the Radnorshire *Blayneys* of Heyop (and later of Kinsham), but were later intermarried with them. 'Blaenau' has somewhat the

---

18 For Blayneys, see S. P. Thomas, 'Branches of the Blayney family in the xvi and xvii centuries', *Montgomeryshire Collections*, 64, 1976, pp.7–38, and 'A Postscript', *Montgomeryshire Collections*, 67, 1979, pp.91–108. I am most grateful to my friend S. P. Thomas for help with this and many other families over the years.

19 For Welsh soldiers at Agincourt, see H. Owen, ed., *The Description of Pembrokeshire by George Owen of Henllys*, 4 vols., London, 1892–1936, pp.4, 588.

appearance of a nickname in origin, for the descendants of Evan Blayney were for several generations uncertain as to their exact surname, some branches taking surnames other than *Blayney*. The Irish title, Lord Blayney, came with the family settling in Ireland.

Pembrokeshire

Ambleston (Ambleston); *Bosher* (probably abbreviated from Bosherston); *Breynangle* (possibly from St Mary-in-Angle, near Angle); *Brody* (Brawdy); *Bryne* (possibly from Dyffryn Breuan, near Llantood and Breidell); *Canaston* (Canaston); *Canton* (possibly Canton, a lost place-name near Roch; *Carew* (Carew); *Castlemartyn* (Castlemartin); *Cawey* (possibly Capel Cawy near Mynachlog-ddu); *Colby* (Colby); *Crabhole* (Crabhall, near Dale); *Filbedge, Filbatch* (Philbeach, near Marloes); *Helott* (Heylett, Haroldston St Issell's); *Hopla, Hopley* (possibly from Hoplass, in Roscrowther); *Hasker, Huskards* (Hasguard); *Johnston* (Johnston); *Keaston* (Keyston); *Killa* (possibly from Ciliau, Llanwnda, or Ciliau, Llanstinan),[20] *Keymer* (possibly from Castell Kymer at New Moat); *Lamphey, Lanfey* (Lamphey); *Lanryan* (Llanrhian); *Lanyon* (possibly Lanion); *Lony, Luny* (Linney, Castlemartin); *Loudeshope* (Lydstep, formerly Loudeshope); *Marlos* (Marloes); *Martel, Martell* (Martel, near Little Newcastle); *Martley* (possibly from Martletwy); *Murthy* (possibly from Mathry, formerly Marthry); *Muselwike* (Musselwick near St Ishmael's); *Nangle* (Angle); *Narberth, Narbett* (Narberth); *Nash* (Nash); *Never* (Nevern); *Newport* (Newport); *Nolton* (Nolton); *Oriel* (possibly abbreviated from Orielton, near Pembroke); *Palmerslak, Palmerslake* (Palmerslake near St Florence); *Pencaer* (Pencaer peninsula); *Pembroke, Bembroke* (Pembroke); *Petrechurche* (Paterchurch); *Picton* (Picton near Slebech); *Pill* (possibly Pill, Milford Haven); *Prendergast, Prengest* (Prendergast); *Puncherston* (Puncheston); *Rath* (unidentified, posibly topographical, 'rath' meaning 'fort' or 'motte'); *Rhigian* (Rhiwgian near Newport); *Roch, Roche* (Roch); *Rossan, Rossent* (possibly Rhosson, St David's); *Slydoghe* (possibly Scleudach, Isclydach in

---

20 I am most grateful to the Revd Stanley Jones of Llangennech, for his help regarding his Killa ancestors, for the evidence for the correct pronunciation, 'Killeh', and for the identification with the Fishguard area. Both Ciliau at Llanwnda and Llanstinan are spelled *Kelle* on W. Rees's map of South Wales in the fourteenth century.

Cemais); *Stainton, Stanton* (Steynton); *Stackpool, Stacpole* (Stackpole); *Stedwell* (possibly abbreviated from Llanstadwell); *Templeton* (Templeton); *Tenby, Temby* (Tenby); *Treawent* (Trewent near Stackpole); *Wallas* (possibly Wallis near Ambleston); *Walterston* (Walterston); *Wathan, Wathen* (Robeston Wathen); *Whitehook* (Whitehook near Bletherston); *Wydelock, Wedlock* (Great Wedlock, near Tenby).[21]

Pembrokeshire has 63 locative surnames to its credit, a far larger total even than Glamorgan, but with around 156 parishes it was in all probability by far the most populous of Welsh counties in the main surnaming period, so the total is not quite so surprising. The county was not only conquered but, at least in its southern half, intensively colonized by the English and Flemings in the Middle Ages, hence the English character of so many of the locative surnames. Even so, some of the locative surnames such as *Rhigian, Cawey, Killa* and *Pencaer* come from areas which are Welsh in speech. The Anglo-Norman conquest of the area was connected with the aim of conquering Ireland, and several of the locative surnames earliest recorded are those involved in the conquest or early settlement of Ireland: *Carew, Castlemartin, Huskard, Nangle, Prendergast, Roche, Stacpoole*, and *Stanton*. It is quite possible that there is no family connection between those early Irish settlers and the later Pembrokeshire families of *Carew, Prengest, Roch*, and *Stackpole*. The ultimate origin of the name *Prendergast* has been disputed, but tradition has always held that Maurice de Prendergast, one of the conquerors of Ireland, came from Prendergast outside Haverfordwest.

A few locative names are those of the estates of the gentry who owned them, such as *Roch* or *Martel*. The great majority of the

---

21 Many Pembrokeshire surnames are discussed in the extensive notes to H. Owen, ed., *George Owen's Pembrokeshire*, but see also H. Owen, *Old Pembrokeshire Families*, London, 1902; H. Laws, *Little England beyond Wales*, London, 1888; and the material printed by F. Green in *West Wales Historical Records*, especially the lay subsidy rolls for Pembrokeshire, 1543 in vol. 4, 1914, and 'Pembrokeshire hearths in 1670', in vols. 9–11, 1920–26. The surname *Stedwell* (Roger Stedwell of Manorbier, 1670 Hearth Tax returns), was omitted from the article on surnames by P. Morgan, *Nomina*, 13. One of the most useful sources for surnames of the sixteenth and early seventeenth centuries is the collection of probate Registers for the diocese of St David's, at the National Library of Wales. See also B. G. Charles, *The Place-names of Pembrokeshire*, Aberystwyth, 1992.

surnames are those of villages, such as Nash, or of large farms such as Great Wedlock, and although the surname must always have been a rare one, *Wedlock* still survives to this day in Tenby. The Anglicized or English nature of so many of Pembrokeshire place-names means that many locative surnames, such as *Martell, Nash, Johnston, Brody*, and others, resemble surnames which arise from quite different geographical locations. *Harford* and *Harfett* represent the general colloquial pronunciation of Haverford (west), but it may be very tentatively suggested here that the surname *Havard*, particularly common in many parts of Pembrokeshire, may represent another attempt to convey the colloquial pronunciation of Haverford. In England, of course, *Havard* may have quite different origins, and the *Havard* surname in Breconshire may be derived from nearby Hereford.

Radnorshire

Badarn (possibly abbreviated from Llanbadarnfawr or Llanbadarn Fynydd); *Blayney* (topographical, 'blaenau' meaning 'hill country'); *Bykeldy* (Beguildy); *Cascoppe* (Cascob); *Hodoll* (Hoddell, Old Radnor); *Radnor* (Radnor); *Rayad, Ryatt* (possibly from Rhayader); *Treylowe, Trillo* (possibly from Maestreylo near Presteigne).[22]

Radnorshire was a thinly populated county with some 54 parishes and so a total of eight locative surnames is not surprisingly small. *Blayney* arises in the later Middle Ages in Heyop, but then moves to Kinsham, near Presteigne. *Radnor* is mostly found in English counties such as Hereford, while *Rayad* was found early on in Pembrokeshire, and so can only be very tentatively connected with Rhayader. The ultimate origin of the place-name Hodell, Hodoll, may lie in a Welsh personal name, but it looks as if the surname is derived from the farm-name.

---

22 For Radnorshire and the border counties, see T. E. Morris, 'Welsh surnames in the border counties of Wales', *Y Cymmrodor*, 43, London, 1932, pp.93–173; but the volumes of the *Transactions of the Radnorshire Society*, Llandrindod, 1933, ff., contain many notes on Radnorshire families, and references to early wills, etc. I am grateful to Commander A. W. Pressdee of New Malden for providing me with material on Radnorshire names, and for the early references to Hoddols at Old Radnor, from P.R.O., E. 179/224/568.

Regional Locative Surnames

Small regions or lordships such as Gower, Deuddwr, Cyfeiliog, and so on, have been mentioned above, and Gwent has been placed under Monmouthshire, because it is so closely identified with that county. But two broad regional names must be mentioned here: *Gwinneth, Gwinnutt* (Gwynedd, North Wales), and *Powis, Powys* (Powys, mid-Wales, or north-eastern Wales).

Conclusion

Clearly, even with a total of over 260 locative surnames in Wales, locative surnames form a very small proportion of the surnames of the Welsh people, and, since such surnames form a high proportion of English surnames, it seems fair to regard locative surnames as a characteristic of England and the appearance of locative surnames in Wales as a sign of English influence. By contrast, one may conclude that an absence of locative surnames is a sign of lack of English influence, or perhaps a resistance to such influences, since the Welsh were quite familiar in the later medieval period with the locative surnames of English settlers such as *Hampton, Salisbury*, or *Bulkeley*, to cite a few examples from North Wales.

The distribution pattern of Welsh locative surnames is irregular, with juxtaposed counties, for example, those of Cardigan and Carmarthen, starkly contrasted with Pembroke. Wales can be divided roughly into two zones: the greater part of Wales being the zone with very few locative surnames — Anglesey, most of Caernarfonshire, west Denbighshire, Merioneth, west Montgomeryshire, Cardiganshire, Carmarthenshire, Radnorshire, Breconshire and Monmouthshire, all areas with few locatives proportionate to the number of parishes. The second zone consists of western Carnarfonshire, Flintshire and eastern Denbighshire, eastern Montgomeryshire, in the north and north-east of Wales, and of Pembrokeshire and Glamorgan along the southern coast, all areas with a fair number of locative surnames.[23]

To some extent this division into two zones reflects the 'inner Wales' and 'outer Wales' model proposed by modern geographers:

23 For Glamorgan surnames, such as Hengott, see E Parkinson, ed., *The Glamorgan Hearth Tax Assessment of 1670*, Cardiff, 1994.

Flintshire, and the eastern corners of Denbighshire and Montgomeryshire forming an area fairly open to influences from Cheshire and Shropshire; and in the south, the Vale of Glamorgan and south Pembrokeshire being areas of early conquest, colonization and Anglo-Norman settlement, a coastal region open to sea contacts with the west of England and Ireland. Given the division into two broad zones, it is clear that there were exceptions: it is somewhat difficult to explain the comparative lack of locative surnames in such an intensively colonized area as the Gower peninsula, and even along the coastline of Carmarthenshire, which was just as open to English influence, penetration, and to some extent, colonization, as other parts of the southern coastlands. It is also somewhat difficult to explain the little corner of locative surnames appearing from the later fourteenth century to the late sixteenth century on the Lleyn peninsula in west Caernarfonshire, since it has the appearance of remoteness, and has remained until the present day an area of monoglot Welsh speech. The only explanation which may be forwarded here is that Caernarfon was the centre of royal administration in north Wales, and that this made the Caernarfonshire gentry more open to this kind of English influence than might otherwise be expected. In another sense, the distribution pattern does not conform to the geographers' concept of 'inner Wales' and 'outer Wales', because of the comparative paucity of locative surnames in the zone running from Radnorshire to Monmouthshire, a borderland area, which one would expect to show close and constant contact with England. If one takes locative surnames as an index, then the southern borderlands were areas of resistance rather than of penetration in this period.

VII

Names in -*kin* in Medieval Wales

OLIVER PADEL

Most works on surnames, including those by our colleague whom we honour here, mention this suffix; and most discuss the problems of its origin and meaning. However, there does not seem to have been much treatment of precisely how names containing the suffix were used. Some recent work, carried out for quite other purposes, on the fine series of court rolls covering the Welsh marcher lordship of Ruthin or Dyffryn Clwyd, part of the later county of Denbighshire, has shown a rather particular usage in that area in the fourteenth century. It is worth recording here, in the hope that others may be able to throw light on the usage, or at least say whether it is particular to Wales, or to the fourteenth century, or to both or neither.

The Dyffryn Clwyd project, during its first two years, involved calendaring the entire contents of the court rolls of that lordship in two periods of the fourteenth century, 1340–52 and 1389–99.[1] The

---

1 The court rolls of the lordship of Dyffryn Clwyd are in the Public Record Office, London. Those covering 1294–1399 are P.R.O. SC2 215/64 to 221/1; the rolls covering the years 1340–52 and 1389–99 are P.R.O. SC2 217/6 to 218/3 and 220/8 to 221/1. The contents of the earliest rolls, 1294–1301, have been published by R. A. Roberts, *The Court Rolls of the Lordship of Dyffryn-Clwydd* [*sic*], London, 1893. The larger project on the court rolls, of which this offering is a minor part, was made possible by a grant from the Economic and Social Research Council (number R000232548). The computerized data have been deposited in the E.S.R.C. Data Archive, Colchester, Study number 2979A, 'Welsh Society in the Fourteenth Century'; this can be consulted by those having the necessary computer software (the package 'Idealist'). I give my warm thanks to my colleagues on the project, Drs Andrew Barrell and Llinos Beverley Smith and Professor Rees Davies.

project has since continued, to embrace further material from the rest of the century, but the following comments are based primarily upon the material collected from those two periods, in the middle and at the end of the fourteenth century, since they are the ones on which I had the opportunity to work in detail. Over 38,500 entries in the 23 years of court rolls were calendared in detail; as far as can be assessed, about 1,200 individuals were active in the lordship, and appear in the rolls, in the years immediately after the Black Death; the number before the Black Death must have been rather higher. Many of these individuals occur only once or a few times in the material calendared; but others occur repeatedly, often many times in single year. One of the advantages of court rolls for studying naming-patterns is that there are often several references which are demonstrably to a particular individual. For instance, if a court-case is held over from one court to the next (usually every three weeks) — as many cases were, often many times — then one can be sure that the individuals appearing in subsequent entries referring to that case are the same as those of the previous entries, even if their names are given in slightly different form. This gives a valuable perspective on the different ways in which a single person could be named. It is worth noting that a surprising number of individuals appear both in the earlier of our two periods and in the later, thus having an active life of 50 years or more. Because of the Welsh patronymic system of naming, one can usually be certain that these are indeed single individuals, and not fathers and sons with the same names, as might be the case in England.

First the origin of the termination should be mentioned. It is an English suffix, generally recognized to be a diminutive ending (as in 'lambkin' and 'catkin'). A very wide variety of forenames was current in fourteenth-century Dyffryn Clwyd, as in the rest of medieval Wales. Most of them were of Welsh origin, but there was also a generous selection of the rather limited stock of forenames which were in widespread use in England in the period following the Norman Conquest — Hugh, Richard, Robert, Walter, William, and the like. These names were used both by the English settlers in Wales and also by the native Welsh, who in the late thirteenth and the fourteenth centuries, if not earlier, borrowed them enthusiastically from their conquerors and made them their own, just as the English themselves had done some two centuries earlier. In the same way, the Welsh also borrowed the English suffix *-kin*, and used it, not only in combination with these new, borrowed, names, but also occasionally with native Welsh names. It became a formative suffix in Welsh.

How it came into use in Wales is a question related to its origins in England. According to both Reaney and McKinley, its first appearance in England is among the names of Flemings in the mid-twelfth century.[2] In that context, the flourishing Flemish settlement in Pembrokeshire in the early twelfth century could well have been partly responsible for its introduction into Wales.[3] More relevant to our area, however, is the fact that the suffix is said to have been common in Cheshire by the end of the thirteenth century.[4] If it was especially popular there, then north-east Wales, including the area covered by the Ruthin court rolls, might have been the route of its adoption into Welsh nomenclature. The choice between the two areas would depend upon knowing where in Wales it first became common; but there does not seem to be much information available on this, and the necessary historical data may not exist on which to base a decision. The suffix was already established in Merionethshire, in central west Wales, by the 1290s; and it was already being used there with native Welsh names as well as English ones, as seen in a lay subsidy roll of 1292–93 for that county, unfortunately one of the few such rolls to survive for Wales. In that source, as well as the names *Adkin, Ionkin* and *Iankin* (from Adam and John), we also find *Meilkin, Iockin* and *Gurkin*, from the Welsh forenames *Meilyr, Iorwerth* and presumably one beginning with *Gwr-*, such as *Gwrgenau*.[5] In fact, the commonest *-kin*-name among the 2,669 named tax-payers in this source is that standardized as *Iocyn* (spelt *Iockin* or *Iockyn* in the roll), with 13 examples; this is the

2 P. H. Reaney, *A Dictionary of British Surnames*, 2nd ed., London, 1976, p.xxxvii; P. H. Reaney, *The Origin of English Surnames*, London, 1967, pp.213–17; R. McKinley, *A History of British Surnames*, London, 1990, p.100.

3 Lauran Toorians, 'Wizo Flandrensis and the Flemish Settlement in Pembrokeshire', *Cambridge Medieval Celtic Studies*, 20, Winter 1990, pp.99–118.

4 P. H. Reaney, *Dictionary of British Surnames*, p.xxxvii.

5 K. Williams-Jones, *The Merioneth Lay Subsidy*, Cardiff, 1976. Forms of *Adkin* appear on pp.9, 34, 63 and 83, of *Ionkin* on p.24, and of *Iankin* on p.14.

-*kin*-form of the Welsh name Iorwerth, often equated with Edward but in fact of native origin.[6] So by 1293 the suffix had already been thoroughly assimilated into the native name-stock in this part of west Wales.

The concern here, however, is not with the route by which -*kin* was adopted into Welsh, but the use that was made of it. In the Dyffryn Clwyd material the suffix is much commoner in the earlier of the two periods, 1340–52, though present in both. The following names formed with it appear in our material. Those derived from names probably borrowed from English are: Adkin (from Adam), Dawkin (from Ralph, not David! See below), Filkin (from Philip), Hawkin (Ralph), Hochkin (Roger), Hopkin (Robert), Iankin (John, or Welsh Ieuan), Ionkin (John), *Rikkyn* (from Richard, presumably), Watkin (Walter), Wilkin (William, or Welsh Gwilym), and the female Malkin (Maud).[7] Those formed from Welsh names are *Blethekyn* (from Bleddyn),[8] Deykin (from Dafydd, or from anglicized David) and Iocyn (from Iorwerth). Two are of unclear origin, *Ieckyn* and *Maykyn*;[9] they look more likely to be from Welsh names than English ones.

The curious feature of these names is the way in which they are used. This is predominantly as patronymics, particularly in the 1340s. If -*kin* is a diminutive suffix, then one might expect to find it used for the younger of a father-and-son pair who bore the same forename. That is to say, an Adam who was son of Adam might have been expected to appear also as *Adkin*, 'little Adam', to distinguish him from his similarly-named father. There is only one such example, in the whole of the material collected — a single reference to a man called *Filkyn ap Philip Vaghan*, 'Filkin son of Philip the little'.[10]

---

6 I. Williams, 'Iorwerth', *Bulletin of the Board of Celtic Studies*, 11, 1941–44, pp.144–5.

7 All forenames from the rolls, including those following Welsh *ap*, 'son', are quoted here in standardized form, with the exception of unique formations, which are quoted in the manuscript form and are italicized. Other surnames, apart from ap-phrases, are given in italics, in the forms found in the manuscript.

8 SC2 217/6, m.11 (1340–41).

9 Dafydd *ap Ieckyn*, SC2 220/8, m.17d (1395); Alice, daughter of *Maykyn*, SC2 217/8, mm.5 and 6 (1343); William, son of *Mayken/Maykyn/Maykin*, William ap *Maykyn*, SC2 218/2, mm.13 (thrice), 13d and m.23 (all one person, 1351).

10 Filkyn at SC2 217/9, m.22d (1344).

(Unfortunately one cannot tell, in this pattern of patronymic-with-epithet, whether the epithet, here *Vaghan*, 'little', belongs to the son or the father — not that it matters for the present purpose; other word-orders, or other references to either individual, can sometimes make it clear.) This same man is also often called Philip ap Philip (*Vaghan*),[11] and the suffix is thus used here in the way that one might have expected: *Filkyn*, 'little Philip', would reasonably have been so named in contrast with his father who bore the same forename. However, this is a unique instance in the material of such a naming-pattern, as well as being the only occurrence, in all the 38,500 entries calendared, of the name *Filkyn*.

There are other instances of -*kin*-names being used as first names. This is particularly true of Dawkin. One surprise regarding this name was the discovery that it was consistently used as a pet-form not of David, as is usually stated in the literature, but of Ralph. Dawkin *de Sotton*, who was essoined for the first time as defendant against Dafydd ap *Barth* and Angharad his wife on 4th December 1347, is unquestionably the same person as Ralph *de Sutton*, essoined for the second time against the same couple at the following court, 8th January 1348.[12] Once this is observed, it can be found that all other instances of the name Dawkin are also equivalent to Ralph. Dawkin *del Wode*, a brewer in Ruthin town in 1344, is to be equated with the man called Ralph *del Wode* in the corresponding list of brewers in 1350;[13] Dawkin son of John *Tibot* is more often referred to as Ralph son of John *Tybot* (or of John *Tybotson*);[14] and Katherine wife of Dawkin *Witton* is also called Katherine wife of Ralph *de Witton*.[15] In each of these three cases, the firm proof seen in the first instance (a case carried over from one court to another, with a change in the way that one party is named) cannot be produced; but since there are no candidates called David or Dafydd who could be the Dawkins referred to, the identification of these Dawkins with the people elsewhere

---

11 For instance, at SC2 217/9, m.24d (1344), SC2 217/10, m.19d (1345), and SC2 217/11, m.24d (1346).

12 SC2 217/13, mm.2 and 2d.

13 SC2 217/9, m.2, and SC2 218/2, m.24.

14 SC2 220/7, m.9 (twice), and SC2 220/8, mm.14B and 16, and frequently.

15 SC2 220/7, m.9, SC2 220/8, m.6, and elsewhere.

called Ralph is in no doubt. Virtually all of the people called Dawkin in our rolls can be identified with assurance with people otherwise called Ralph, and there is no instance of a Dawkin who is elsewhere called David or Dafydd. The origin of this equation is easy to see, once it is known. The *l* in Ralph would have been vocalized to *u* or *w*, as so often, giving *Rauf*; and the initial *D* replacing *R* in the pet-form (*Daw* for *Raw*) is paralleled by other similar forms, such as Dick for Richard and Dobb for Robert, and (less closely) by Ted or Ned for Edward. It would be interesting to know whether the widespread acceptance of Dawkin as a supposed form of David is based on proven examples, which could counter those in the Dyffryn Clwyd material, or whether it is an assumption which has been repeated from authority to authority. It is possible that all instances of Dawkin, in England as well as Wales, are in fact forms of Ralph. The corresponding pet-form for David or Dafydd, in this material at least, was Deykin.

However, the name Dawkin is unusual in the Ruthin court rolls, in that it is used regularly as a first name. Most of the other *-kin*-formations are used predominantly as patronymics, and occur especially after Welsh ap, 'son'. The most striking example is Wilkin. In our rolls this name occurs 35 times, as a substitute for William or Welsh Gwilym; in none of these is it a first name, and it occurs only in phrases such as Gronw ap Wilkin, Dafydd ap Wilkin, Hugh ap Wilkin, Ieuan ap Dafydd ap Wilkin, Dafydd *Loid* ap Wilkin, and the like. Similarly with Adkin, from Adam or Welsh Adda: it occurs 50 times in the rolls calendared, and except for one individual, Adkin ap Heilyn, who accounts for three of those 50 occurrences, all instances are again in patronymic phrases such as Madog ap Adkin, Hywel ap Adkin, Einion ap Adkin, John ap Adkin, Ieuan ap Einion ap Adkin, and the like. So also with Watkin, where there are again no instances of its use as a first name, but 37 of its use as a patronymic. *Iankin* occurs 31 times, nearly always in the phrase *ap Iankin* and only twice as a first name.

The use made of other *-kin*-names is less clear-cut. Hopkin (from Robert) is found primarily in two patronymic names, Dafydd ap Hopkin and Gronw Hopkin, but occurs also as the name of an individual, Hopkin *Taylor* or *le Taylor*. It is interesting that Gronw Hopkin, on one of his occurrences, is seen to be making a living as a tailor: could this suggest that he was the son of Hopkin *le Taylor*, and had inherited the craft, though not the occupational surname, of his father? So also Hochkin (from Roger) occurs predominantly in patronymic phrases such as Iorwerth ap Hochkin, Bleddyn ap Hochkin, Gwyn ap Hochkin *Cragh* ('scabby'), and Angharad ferch Hochkin ('daughter of Hochkin'), also known as Angharad ferch Hochkin ap *Dollam* (the patronymic here is unexplained, for it does not seem to be a normal forename). There is just one instance of Hochkin used as a first name, a man referred to as Hochkin ap . . ., the father's name, sadly, lost on the manuscript.

With other names in -*kin*, the balance is in the other direction. Deykin (from David or Dafydd) occurs nearly always as a first name, of nine or more individuals, but also as a patronymic for two men, Iorwerth ap Deykin and Ieuan ap Dafydd Deykin (where Deykin, or Dafydd, must have been the name of Ieuan's grandfather, or of a more distant ancestor, as well as that of Ieuan's father). *Ionkin*, in the earlier decade, occurs 127 times, of which 121 are as a first name and only six in the phrase 'son of Ionkin' (in Latin, rather than Welsh, with this name): contrast *Iankin*, which is nearly always used as a patronymic. Finally, the name here standardized as Iocyn functions very much as an ordinary first name: in our rolls it occurs 70 times, of which 47 are as a first name, and 23 in the phrase *ap Iocyn*; in the former role it often interchanges with *Iorwerth* for a given individual.

Thus most of the names in -*kin* in our material occur solely or primarily as patronymic names, while a few, such as Dawkin, occur solely or primarily as first names. Those which occur equally as first names or as patronymics are very much a minority.

It will be seen from the names cited that many of these names in -*kin* are those of Welshmen, at least in the sense that they occur in Welsh phrases and in combination with Welsh names. The suffix was indeed taken up enthusiastically by the Welsh, not only in these names based upon forenames in the 'common stock', shared with the English by this date, but also to make fresh formations from Welsh first names, as mentioned above. That being so, it is slightly surprising to find that the Welsh poet Dafydd ap Gwilym, writing in the mid-fourteenth century, about the time of the earlier of our two periods, employed names containing the suffix when he wished to use typical English forenames. In his poem known as 'Trafferth mewn Tafarn' ('Trouble at an Inn'), Dafydd refers to three

Englishmen who were staying at an inn where he caused a disturbance during the night. He presumably chose names which would seem typically English to his audience; these were 'Hicyn, a Siencyn, a Siac', the latter two being equivalent to Jenkin and Jack, while the first is formed from Hick (a pet-form of Richard) plus the -kin suffix. Two of Dafydd's 'English' names are thus of the type discussed here, although the evidence is that such names were also common among Welshmen by this date.[16]

A preliminary look at material outside the two periods covered in the initial stage of the Dyffryn Clwyd project suggests that this preference for using *-kin*-names as patronymics may have developed in Wales during the course of the fourteenth century. In the earlier rolls, some of which are now available in computerized form, these names are used quite differently. Before the 1340s they generally occur in first position, not in the patronymic position which was later preferred. In the selective material calendared from before 1340, the name Wilkin occurs only once, not as the patronymic which it always is later on, but as a first name, Wilkin *Gam* ('crooked').[17] So also men such as Ionkin *Lingard* and Ionkin *de Mungomer'*,[18] Iankin ap Gronw and Iankin *Duy de Glascoit*,[19] and Adkin *de Cartheneua*[20] all show these formations being used in exactly the way in which they tend not to occur in the later material. Only in the 1320s do hints of the later usage start to appear, with men such as Ieuan ap Adkin and Cadwgan ap Iankin, both of whom first appear in 1325.[21]

Why should this change have occurred? One obvious answer

---

16 *Gwaith Dafydd ap Gwilym* ['The Work of Dafydd ap Gwilym'], edited by Thomas Parry, 2nd ed., Cardiff, 1963, no. 124, pp.327–30; for a translation, see *Dafydd ap Gwilym: a Selection of Poems*, edited and translated by Rachel Bromwich, Llandysul, 1982, no. 40, pp.142–4. Two of the names begin with Welsh *si*, a Welsh sound-substitution for the English 'J', as that is not a Welsh sound. This would have given the names a foreign feel, and might be partly why they were chosen.

17 SC2 215/74, m.18d (1316).

18 SC2 215/74, m.11 (1314); 215/64, m.3 (1295), printed as *Ioukin de Mungomer'* in *Court Rolls of Ruthin*, edited by R. A. Roberts, p.9, perhaps correctly, as this man appears elsewhere in the same year as *Iowkin de Mongomr'* (*ibid.*, p.23).

19 SC2 215/67, m.2 (1299); 215/69, m.13 (1306).

20 SC2 215/75, m.11 (1316; spelt Adekyn).

21 SC2 216/5, m.23d (spelt *Atekyn*); 216/5, m.24.

might be 'scribal usage'. Various other changes occur in the rolls in about 1340 — changes of method in recording the material, and also changes in the administrative practices recorded. However, while scribal practice might provide a partial answer, it certainly is not a complete one, for the administrative changes recorded in the rolls at this time are ones more fundamental than scribal practice alone can explain; many of them must have been changes in practice, as English rule and law became consolidated in the lordship. As far as can be ascertained, there is more than one scribe responsible for the material covering the period 1340–52, when the use of -*kin*-names as patronymics becomes particularly noticeable; and the distinctive usage, once it had become established, remained in force, though less markedly so, throughout the rest of the century.

A fuller explanation for the change in use of -*kin*-names may perhaps be that it was part of a larger change in the method of recording the names in the rolls. At first there is a weird variety of names and a greater proportion of hypocoristic forms, such as *Madyn*, which appears very rarely later on.[22] It may be that the lack of -*kin*-names in first position after about 1340 was partly due to a more formal, and more formulaic, approach to recording names, as the English administration became better established. In the later rolls (from about 1340 onwards) the first names of people featuring in the rolls were recorded in a stylized way, which would reduce the occurrence of hypocoristic and derivative forms, including the -*kin*-names. However, this would not explain why these formations continued to be recorded as patronymic forms, and one is left with a distinct impression that they were in some way thought suitable to appear at final position in a name, as if they carried with them a patronymic flavour.

This is not to say that they were thought of as true patronymic forms, like English *Henryson, Robertson*, and so on, for then they would not be found after Welsh *ap*, 'son', which would be tautologous; it appears rather that they were felt to be forms which were more appropriately used in a patronymic context. For those in the lordship who knew some English, the similarity of the suffix -*kin* to the English word *kin* meaning 'kindred' may have helped in this process, even though that similarity is presumed etymologically to

22 E.g. SC2 215/69, mm.3 (1306; thrice), 4 (1307) and 14 (1307); 215/76, m.11 (1317); 216/1, m.17 (1318).

be mere coincidence. That this feeling was present is suggested in an English context by names such as (to cite an extreme example) that of Roger *Almarison Williamson Watkyn* (1395), who occurs in various guises.[23] His great-grandfather was Walter de Blakeney, who died in 1342,[24] and whose son William, Roger's grandfather, must have been known as William Watkin, though he is not so recorded in the rolls as far as is known. In that longest form of his name, Roger *Almarison Williamson Watkyn*, the English patronymic system gives a true account of Roger's ancestry; but the name ends, not with a third form in -son, although it could have done so, but with a *-kin*-name, just as do so many Welsh names such as that of Ieuan ap Einion ap Adkin, mentioned above. It is as if 'Watkin' itself was, to some extent, felt to mean 'son of Walter', so that it was not necessary to express the idea 'son' when it was used in English. That cannot always have been so, of course, or we should not find forms such as Atkinson; one can only suggest that at some time, or in some context, it was so felt. If so, this also suggests that it was not a specifically Welsh distortion that gave an extra dimension to these *-kin*-names, but one present also among the English-speaking population, to which Roger *Almaryson* must certainly have belonged.

To conclude, the English suffix *-kin* was taken up enthusiastically by the Welsh in the late thirteenth and early fourteenth centuries. They used it both in forms based on Welsh names, and in a good number of names drawn from the common European stock in use in England. But there appears to have been a change in its use during the fourteenth century, and it cannot entirely be accounted for by scribal practice. It was used in the opposite way to that which might have been expected — to refer not to sons, but to fathers; and it came to be felt as a semi-surname, suitable to be used in final position in a composite name, especially in a patronymic context. The material shows a difference in usage between the several names, with some showing a more patronymic tendency than others. A confusion of meaning with the English 'kin' (relations) may have been partly responsible for this usage.

23 In that form, SC2 220/10, m.10d; also as (Roger) 'son of Almary', 'son of Almary son of William', 'son of Almary son of William Watkyn', and 'son of Almary Watkyn'.

24 SC2 217/8, m.19d.

Part Two

Essays by colleagues
associated with the
Department of English Local History

VIII

---·•⧈⧈•·---

Farmworkers' Accommodation in later Medieval England: Three Case Studies from Devon[1]

HAROLD FOX

To RECREATE THE QUALITY of life in the past becomes all the more difficult as the historian turns to focus on the margins of society and this applies not least to those seemingly fleeting countrymen and countrywomen who depended for the greater part of their livelihoods upon wage labour. 'No one', says Alan Everitt of the Tudor farmworker, 'has written his signature more plainly across the countryside . . . no one has left more scanty records of his achievements', while for the Middle Ages, L. R. Poos has noted the shortage of evidence about 'the qualitative or experiential details of labourers' lives'.[2] Despite these difficulties my essay attempts to examine one aspect of the quality of life among farmworkers, namely their accommodation. It focuses squarely upon the Later Middle Ages, broadly speaking

---

1 Richard Smith and Keith Snell have helped me to turn my mind towards this theme. Some of the ideas explored here were presented in undeveloped form to the seminar on English Economic and Social History at All Souls College, May 1989, and I am grateful to the audience, especially Chris Dyer, Zvi Razi and Tony Wrigley for comments then. Margery Rowe with all of her Staff at the Devon Record Office and Audrey Erskine (latterly Angela Doughty) tolerated my incessant demands for Ashwater and Sidbury court rolls. Additional references and help have come from Keith Davis, Greg Finch, Ken Smith and David Postles. I owe thanks, for their hospitality, to Bob Roberts of Stokenham and Margaret Meeres of Exeter.

2 A. Everitt, 'Farm labourers', in J. Thirsk, ed., *The Agrarian History of England and Wales, iv, 1500–1640*, Cambridge, 1967, p.396; L. R. Poos, *A Rural Society after the Black Death: Essex 1350–1525*, Cambridge, 1991, p.207.

the period between 1348 and the early sixteenth century. The three case studies presented are all from Devon, all employ surveys and related documents, while the train of thought which sparked off this essay came during a nominal analysis of a late fourteenth-century survey. The essay is offered as a tribute to a scholar who once presided over the City of Exeter Record Office, who spent many hours with the surveys contained in the Hundred Rolls and who, above all, was a master of nominal studies.

Despite the difficulties of evidence mentioned above, several historians have recently made very significant contributions to our understanding of the quality of labouring life in the countryside in the centuries before it was thrown into stark relief by reports to the Select Committees and Royal Commissions of the Victorian era. Alan Everitt has sympathetically reconstructed the lives of farmworkers in the sixteenth century and the early seventeenth, with especial reference to a range of influences on their quality of life: access to land, common rights, ownership of animals, by-employments, living space, diet. Everitt's survey comes to an end towards the middle of the seventeenth century just at a time when, according to another important contribution — by Ann Kussmaul — there took place a quite dramatic change in the preferences of farmer-employers, from a tendency to hire a good deal of their work-force more or less casually on a daily or weekly basis towards employment on yearly terms, the employee then becoming a 'servant in husbandry' living in the farmhouse as part of the family of the farmer. She sees two influences at work behind the trend towards greater reliance on a resident labour force on farms: first, under late-seventeenth-century conditions of falling population, farmers attempted to secure an ever more scarce commodity, labour, by binding young people to annual contracts and keeping them on the farm (thereby also saving on labour costs); second, the tendency towards greater involvement with pastoral farming, a product of relative price movements, meant that resident labour was all the more desirable in order to cope with the constant daily needs of farm animals as well as crises of birth and death which could come at any time of the day or night.[3] The contribution of Poos is in some senses an extension of Kussmaul's arguments but

---

3 A. Everitt, 'Farm labourers', pp.396–465; A Kussmaul, *Servants in Husbandry in Early Modern England*, Cambridge, 1981, pp.97–119.

applied to another period when labour was costly and in scarce supply and when the balance in the farming economy tipped towards the pastoral: the Later Middle Ages. In a regional monograph of unparalleled depth (on later medieval Essex) he argues that 'economic logic, albeit not empirical demonstration, suggests that . . . [servants] played a role at least as important in the district's workforce as before 1350 or after 1520, and quite likely rather more.'[4] Both Kussmaul and Poos elaborate the connections between declining population, scarcity of labour, increasing recourse to hiring servants in relatively young age groups, delayed age of marriage and further population decline.

These last authors formally recognize two contrasting systems of farmworkers' accommodation associated with two very different forms of lifestyle for the employee. Service in husbandry was associated with the early years of the life-cycle and among some groups of servants there developed elements of a distinctive culture of youth; employment, when it was found, was relatively secure for the term of service, usually a year; to be a servant meant movement away from the family and often away from the native settlement; it meant submission to the regime of another household, be it paternal or autocratic.[5] By contrast, the labourer living in a rented cottage was more likely to be older, married and relatively less mobile; he has been portrayed as working uncertainly for a variety of employers, at their whim and at the weather's whim; he was in some senses more independent than a servant in husbandry although, as Alan Everitt showed, there were degrees of independence engendered by differences from place to place in the structure of authority.[6] Probably at all periods the two systems co-existed side by side although there were changes over time in the predominance of one over the other, the last of these

---

4 L. R. Poos, *op. cit.*, p.225. For an early statement of this view see R. M. Smith, 'The people of Tuscany and their families in the fifteenth century: medieval or Mediterranean?', *Journal of Family History*, 6, 1981, pp.123–5.

5 For culture see, for example, D. Buchan, 'The expressive culture of nineteenth-century Scottish farm servants', in T. M. Devine, ed., *Farm Servants and Labour in Lowland Scotland 1770–1914*, Edinburgh, 1984, pp.226–42; B. Munro, 'The bothy ballads: the social context and meaning of the farm servants' songs of north-eastern Scotland', *History Workshop*, 3, 1977, pp.184–93; A Howkins, *Reshaping Rural England: a Social History 1850–1925*, London, 1991, p.22.

6 A. Everitt, 'Farm labourers', pp.462–3.

changes being the final decline (though not complete extinction) of service, especially acute during the last decades of the eighteenth century and the early decades of the nineteenth.[7]

As we move into the nineteenth century we become fully aware of yet other types of accommodation for farmworkers, revealed to us by a superior documentation born out of social concern over the various kinds of relationships which existed between employer and employed.[8] One variant was the bondager system, reported from the North-East, on both sides of the Tweed; a cottage labourer was obliged to accommodate an extra pair of hands to work on his employer's farm and in return for the cottage.[9] The system may have had a near equivalent in the Middle Ages in heavily manorialized villages where labour services for the lord were so heavy that villeins were obliged to hire servants in order to acquit them.[10] Another variant

7 A. Kussmaul, *op. cit.*, pp.120–34; K. D. M. Snell, *Annals of the Labouring Poor: Social Change and Agrarian England 1660–1900*, Cambridge, 1985, pp.67–103 and especially pp.81–2 for a 'variety of practices . . . within the system of service, which became more evident during its decline' in the nineteenth century.

8 A good introduction to the variety in farmworkers' accommodation in the nineteenth century, and to some of the evidence, is to be found in A. Howkins, 'The English farm labourer in the nineteenth century: farm, family and community', in B. Short, ed., *The English Rural Community: Image and Analysis*, Cambridge, 1992, pp.85–104 and in A. Howkins, *Reshaping Rural England*, pp.7–60. See also A. Armstrong, *Farmworkers: a Social and Economic History, 1770–1980*, London, 1988.

9 For bondagers north of the border see M. Robson, 'The border farm worker', in T. M. Devine, ed., *op. cit.*, pp.74–5, 82–3. For south of the border, P. Brassley, *The Agricultural Economy of Northumberland and Durham in the Period 1640–1750*, New York and London, 1985, p.35. Robson makes the points that some contemporaries believed that the origin of the term had to do with 'the form of slavery' which the ancillary worker laboured under but that in all probability it derived from the 'bond' or contract to provide extra labour entered into between master and cottager. The system itself is said to have originated from the obligation of a cottager to provide his employer with the labour of his wife at harvest time, an obligation which came to be more and more extended, and less and less often applied to the spouse, at a time when 'the whole trend of the new agriculture was to extend the busy season by raising, and tending, a greater variety of crops': J. P. D. Dunbabin, *Rural Discontent in Nineteenth-century Britain*, New York, 1974, p.135.

10 In thirteenth-century custumals a villein tenant is often said to have to perform certain works 'with one man' and, more occasionally, it is stated that the attendant will be the *famulus*, *serviens* or *ancilla* of the tenant; moreover, a theoretical case

for which there is good evidence in the nineteenth century was the practice of boarding farm servants not in the farmhouse but in common barracks, like the one near the deserted village of Wharram Percy on the Yorkshire Wolds which housed 10 male labourers, most of them young, in 1841. They are said to have been associated with regions where, by the nineteenth century, available pools of day labour were few and far between and where farms were of some size, requiring a large male workforce.[11] Again, they had earlier antecedents: there is evidence for barracks on large farms in the seventeenth century, and on some medieval demesnes some agricultural servants appear to have been housed in their own quarters within the *curia*.[12]

may be made for the employment of servants by villeins whose total work-load (for themselves on their own holdings and for the lord on the demesne) was pushed above a certain threshold by excessive labour services. The situation is discussed in detail in H. S. A. Fox, 'Exploitation of the landless by lords and tenants in early medieval England', in Z. Razi and R. M. Smith, eds., *Medieval Society and the Manor Court*, Oxford, 1996, pp.518–68.

11 M. W. Beresford, 'Documentary evidence for the history of Wharram Percy', in D. D. Andrews and G. Milne, eds., *Wharram: a Study of Settlement on the Yorkshire Wolds*, London, 1979, p.15; A. Howkins, 'English farm labourer in the nineteenth century', p.92. The system was perhaps most fully developed in parts of Scotland, where barracks were called bothies, a demoralizing type of housing condemned by William Cobbett and many later writers: I. Carter, *Farmlife in Northeast Scotland 1840–1914: the Poor Man's Country*, Edinburgh, 1979, pp.121–7 and (for Cobbett) E. Gauldie, *Cruel Habitations: a History of Working-class Housing 1780–1918*, London, 1974, pp.66–7.

12 For the sixteenth and seventeenth centuries: A. Everitt, 'Farm labourers', p.434 (a 'convenient house' for the accommodation of extra harvest hands); E. Kerridge, ed., *Surveys of the Manors of Philip, First Earl of Pembroke and Montgomery 1631–2*, Wiltshire Archaeological and Natural History Society Records Branch, ix, 1953, pp.72, 109 ('an out-chamber for servants to lodge in'; '1 ground room, being a lodging chamber for servants, standing in the backside'); R. H. D'Elboux, ed., *Surveys of the Manors of Robertsbridge, Sussex, and Michelmarsh, Hampshire, and of the Demesne Lands of Halden in Rolvenham, Kent 1567–1570*, Sussex Record Society, xlvii, 1944, p.125 ('one long lowe house standinge nere unto the kytchen . . . wherein are iiii or severall lodginges for servantes of husbandry'); A. Hassell Smith, 'Labourers in late sixteenth-century England: a case study from North Norfolk, part I', *Continuity and Change*, 4, 1989, p.15 ('discrete lodgings . . . in the estate yard'). It must be added that all of these examples are from exceptionally large holdings on which social relations between master and men would have been of a less domestic, less familiar kind than those on smaller farms. For the Middle Ages: D. Oschinsky, ed., *Walter of Henley and other Treatises on Estate Management and Accounting*, Oxford, 1971, p.283 ('Every carter ought to

Finally, though not exhaustively, there is good nineteenth-century evidence for another variant, the tied cottage system, whereby the labourer was provided with accommodation by his farmer-employer in return for work, but in married quarters so to speak. Farmworkers living in tied cottages were half labourers, half servants. Bound to serve throughout their tenure of the cottage, their conditions of work were those of a servant but unlike the traditional servant in husbandry they could be married and with a family, to the considerable advantage of their employers. The institution has aroused much controversy in the present century and has been criticized for restricting mobility of labour and tending to instil deference among labourers. Yet despite this contemporary interest little serious work has been done on its early history.[13] Most historians see it as 'a quite recent development of mid-Victorian agriculture', associated with decline in farm service and 'the desire of farmers to control labour supplies'; Hasbach, writing at a time when the nineteenth century was still fresh in men's minds, linked the building of tied cottages to a decline in gangs of itinerant independent workers; Newby makes

sleep every night with his horses'); M. Hollings, ed., *The Red Book of Worcester*, Worcester Historical Society, 4 pts., 1934–50, iii, p.277 (*domus bovariorum*); D. J. H. Michelmore, *The Fountains Abbey Lease Book*, Yorkshire Archaeological Society Record Series, cxl, 1981, p.227 (demesne lessee 'to keep at bed and board four menservants called hynes'); P. D. A. Harvey, *A Medieval Oxfordshire Village: Cuxham 1240 to 1400*, Oxford, 1965, p.77 ('*famuli* at Cuxham . . . referred to as a household, or *familia*, and they were certainly expected to live in the *curia*'); I. Kershaw, *Bolton Priory: the Economy of a Northern Monastery 1286–1325*, Oxford, 1973, p.53 ('the alternative name for the *bovaria*, or oxhouse, at Bolton was *le hinehouse* — the home of the hinds or agricultural workers'); F. G. Davenport, *The Economic Development of a Norfolk Manor 1086–1565*, Cambridge, 1906, p.21 n.9 (*domus famulorum* at Forncett); Longleat House MSS, 11216 and other Uplyme accounts referring to the *inhyne*, possibly 'living-in hind', though the word is not in *O.E.D.*; F. M. Page, ed., *Wellingborough Manorial Accounts A.D. 1258–1323*, Northamptonshire Record Society, viii, 1936, p.18 ('*famuli* staying in the *curia*'). Although *some* demesne *famuli* resided in barrack-like accommodation, perhaps especially those concerned with horses, oxen and other cattle (except cows), the majority probably did not, as Postan argued: M. M. Postan, *The Famulus: The Estate Labourer in the xiith and xiiith Centuries*, Economic History Review Supplements, ii, Cambridge, 1954, pp.39–41.

13 The best introduction to the tied cottage in the twentieth century is H. Newby, *The Deferential Worker: a Study of Farm Workers in East Anglia*, Harmondsworth, 1979 edn., pp.40–1, 178–94. See also A. Armstrong, *op. cit.*, pp.236–9.

an even more specific link with the act of 1867 which banned women and children from the gangs, with the implication that tied cottages were provided as an enticement to the labour of whole families. Barley was more cautious but more perceptive. He saw that 'the beginning of the tied cottage . . . is of great social importance' but, suspecting an earlier origin than is generally believed, wrote that it is 'singularly difficult to date from the documents'.[14] He was correct on all counts although, as this essay will show later, close inspection of manorial sources reveals that the institution was already present in the Middle Ages when and where the circumstances were ripe.

It is with these types of nineteenth-century farmworkers' accommodation in mind that we may now turn to the Middle Ages in the hope that the variations and changes described in detail by Victorian official inquisitions will help us in our understanding of earlier periods when the labourer is a more fleeting figure in the farming landscape.

'Separated from the rest of the world'[15]

Our first case study comes from the manor of Ashwater in what has long been the remote and peacefully pastoral countryside between Dartmoor and the northern coastline of Devon. On this manor, cottage accommodation disappeared totally during the Later Middle Ages. A rental made a few years before the Black Death reveals some cottage holdings[16] but relatively few compared with some other Devon

14 H. Newby, *Green and Pleasant Land? Social Change in Rural England*, London, 1979, p.137; W. Hasbach, *A History of the English Agricultural Labourer*, London, 1908, p.203; H. Newby, *Deferential Worker, op. cit.*, p.40; M. W. Barley, *The English Farmhouse and Cottage*, London, 1961, p.247. For the dating of the tied cottage to the nineteenth century see also A. Kussmaul, *op. cit.*, p.169.

15 'Farmhouses . . . scattered and farm servants . . . separated from the rest of the world': a description of parts of the East Riding of Yorkshire, given to the Commission on the Employment of Children, Young Persons and Women in Agriculture and quoted in A. Howkins, *Reshaping Rural England*, p.22.

16 Throughout this essay I define a cottage or 'cottage holding' as a cottage and curtilage only and no other land; 'farm holdings' are those with over one acre. The distinction is obviously too precise but the evidence unfortunately does not allow me to draw a line between smallholders with, say, three acres who on occasion hired themselves to others and larger farmers who did not.

manors of about the same size, so perhaps we can say that the decline had already begun in the early fourteenth century; thereafter further decline took place, with several decayed cottages mentioned in an account roll of 1377 and none remaining by the time of a rental of 1464. Comparison of a rental of 1523 and the subsidy return of 1524 confirms that the cottage labourer had disappeared from the social landscape of Ashwater during the Later Middle Ages.[17]

Developments during the latter part of the fourteenth century were crucial in giving Ashwater and other North Devon manors the empty, pastoral air which the region still wears today. The unattractive soils of the Culm Measures, when cultivated, yielded crops of low price — largely rye and oats — so that arable land here was assessed at the lowest possible valuations in the early fourteenth century.[18] With a reduced local demand for grain after 1348 the region experienced a sharp fall in cultivation, some land reverting to rough moor and much of the rest tumbling down to pasture. During the Later Middle Ages the speciality of the region came to be the breeding and rearing of what Leland described as a 'very good . . . broode of catell', to be traded off at fairs on its periphery and ending up in distant urban meat and leather markets.[19] This specialization

17 In this section all references to Ashwater are, unless otherwise stated, from the Devon Record Office (hereafter D.R.O.), Cary MSS. These documents were still being catalogued when I consulted them, so I am unable to give reference numbers, though I try to mention the type and date of the manuscripts used for most statements here. For the subsidy of 1524 I have used T. L. Stoate, ed., *Devon Lay Subsidy Rolls 1524–7*, Bristol, 1979, p.134; comparison with the rental of 1523 reveals that the men who were assessed at the lowest rates in this subsidy were occupiers of farm holdings, not cottagers. My earlier interpretation of the subsidy is incorrect, and I withdraw it: H. S. A. Fox, 'Tenant farming and tenant farmers: Devon and Cornwall', in E. Miller, ed., *The Agrarian History of England and Wales*, *iii, 1348–1500*, Cambridge, 1991, p.736. A useful church rate of 1752 (D.R.O. 2466A/PW/2) shows that cottagers were still virtually absent from the parish at that time, but the tithe map (also D.R.O.) indicates that some of the roadside cottages, still visible behind the verges today, were there by the 1840s.

18 H. S. A. Fox, 'Medieval farming and rural settlement', in R. J. P. Kain and W. L. D. Ravenhill, eds., *Historical Atlas of South-West England*, Exeter, 1999, p.275, map of land values based on inquisitions *post mortem*.

19 H. S. A. Fox, 'The occupation of the land: Devon and Cornwall' and 'Farming practices and techniques: Devon and Cornwall', in E. Miller, ed., *op. cit.*, pp.157–8, 317; L. Toulmin Smith, ed., *The Itinerary of John Leland*, London, 5 vols.,

in a commodity whose marketing did not involve high transport costs was ideal for farmers in a region which had no large urban markets itself and no local concentrations of consumers engaged in rural industry: markets were at a distance, so the speciality chosen was one which could walk to the source of demand.[20] Ashwater was absolutely typical of its region. Some grain was cultivated there in the Later Middle Ages, but, one suspects, for domestic consumption only. Most cases of trespass recorded in court rolls took place on pasture land where bovines were overwhelmingly the most frequent trespassers, horses and pigs being equal as poor seconds and sheep third. Within the cattle herds, cows were obviously present for breeding but calves and *boviculi* are far more commonly mentioned than the older *bovetti*, suggesting that cattle were sold off at three years of age, possibly to be fattened for a further year in the lusher vales of East Devon.[21] Rustling the steers was not uncommon, as in 1422 when John Antony entered the meadow of Thomas Jagoe and drove away three cows and a *boviculus*; tenants with surplus pasture took in the stock of neighbours, as in 1441 when there was a broken convention over the accommodation of six *boviculi*; strays included red oxen and young bovines, also red; tenants were frequently in debt with one another over sales of cattle. The very landscape of Ashwater was designed for the lowing herds: tenants had steer houses in their yards, beyond which were closes with hedges for

1907–10, i, p.172. Maryanne Kowaleski tells me that Crediton, significantly at a junction between two types of farming region, was an important trading place for cattle during the Later Middle Ages. According to account rolls of the 1460s and 1470s the lord of Ashwater sold off stock at fairs at Tavistock, Launceston, Holsworthy, Brentor and Week St Mary.

20 The *isolation* of parts of the region is to be stressed: Great Torrington was the only town of significance (in terms of tax wealth) within the region; Barnstaple, on the northern coast, was served by its own fertile hinterland, of a different character from the rest of North Devon.

21 Statements about crops and livestock are all from incidental references in court rolls, sampled between 1403 and 1489. Oats and rye, both grains of low value, were the principal crops. For the suggestion of movement of cattle to East Devon for a final fattening see H. S. A. Fox, 'Farming practices and techniques', p.320. For the meat and hide trade in later medieval Exeter, where many North Devon carcasses may have ended up, see M. Kowaleski, 'Town and country in late medieval England: the hide and leather trade', in P. J. Corfield and D. Keene, eds., *Work in Towns 850–1850*, Leicester and London, 1990, pp.59–62.

shelter and beyond them many patches of rough moor, most of them appropriated to particular farms.[22]

During the Later Middle Ages, Ashwater became a manor dominated by large farms. By about 1400 there were no small holdings and no landless cottage holdings. The evidence is not precise but it suggests that in the fifteenth century the manor boasted some farms of between 80 and 100 acres and many of between 40 and 80 acres, enlarged by engrossing and by the acquisition of demesne.[23] The presence of large pastoral farms, combined with an absence of small-holdings and cottage accommodation, implies that those farmers who were not able to call on the services of sons must surely have employed living-in servants in husbandry, the type of labour which was usually preferred when constant attention to livestock was necessary and crises (of birth, of death in the herd) often occurred at night. The very isolation of many of the farms on the manor (a product of ancient settlement pattern and later medieval settlement contraction) rendered living-in servants all the more necessary.[24] The case may be made from the standpoint of supply as well as demand: for 'surplus' sons not wanted on their fathers' holdings there were no cottages or smallholdings — niches from which they might have begun to ascend the ladder of landholding — so that the only way (locally at least) in which to accumulate enough capital to take on and stock a large farm was through employment as a servant, a celibate on a wild, lonely farm. And servants are certainly visible in Ashwater's court rolls as, for example, in a case of 1444 when two tenants bicker over the enticement of a servant and a retaliatory

22 Statements from the sample of court rolls, as in n.21 above. The reference to a steer house is in a court roll of 1489. References to tenants who allowed the hedges of their closes to decay are fairly frequent in the court rolls. The best evidence for large acreages of moorland held by individual tenants is a detailed survey with field names, undated but probably from the first half of the sixteenth century. Many of the patches of moorland in the region were not strictly commonable but were 'attached to particular estates' or belonged 'exclusively to particular estates': C. Vancouver, *General View of the Agriculture of the County of Devon*, London, 1808, pp.277, 290.

23 Early rentals of Ashwater are couched in terms of 'tenures' and do not therefore help over the question of size of holding. The exception is an early sixteenth-century survey for which see above n.22. My figures are based on collation of that survey with earlier rentals.

24 See n.30 below.

theft of cattle or in the same year when a youth is reported as living on the manor yet outside his parents' home.

From other manors in the countryside of North Devon there is ample evidence, similar to that from Ashwater, for the decline of cottage accommodation and for the employers' preference for servants during the Later Middle Ages. At Fremington there were 39 cottages in 1326 but 'diverse destroyed cottages' by 1388. A detailed survey of Brendon drawn up in 1525 for the Marchioness of Dorset lists many large farms of over 50 acres each with grazing for 30 large beasts on the flanks of Exmoor, but no landless cottagers. At Werrington, a few miles west of Ashwater, cottages seem to have disappeared by the 1360s.[25] Many large pastoral farms and few cottages imply living-in servants and there is good evidence for them throughout the region, for which Great Torrington may have been the hiring fair.[26] The court rolls of Monkleigh, from 1438 into the early sixteenth century, regularly record the names of males sworn into tithing and the names of heads of households with whom they were residing; many (24 out of 31 recorded cases) were in households which were not their parents' and were almost certainly servants.[27] At Braunton it was the custom 'for every tenaunte . . . haveyng ther chyldern in houshold . . . not to be presented for a censur tyll tyme that they do be of full age by Statute and put oute . . . for waygs'. A late-fourteenth-century listing for *censura* (an obscure West Country tax) survives for Bratton Clovelly, a few miles from Ashwater and seems to differentiate between landless males in the parental home and those who were living with others; 13 out of 38 landless males appear to have been servants.[28] Finally, a fascinating

25 P.R.O. C. 134/99 and *Calendar of Inquisitions Miscellaneous, 1387–93*, London, H.M.S.O., 1962, p.89; P.R.O. E. 315/385; D.R.O. 1258M/D/70, court rolls of Werrington in which transfers of cottage holdings are noticeably absent.

26 The evidence is suggestive but not conclusive: B. H. Putham, *The Enforcement of the Statutes of Labourers*, New York, 1908, p.167*.

27 D.R.O. C.R. 1094 and subsequent numbers. One of the servants was stated to have been an immigrant, and there are two cases of farmers with two servants. There is similar (but not identical) material in the court rolls of Werrington: D.R.O. 1258M/D/70.

28 R. Dymond, 'The customs of the manor of Braunton', *Transactions of the Devonshire Association*, 20, 1888, p.280; D.R.O. 314M/M/2, listing perhaps to be dated to 1397–8. For *censura* see N. Neilson, *Customary Rents*, Oxford Studies in

glimpse of contemporary perception of the expertise in livestock management which grew up among the farm servants of the region comes from a late fourteenth-century episcopal account roll which records that the bishop sent over 35 miles to North Devon in order to hire a bullock-herd to add to his team of *famuli* at Clyst near Exeter.[29]

It is easy to see why the evolving later medieval farm economy of Ashwater should make the manor (and others like it) a classic locality for the development of service in husbandry: the trend towards pastoralism encouraged farmers to employ living-in labour which was always at hand — day, night and early morning — to attend cattle; the isolation of many of the farmsteads of the region, an isolation which increased as hamlets dwindled to become single farms and as some settlement sites became deserted, also encouraged the institution.[30] It seems likely that the servant labour force was

Social and Legal History, ii, Oxford 1910, p.106. Finberg produced evidence to show that *censura* could on occasion be used as a term for tithingpenny: H. P. R. Finberg, *Tavistock Abbey*, Cambridge, 1951, p.208. More often, though, it appears to have more affinity with a family of manorial taxes which fell upon landless males, discussed in detail in H. S. A. Fox, 'Exploitation of the landless'.

29 D.R.O. 1258M/G/3, account of 1378–9.

30 For isolation from pools of village labour as one factor which encouraged employment of servants in husbandry see A. Howkins, *Reshaping Rural England*, p.22 and A. Kussmaul, *op. cit.*, pp.23–4. For an example of later medieval changes in settlement patterns which led to the increasing isolation of remaining farmsteads in North Devon see H. S. A. Fox, 'Contraction: desertion and dwindling of dispersed settlement in a Devon parish', *Medieval Village Research Group Annual Report*, 31, 1983, pp.40–2. For the case of Ashwater manor see A. E. Baker, 'Insular farms and muddy lanes: pre-Conquest and medieval settlement on the Culm Measures of Devon', unpublished M.A. dissertation, Department of English Local History, University of Leicester, 1985, pp.44–9. It is interesting to note that the isolation of so many farms in the region, as well as a continuing pastoral farming type, meant that male living-in servants remained common well beyond the 1850s; some were still employed in this way when W. M. Williams made his classic study of the pseudonymous Ashworthy, a parish just a few miles away from the real Ashwater: *A West Country Village, Ashworthy: Family, Kinship and Land*, London, 1963, p.47 and see also p.15. M. Bouquet, *Family, Servants and Visitors: the Farm Household in Nineteenth and Twentieth Century Devon*, Norwich, 1985, p.76 gives another example of the late persistence of farm service in the region. North Devon was clearly one of those 'obscure districts of merry England' where, according to William Howitt, servants in husbandry remained common long after the institution had died out elsewhere: quoted in A. Kussmaul, *op. cit.*, p.130.

largely male, for many tasks associated with cattle rearing were in the male domain: rounding up frisky steers which became 'wild' if uncared for, according to an inquisition of 1388,[31] moving them from close to close, droving them to market, taking the bull to the cow, carting hay in early summer and forking it in winter.[32] Under these circumstances the labour of a cottager's wife and children was little needed and the class was all but extinguished from many North Devon manors.

'Independence and mild animosity'[33]

Forty miles away from Ashwater, and in the very different countryside

31 *Calendar of Inquisitions Miscellaneous*, 1387–93, London, H.M.S.O., 1962, p.45.

32 Droving was one occupation, involving large and often difficult-to-manage animals, which was wholly in the male domain. See, for example, K. J. Bonser, *The Drovers*, London, 1970, p.39 for the act which gave powers to Quarter Sessions to limit the occupation to males over 30 years of age. For the dangers of the occupation and the qualities of endurance required, see A. R. B. Haldane, *The Drove Roads of Scotland*, London, 1952, p.23 and R. J. Colyer, *The Welsh Cattle Drovers*, Cardiff, 1976, p.61. For work among farm horses, likewise, see S. Caunce, *Amongst Farm Horses: the Horselads of East Yorkshire*, Stroud, 1991, *passim*, where the heaviness of the work, its strenuous nature and occasional dangers are stressed. Caunce also makes the point that the length of the working day rendered the occupation of looking after a horse unsuitable for married labourers. There is of course some gap between the undoubtedly male-orientated occupations described in these works and our assertion that male servants were preferred by North Devon cattle rearers in the Later Middle Ages, so an examination of the sexual composition of the farmers themselves is interesting and suggestive. At Ashwater, according to a rental of 1464–5, only one out of 38 conventionary tenants of farm holdings was a woman (about 3 per cent), which could suggest that women found it difficult to manage these holdings (and therefore, by implication, that male servants were preferred). Other comparable figures from manors in the region are no female tenants at Umberleigh in 1441–2 and none at Brendon in 1525: Royal Institution of Cornwall, HD/20/12 and P.R.O. E. 315/385. They may be compared with figures from manors in East Devon, discussed in the next section of this essay, where small farm holdings were common and where dairying, in the female domain, rather than rearing was the speciality. There 13 per cent of the occupiers of farm holdings at Sidbury in 1394–5 were women, 22 per cent at Dawlish in *c.*1385 and 20 per cent at Lympstone in 1525: Dean and Chapter Archives, Exeter (hereafter D.C.A.), 2945; D.C.A. 2937; P.R.O. E. 315/385. Of course, factors other than those suggested here may have contributed to this intriguing regional contrast

33 A. Everitt, 'Farm labourers', p.464, a description of the cottagers of Flora Thompson's Lark Rise.

of East Devon, surveyors for the Chapter of Exeter made two rentals of their manor of Sidbury, in 1350–51 and 1394–95. The first reveals a large population of cottagers (38 in all, slightly fewer than the number of farm tenures, which stood at 47) and very few vacant cottages. The second shows only a slight decline in the number of occupied cottages and although some vacancies are recorded in the fifteenth century, the independent landless cottager remained an important element in the manor's social structure.[34]

We may explore the resilience of Sidbury's cottage population by looking first at opportunities for making a living there other than by farm labouring. The geological map will suggest that as much as half of the face of the parish would have been uncultivated during the Later Middle Ages, the steep slopes of the infertile Greensand hills on either side of the river Sid and their flat, wet tops covered by clay-with-flints. Some of this uncultivated land was occupied by the Chapter's woods but the rest was common pasture upon which occupiers of farm holdings were allowed as many animals as their tenements could support.[35] How these generous rights enjoyed by farmers were translated for the cottage population is uncertain. At close-by Northleigh a fourteenth-century lease of a single acre gave the lessee the right to pasture as many animals as he wished *in montibus*; an early-sixteenth-century survey of Churchstanton, to the north, allowed cottagers stints of 15 sheep and a cow on the rough pastures.[36] The evidence of heriots shows that some Sidbury cottagers kept cows, horses and sheep which would certainly have

34 D.C.A. 2944, 2945. 'Cottager' and 'farm holding' or 'tenure' defined as in n.16 above. In addition to the 38 independent cottagers of the first rental and the 31 of the second, there were respectively three and two additional *cottages* rented by individuals who also rented farm holdings, an arrangement discussed in the next section of this essay. For some fifteenth-century cottage vacancies see, for example, D.C.A. 4805. The documents make it clear that many of these cottages were grouped around the church, where their successors still stand today.

35 There was dispute between the Chapter and its tenants over common pasture on the wastes in the thirteenth century; by the fifteenth the discord seems to have disappeared, either by resolution or by a lessening of interest on the part of the lord, and by 1490 the steward admitted that tenants could occupy the commons with as many animals as their tenements could support: D.C.A. 3672A, 4830.

36 D.R.O. 123M/TB/349; P.R.O. E 315/385.

run on the common wastes, for these were landless tenements with no more than a curtilage.[37]

The common wastes of the manor provided cottagers with ferns, cut in the fourteenth century on 'the great heath or waste' lying between Sidbury and Ottery St Mary; with rabbits, the game rights to which were leased by the Chapter to tenants; and probably with turf, for medieval turbaries are well evidenced on many of the flat, wet hill-tops of East Devon.[38] The medieval cottager at Sidbury had access to resources far more diverse than those available to his fading counterparts at Ashwater where the monotonous moors were appropriated to particular farms, and he cannot be described in George Bourne's phrase coined for the nineteenth-century cottager after enclosure — 'a peasant shut out from his countryside and cut off from his resources'.[39]

The landless cottager at Sidbury could also earn an income from cloth working for which there is good evidence throughout East Devon during the fourteenth and fifteenth centuries. In 1499 Sibil Pounde of Sidbury, who reputedly combined the by-employments of spinster and prostitute, broke into a neighbour's house and took away

37 Heriots of cottagers recorded in D.C.A. 4798–4835, court rolls between 1421 and 1500. The curtilages of these cottages were small (as is clear from inspection today and from D.C.A. 2945 which singles out an especially large one for special mention); it is unlikely that they could have supported cows.

38 D.R.O. C.R. 1288 m.17 and P.R.O. E. 134/5 Jas I Mich 1; D.C.A. 5065; for examples of turbary in the region see P.R.O. C. 133/43 (Hemyock), 133/54 (Woodbury), 133/62 (Colyton), D.R.O. T. 42, f.53 (Venn Ottery); Longleat House MSS, account rolls of Uplyme (Uplyme). 'Dunkeswell Turbary' is marked on modern O.S. maps.

39 G. Bourne, *Change in the Village*, London, 1920 edn., p.133. For the large contribution of common rights to the standards of living and independence of cottagers see A. Everitt, 'Farm labourers', pp.403–6; A. Armstrong, 'Labour', in G. E. Mingay, ed., *The Agrarian History of England and Wales, vi, 1750–1850*, Cambridge, 1989, pp.721–8; and, most recently, J. M. Neeson, *Commoners: Common Right, Enclosure and Social Change in England 1700–1820*, Cambridge, 1993, *passim*, but especially the chapter on 'The use of wastes'. The small number of Ashwater cottagers who survived for a few decades after 1348 would have been especially the poorer, compared with their counterparts at Sidbury, for lack of ownership of a small flock of sheep. Not only was their access to wastes restricted, but also some of the soils of North Devon tended to induce foot-rot and other diseases in sheep: C. Vancouver, *op. cit.*, pp.339–41, 343.

two-and-a-half pounds of wool dyed sanguine ready for spinning. In the same year among the chattels of a Sidbury labourer was a 'turne' or spinning wheel and 'a payre of cardez' used to tangle and interlock wool ready for spinning. The existence of a clothing industry almost certainly explains the numerous references to 'shops' at Sidbury, probably weavers' sheds, precursors of the wooden structures which can still be seen tucked away in the backs of yards in East Devon settlements.[40] The manor's diversified economy was also enhanced by the presence since 1291 of a formally licenced market and fair, the latter possibly for cheese and cattle.[41] A grant of the right to hold a periodic market often generates (sometimes post-dates) permanent commercial activity and Sidbury surnames from the fourteenth century reveal a smith, two wood-related trades (hooper, turner), two related to hides (skinner, cobbler) and a soaper, who possibly used the ashes of burnt ferns gathered from the commons. The occupations of butcher, spinster, glover, fisher and prostitute are mentioned in the fifteenth century and surname evidence for the same century reveals a possible hatmaker, a tavern keeper, a baker, a smith, a juggler and a carpenter.[42] The 'diverse craftsmen (*artificiarii*) and labourers and their servants' at work about the Chapter's tithe barn in 1496 were no doubt drawn in part from a pool of cottage labour at Sidbury.[43]

With many opportunities for earning a living, Sidbury's cottagers enjoyed an independence denied to their counterparts on manors with less diverse resources. Their sons could accumulate enough

40 H. S. A. Fox, 'Rural industry', in R. J. P. Kain and W. L. D. Ravenhill, eds., *op. cit.*; D.C.A. 4835. For a medieval illustration of a pair of cards being used to tangle and interlock wool see L. F. Salzman, *English Industries of the Middle Ages*, Oxford, 1923, p.213. The earliest reference to a *shoppa* at Sidbury is in a rental of 1394–5 (D.C.A. 2945) and thereafter there are frequent references in the court rolls. For 'a shoppe to work in', bequeathed by an Essex fuller, see L. R. Poos, *op. cit.*, p.69.

41 *Calendar of Charter Rolls*, ii, London, H.M.S.O., 1906, p.403; W. White, *History, Gazetteer and Directory of Devonshire*, Sheffield, 1850, p.244. The fair was at Michaelmas, the end of the cheese-making and fattening season: see, for example, D.C.A. 5054 and later accounts.

42 Names and occupations from rentals (above n.34), court rolls (above n.37) and a few from account rolls (also at D.C.A.). For balls made of the ashes of ferns, and used in washing, see J. Nichols, *The History and Antiquities of the County of Leicester*, London, 4 vols., 1795–1811, iii, p.132, n.1.

43 D.C.A. 5068.

cash, through various kinds of work including day labouring, to be able to afford the entry fine for one of the numerous small niches which existed on the manor, cottage holdings and smallholdings; they thus may never have experienced subservient contractual labour relationships as servants or tied cottagers. Sidbury's independent cottagers would have been able to take their labour where they willed and indeed in the manor's court rolls there are frequent references to *laborarii* who earned excessive wages on the manor and who went 'eastwards' at harvest time (presumably to the more arable parts of Somerset and Dorset or even further afield) contrary to the wishes of those landlords who liked to restrict circulation of labourers to the *pays propre*.[44]

It could be argued too that there was but limited *demand* among the farming population of Sidbury for living-in servants. Farms there were on the small side during the Later Middle Ages; the mean size was 24 acres and there was a remarkably persistent five-acre class.[45] As cultivation declined (the value of the Chapter's tithe sheaves fell by well over 25 per cent between 1425 and 1460) grain farming was replaced by a well-rounded type of pastoral husbandry typical of East Devon.[46] The region's alternating hill and vale countryside was ideal for both intensive and extensive livestock management, while urban markets for meat, dairy products and leather were close to hand at Exeter and in numerous resilient small towns.[47] It was a region of pastoral smallholdings with much dairying in the vales

---

44 D.C.A. 4798, 4799, 4800, 4801, 4802, 4803, 4804, 4805, 4806, 4808, 4810; *Rotuli Parliamentorum*, ii, pp.340–1.

45 Based on D.C.A. 2945, the rental of 1394–5. The figure includes leased demesne. The manor was still notable for small farms and independent cottages in the seventeenth century: D.R.O. 906M/M/16.

46 D.C.A. 5054, 5055. There is no means of telling the extent to which the value of the tithe sheaves had already fallen by 1425. The level remained low in the late fifteenth century: D.C.A. 5068 and D.R.O. 906M/M/1.

47 H. S. A. Fox, 'Farming practices and techniques', pp.318–9. For the burgeoning towns of the region see E. M. Carus-Wilson, *The Expansion of Exeter at the Close of the Middle Ages*, Exeter, 1963, pp.18–19 (for Tiverton and Cullompton), and H. S. A. Fox, 'Tenant farming and tenant farmers'. For meat and leather markets see M. Kowaleski, 'Town and country in late medieval England', pp.59–61. For the commercialization of some aspects of dairying see D.R.O. 1258M/G/3, account of 1378–9 (sale to a 'merchant' of the whole of the season's milk from the demesne cows at Bishop's Clyst).

(reflected at Sidbury in the frequency with which the heriot was a cow) and flocks roaming with little human attendance on the hilltops, described in the sixteenth century as 'verye good sheepe pasture mixed with ffernes'.[48] With nineteenth-century parallels in mind we can envisage at medieval Sidbury the type of small-scale mixed pastoral farming which relied for the most part on family labour, with wives and daughters important in the dairy, aided occasionally by work contracted on short terms from the manor's population of resilient cottagers; some farm holdings, indeed, were run by women.[49]

In East Devon generally we should expect to find many other manors, like Sidbury, with relatively large populations of independent cottagers surviving through the Later Middle Ages. A brief examination of a rental of Dawlish in 1513, part of a long-term study of the manor still in progress, reveals a large number of independent cottagers (34 cottages alongside 59 farm holdings) and, moreover, there was an increase in the number of occupied cottages during the Later Middle Ages.[50] The profile of Dawlish is very similar to that of Sidbury: there were extensive common wastes; opportunities existed for non-agrarian employment in fulling and weaving and on an accessible shoreline with salterns and oyster beds; many farms were smallholdings of 15 or seven acres or less, the great majority being below 31 acres, so that demand for living-in servants in husbandry was probably slight. Finally, a rather bland extent of Uffculme in

---

48 In court rolls between 1421 and 1500 (above n.37) the heriots appearing with the greatest frequency (for farm holdings) were cows, followed by horses, the latter perhaps reflecting the tenants' involvement in marketing; oxen appear rarely; sheep are infrequent, but this is only because the best beast would not be a sheep if larger beasts were present on the holding. Description of the hilltops from a survey of the manor of Northleigh, a few miles from Sidbury: D.R.O. 123M/E/31.

49 A. Howkins, *Reshaping Rural England*, pp.41–2. For women landholders at Sidbury see above n.32.

50 D.C.A.3684. Comparison with an earlier rental of *c.*1385 shows an increase in the number of cottages between that date and 1515, while late fifteenth-century account rolls have reference to new-built cottages. All other information on Dawlish in this paragraph is from documents at D.C.A. on which I am currently working. The importance of employment along the Exe shoreline is dealt with in H. S. A. Fox, *The Evolution of the Fishing Village: Landscape and Society along the South Devon Coast, 1086–1550*, Oxford, 2001, pp.116–18.

1420 mentions 21 cottages and 21 tenants of farm holdings, a ratio of 1:1, the highest yet encountered. Unfortunately the medieval documentation for Uffculme is rather sparse, but the extent does hint at one of the reasons for the survival of so many cottagers in this pastoral vale: the river Culm drove no fewer than three fulling mills on the manor, indicating a clothing industry of some size.[51]

'By a tenure of entire dependence'[52]

The third case study in this essay comes from the coastal manor of Stokenham in the deep South Hams of Devon, seen by Francis Hastings in about 1583 as 'the uttermost south poynte of England'. Luckily for the student of the manor's tenemental structure in the fourteenth century, there exist two very detailed rentals, one made before the Black Death (possibly in 1347), the other made several decades later, possibly in 1390 when Stokenham came into the hands of John de Montecute, poet, soldier and Lollard.[53] The first rental lists 147 farm holdings and 89 cottages. Analysis of the second shows that the number of farming units had fallen to 120 and the number of occupied cottages to 61. This is as we should expect, for declining population was accompanied by some promotion of cottagers into the ranks of occupiers of farm holdings and a good

---

51 P.R.O. C. 138/52. For the activities of the aulnager in the Culm valley see H. S. A. Fox, 'Rural industry'.

52 Description of the tied cottage by the Revd J. M. Wilson, writing in his mid-nineteenth-century *Rural Cyclopaedia*, quoted in A. Armstrong, 'Labour', p.810. For tied cottages in the South-West in the nineteenth century and later see F. G. Heath, *Peasant Life in the West of England*, London, 1881, p.83, a description of a tied cottager in which the notorious Canon Girdlestone had an interest; H. Rider Haggard, *Rural England*, London, 2 vols., 1902, i, pp.201–3, provision by a South Hams farmer of free cottage accommodation as an inducement to scarce labour; P. Fletcher, 'The agricultural housing problem', *Social and Economic Administration*, 3, 1969, pp.155–66, a survey of tied cottages in Tiverton Rural District.

53 C. Cross, ed., *The Letters of Sir Francis Hastings 1574–1609*, Somerset Record Society, lxix, 1969, p.28; P.R.O. S.C. 11/765; Huntington Library, San Marino, HAM box 64, rental of '1577'. *The List and Index* produced by P.R.O. misdates and wrongly locates the first of these rentals while the Huntington Library's catalogue attributes the second to the sixteenth century not to the fourteenth where it rightly belongs.

deal of amalgamation of tenures into larger farms. But a closer examination of the second rental, made during a study of the turnover of surnames on the manor, reveals an unexpected finding: a very high proportion (59 per cent) of the cottage rents were being paid by individuals who were also occupiers of farm holdings. For example, William Janet occupied two farm holdings with their appurtenant farmhouses and he also paid the rents for two cottages. That this is not a quirk of the documentation is shown by comparison with the earlier rental of *c.*1347 when almost all of the cottages were occupied by what we may call 'independent' cottagers with names not found among the tenants of farm holdings.[54] Given the parallels from the nineteenth century it is tempting to see the cottages which can be nominally linked to farm holdings in 1390 as tied cottages which had been acquired by farmers, now with more land on their hands, in order to gain control of farmworkers' accommodation and, thereby, of their labour.

An examination of the economic development of Stokenham in the Later Middle Ages will lend some support to this interpretation. The manor lies in the deep South Hams of Devon, the county's 'frutefulest part' or 'golden fringe'.[55] During the Later Middle Ages the region retained its predominantly arable character; indeed, if we view Devon as a whole, we can see that market-oriented grain

54 There is, likewise, a complete contrast between the large amount of duplication of names in the second Stokenham rental and the very few cases of duplication in later medieval rentals of Sidbury where cottagers were independent, not tied. Our analysis of the second Stokenham rental is of course entirely dependent on the pairing of the name of the occupier of a farm holding with an identical name (both forename and surname) in the cottage section of the rental: identical people or simply identical names of different people (e.g. a cottager son who bore the same forename as his farmer father)? Sons with forenames identical to their fathers' were certainly to be found in our period: D. Postles, 'Personal naming patterns of peasants and burgesses in late medieval England', *Medieval Prosopography*, 12, 1991, pp.29–56. But see below, p.153, for arguments suggesting that, in general, farmers did not acquire cottage accommodation especially for the use of kin, though on any particular manor, of course, a small proportion of the cottages which I have identified as tied cottages may have been occupied by a son with the same name as his father.

55 *The Itinerary of John Leland*, i, p.224; Alexander Gosse of Plympton St Mary, quoted in T. Gray, ed., *Harvest Failure in Cornwall and Devon*, Sources of Cornish History, i, 1992, p.xix.

production came to be concentrated in the South Hams where natural conditions rendered it most profitable and where there were many ports at which ships could be loaded and victualled. Dairying, flock-keeping and cider production complemented arable production.[56] In 1309 the demesne arable at Stokenham was valued at a relatively high price by Devon standards; grains grown in the later fourteenth century were wheat, barley (a crop which, in the South West, was found only in the prime arable regions) and oats; the demesne supported a large sheep flock and a significant number of cows, probably for dairying.[57] Markets were to be found close by at the ports of Kingsbridge, Dartmouth and Totnes, places with which Stokenham tenants were certainly familiar because those who owned boats were obliged to visit them to do the lord's business.[58]

The greatest difficulty facing arable farmers at Stokenham during the Later Middle Ages must have been a shortage of labour. Farms were being enlarged through amalgamation of tenures (to produce a mean size of 45 acres by the late fourteenth century); their cultivation must have required a good deal of labour at many times of the year, and involvement in dairying further spread the workload; yet family size was probably smaller than before 1348, as elsewhere in England,[59] and the pool of cottage workers was diminishing. Under these circumstances competition for labour must have been acute and a rational way in which farmers could secure it would have been to gain control over farmworkers' accommodation so that there was always a working family to hand close by the farm door. Presumably when a cottage became vacant it might then be rented by a farmer who already occupied a farm holding. How a labourer

---

56 H. S. A. Fox, 'Occupation of the land', pp.154–6; H. S. A. Fox, 'Farming practices and techniques', pp.306–7, 315–17, 322–3.

57 P.R.O. C. 134/16/9; *Calendar of Inquisitions Miscellaneous, 1399–1422*, London, H.M.S.O., 1968, p.71. For similar combinations at nearby Sherford and South Pool see B.L. Add. Ch. 13091 and Cornwall Record Office, Arundell collection, executors' account for Thomas Courtenay.

58 Huntington Library, San Marino, HAM box 64, rental of '1577'.

59 The best, though not ideal, is that of replacement rates: see the summaries of such work, and of the difficulties involved, in J. Hatcher, *Plague, Population and the English Economy 1348–1530*, London, 1977, pp.26–9, and Z. Razi, 'The myth of the immutable English family', *Past and Present*, 140, 1993, pp.36–7.

was then enticed into it is open to surmise, but it is not difficult to imagine that a young male immigrant or resident who wished to set up a family, and yet without the capital to stock a large farm holding, may have welcomed access to the perquisite of a cottage with no fine. The advantages to the farmer are obvious: he had a secure supply of male labour close to hand and moreover, as was to be the case with owners of tied cottages in the nineteenth century, he had ready access to the work of the cottager's wife and children, the former perhaps in the dairy, the whole family at harvest time when we know that there could be severe labour shortages in the South Hams.[60] The advantages to the cottage occupant were: first, the accommodation, second, the opportunity of family formation which was denied to living-in servants, and thirdly, employment and a wage, all at the expense of total dependence upon the employer. On the manor of Stokenham, and others like it in the South Hams, a guarantee of wages for farm work was important for the cottager because opportunities for making a livelihood by other means were few. Services for the rural population were concentrated in the borough of Chillington nearby and it is significant that very few indeed of the cottagers in the rental of 1347 bore names indicating a craft or trade.[61] Stokenham was a manor without extensive common wastes, typical of the South Hams in this respect. Fishing at the few small beach toeholds on the manor's largely cliff-bound coastline was, in the fourteenth and fifteenth centuries, a by-employment among the occupiers of farm holdings; cottagers may have assisted them, indeed laboured for them, at the boats but they did not gain an independent livelihood from the sea.[62] A few cottagers may have worked on the demesne throughout the year as *famuli* but most were not demesne-oriented workers, for the Montacute acres were well provided, exceptionally so by Devon standards, with labour services.[63] One may conclude that farm work on

---

60 The region attracted immigrant workers at harvest time: D.R.O. Cary MSS, Ashwater court of October 1436.

61 P.R.O. S.C. 11/765. Out of 89 cottagers only two have names indicative of a non-agricultural occupation: hooper and tailor.

62 The evidence is discussed in detail in H. S. A. Fox, *Evolution of the Fishing Village*, pp.122–9.

63 Rentals as in n.53 above.

the holdings of tenants provided more or less the only employment niche for the landless and that this, combined with the tenants' control of the manor's cottage accommodation in the years after 1348, created a labouring class of an especially dependent character.

The tied cottage: further perspectives

Examples of the phenomenon which has been revealed for Stokenham — cottages becoming attached to farm holdings during the Later Middle Ages — may easily be found elsewhere. For example, a rental of the Devon manor of Axmouth shows that 80 per cent of all cottages were held in this way.[64] The rental, drawn up for Syon Abbey in 1483, reveals a remarkable polarized structure of land-holding. At one end of the scale were 16 large farms, all over 60 acres in size and most of them rented by tenants who also rented tied cottages. At the other end of the scale were seven independent cottagers holding their cottages directly from the lady of the manor. It is worth pondering the question of labour demand and supply in such a situation. One of the largest of the large farms, John Seward's empire of two customary tenures and two huge demesne closes (approaching 200 acres in all) might have required, by eighteenth-century standards, the work of about seven male hands as well as employment of extra women and children at certain seasons.[65] Cultivation would inevitably have been less intensive in the fifteenth century but even so it is difficult to imagine how Seward could have coped with family labour alone. From the point of view of supply of labour, that from the seven independent cottage holdings (all rented by men though some, no doubt, with spouses available for work) must have been inadequate for the needs of the 16 large farms. The shortfall could well have been met from labourers and their families living in the 'tied' cottages rented by farmers: Seward, as it happens, rented seven.

64 P.R.O. S.C. 11/163. The core of Axmouth manor is on red marls which were usually used for the cultivation of crops of high value in the Middle Ages; moreover, the manor had an outlet for coastwise shipment of grain, an asset which always encouraged arable farming.

65 Based on figures in R. C. Allen, 'The two English agricultural revolutions, 1450–1850', in B. M. S. Campbell and M. Overton, eds., *Land, Labour and Livestock: Historical Studies in European Agricultural Productivity*, Manchester, 1991, p.250.

Beyond the county of Devon isolated cases of the phenomenon can be readily culled from the literature: from Kibworth Harcourt in Leicestershire in the 1350s where William de Marnham, a substantial tenant, took five cottages for a life term; or from Woodeaton, Oxfordshire, in 1366, where John Osyat held a messuage and virgate and also 'two small cottages' which 'belonged to' the tenement.[66] Beyond Devon, too, some later medieval rentals reveal manors on which a good proportion of cottages were in the hands of tenant farmers. On the Peterborough manor of Eye in the Soke, three-quarters of the tenants with virgated holdings also rented cottages according to a rental of 1399, and at Brigstock in Northamptonshire, a little later, six of the half-virgates had cottages attached to them. At South Stoke in Oxfordshire all of the cottages, except two held by women, were in the hands of the virgators by 1366. The term 'sub-cottage' seems appropriate for a small dwelling dependent on a larger farm, and it so happens that the term has been found in one later medieval rental. On the Oxfordshire manors of Murcott and Fencott six *sub cotagia* are listed, all held by half-virgators with *messuagia* of their own and, in the mind of the compiler of the rental, somehow different from the (more independent?) cottages listed without the prefix.[67] Very occasionally the documents allow us to see more clearly the farmworker inhabitant of the tied cottage. At Ombersley, Worcestershire, in 1417, John Tandy, 'werkmon', occupied two cottages which were part of the holding of one of the tenants. At Writtle in Essex, also at the beginning of the fifteenth century, William Johann promised to enfeoff his servant with a cottage in reward for long service; it is tempting to suggest that the servant may already have occupied the cottage while he worked for William. The lord of Foxearth, Essex, granted a cottage to John Dryvere 'on

---

66 C. Howell, *Land, Family and Inheritance in Transition: Kibworth Harcourt 1280–1700,* Cambridge, 1983, p.43 (and see also p.135); H. E. Salter, ed., *Eynsham Cartulary,* ii, Oxford Historical Society, li, 1908, pp.21–2.

67 E. King, 'Tenant farming and tenant farmers: Eastern England', in E. Miller, ed., *op. cit.,* pp.633, 635; *Eynsham Cartulary,* ii, pp.128–33; 'Custumal (1391) and bye-laws (1386–1540) of the manor of Islip', being part of Oxfordshire Record Society, xl, 1959, pp.96–103.

condition that the same John will serve . . . for the whole of his life . . . as a common labourer'.[68]

Because the farmworkers who, we are suggesting, inhabited cottages accumulated by tenant farmers are inevitably very poorly documented in the Later Middle Ages we must ask if there could have been other motives behind the acquisition of cottage property by tenants. Could tenant farmers have rented cottages for the uses to which the cottage garden might be put? Luckily we know something about the profits to be had from vacant or decaying cottage gardens because reeves were made to answer for them in their annual accounts. At Clayhidon in 1411 the 'issues' of several vacant cottages — presumably profits from sale of the herbage and fruit — came to a mean of 7d. per cottage, far less than the rental value; and at Dawlish in 1419 the reeve managed to make 12d. and 15d. 'from the curtilage' of two vacant cottages which should have rented at 26d. and 18d. respectively.[69] Clearly the profits which a tenant farmer might have made from these minute gardens would have been less that the rents which would have to be paid. Might farmers have rented cottages as accommodation for sons waiting to enter into a holding, or for other kin?[70] This cannot be ruled out in some cases but in general the circumstantial evidence is against such an

---

68 R. H. Hilton, *The English Peasantry in the Later Middle Ages*, Oxford, 1975, p.52; L. R. Poos, *op. cit.*, p.204; C. Dyer, 'The social and economic background to the rural revolt of 1381', in R. H. Hilton and T. H. Aston, eds., *The English Rising of 1381*, Cambridge, 1984, p.25.

69 Cornwall Record Office, Arundell collection, Clayhidon court rolls; D.C.A. 5031. For other examples where the issue of a vacant cottage is clearly less than the rent see D.R.O. C.R. 521 (Aylesbeare) and D.C.A. 5056 (Sidbury).

70 For sub-cottages provided for kin in the thirteenth century see R. M. Smith, 'Rooms, relatives and residential arrangements: some evidence in manor court rolls 1250–1500', *Medieval Village Research Group Annual Report*, 30, 1982, pp.34–5 (including references to kin assigned to 'a little room in the garden', to 'a small place for habitation at the far end of the messuage' and even to the bakehouse; and Z. Razi, 'Myth of the immutable English family', pp.8–9. In an earlier, extended version of this paper, kindly lent to me by the author, there is even reference to a 'moveable' structure provided for the accommodation of kin.

interpretation. Under the demographic conditions of the Later Middle Ages, and given the over-supply of land then, sons did not have to wait long for a vacant holding. In Devon, as I have shown elsewhere, sons found it easy to pick up vacant land (perhaps after a period as a labourer or servant) without having to wait for the patrimony to become available and seem frequently to have moved to another manor in order to do so, a practice which gave rise to high turnover rates in the stock of families on particular manors; Stokenham, studied in the previous section, is a case in point.[71] Might cottages have been forced upon tenants by lords eager to safeguard their rentals? There may well have been an element of seigneurial compulsion in the immediate aftermath of the Black Death when lords hoped for a return to the old, better days. But compulsion cannot be seen as the reason behind the renting of additional cottages by tenant farmers well into the fifteenth century. By then we find seigneurial authorities lessening the burdens on holdings, subsidizing rather than penalizing tenants, even sanctioning decay of some structures on a manor rather than enforcing maintenance of the total building stock.[72]

While a few tenant farmers, here and there, may have engrossed cottages for the reasons discussed in the previous paragraph, each can be found to be wanting as a general explanation. We return, therefore, to our earlier interpretation of the sub-cottage as a tied cottage used to entice a workforce. Some support for it is given by the finding that such cottages were usually attached to the larger holdings which would have been most in need of drawing labour towards themselves. On the manor of Stokenham, discussed in the previous section, the mean size of farm holdings with cottages attached was 58 acres in *c.*1390, as compared with a mean size for all farm holdings of 45 acres. At nearby Stoke Fleming, according to a rental of 1523, those farmers who also rented cottages were

71 H. S. A. Fox, 'Tenant farming and tenant farmers', pp.726–9.

72 C. Dyer, 'English peasant buildings in the Later Middle Ages (1200–1500)', *Medieval Archaeology*, 30, 1986, p.23. An instructive case is recorded before a court at Stoke Fleming in 1468, where John Foterell took four holdings from the lord yet was required to repair only 'a hall, a bakehouse and a barn': D.R.O. 902M/M/22.

assessed well above the mean for the manor in the subsidy taken a year later.[73]

To interpret the acquisition of cottage accommodation by substantial tenant farmers as a move to gain as much command as they could over labour supplies makes a good deal of sense in the context of other measures which were adopted to meet the same ends. Employers enticed labourers by giving them additional perquisities such as food or clothing: the provision of a cottage may be seen in the same light, and it likewise allowed the employer to make a small saving in labour costs.[74] In addition various forms of social control over labour were attempted by employers. An immediate reaction to turmoil in the labour market after the Black Death was the Statute of Labourers of 1351, a measure with the outward appearance of a move by landlords to maintain the running of their demesnes but which, as Poos has convincingly argued, soon came to be used by tenant farmers to maintain the running of their holdings.[75] Another form of social control of labour during the Later Middle Ages was exercised before the manor court: here by-laws were passed by potential employers in order to compel farmworkers to labour within the vill. Even during the thirteenth century when local population densities were high, by-laws were passed to secure all available labour at harvest, when there was much to be done and when time was short. Such injunctions continued and, one suspects, were more frequently made when labour came to be in short supply after the Black Death: for example, the famous Wymeswold by-laws of the early fifteenth century instructed labourers 'not to go to other townes' at harvest time. And now there were also stricter laws

---

73 Huntington Library, San Marino, HAM box 64, rental of '1577'; D.R.O. Cary MSS, rental of 1523 and *Devon Lay Subsidy Returns*, pp.194–5.

74 For perquisites see S. A. C. Penn and C. Dyer, 'Wages and earnings in late medieval England: evidence from the enforcement of labour laws', *Economic History Review*, 2nd series, 43, 1990, p.371. In the nineteenth century it was common for there to be a reduction, in return for the tied cottage, in wages paid by the farmer to its occupant.

75 L. R. Poos, 'The social context of Statute of Labourers enforcement', *Law and History Review*, 1, 1983, pp.27–52. Labourers were sometimes presented before the justices for refusing to work 'for their neighbours' or 'for the community'.

which attempted to prevent labour migration at any time of the
year. At Stainburn in Yorkshire all labourers had to work with the
lord and the tenants whenever they were needed; on a manor on
the estate of the Bishop of Durham no cottager was allowed to leave
so long as any tenant had work for him to do.[76] These local by-laws
and ordinances were, in effect, mirroring and extending the prohibition,
in the Statute of Labourers, of movement away from home 'in the
summer', presumably a reference to men and women who left first
for the mowing of the meadows, and then went on from vill to vill
to reap the grain, drawn hither and thither as if by the great clouds
which heralded the harvest-threatening rain.

Finally, we find by-laws and ordinances which enforced the
maintenance of a manor's cottage accommodation, presumably with
a view to maintaining a resident pool of labourers. One comes from
Stokenham where, following the Black Death, an ordinance passed
by the whole homage dictated that the men of each hamlet should
communally maintain any cottage which fell vacant within their
settlement.[77] This ordinance helps to explain a curt entry in an
account roll (1422) for Sampford Courtenay, also in Devon, which
states that the tenants, all with houses of their own, 'hold among
themselves 24 cottages'.[78] Another relevant ordinance was made by

---

76 *Report on the Manuscripts of Lord Middleton*, Historical Manuscripts Commission,
   lxix, p.108, and W. O. Ault, *Open-field Husbandry and the Village Community: a
   Study of Agrarian By-laws in Medieval England*, Transactions of the American
   Philosophical Society, new series, 55, pt. 7, 1965, pp.12–16 for by-laws, both
   before and after 1348, which controlled labour, including would-be gleaners, at
   harvest time; E. Miller, 'Tenant farming and tenant farmers: Yorkshire and
   Lancashire', in *idem*, ed., *op. cit.*, p.599; J. Booth, ed., *Halmota Prioratus
   Dunelmensis*, Surtees Society, lxxxii, 1889, p.126; and, for another reference similar
   to that from Stainburn (in this case to a lord demanding the option of the labour
   of those tenants' sons who were not needed in the parental home) see P.R.O.
   C. 145/208/4 (Bincombe, Dorset, in 1376).

77 Huntington Library, San Marino, HAM box 64, rental of '1577'. For attached
   cottages on Stokenham manor, see the previous section of this essay.

78 P.R.O. S.C. 6/1118/6. There are similar entries in a late-fourteenth-century
   rental of Hartland, for example, where all the tenants of the now deserted hamlet
   of Hendon are said to hold between them 'one house and orchard' (which
   sounds like a cottage tenement): Cornwall Record Office, Arundell collection,
   undated Hartland rental.

the Bishop of Durham when, in 1353, he ordered the community of the vill of Easington to ensure that vacant cottages were leased by tenant farmers 'to their servants and to other people without houses'.[79] The Bishop wanted full cottages because cottagers on this manor did labour services; the reference is also of interest because it suggests fairly strongly that in this case the tenants' preference (perhaps associated with the local farming economy, as in the examples given in the second section of this essay) was for servants. One can imagine, in different economic circumstances, a similar ordinance passed by tenant farmers anxious themselves to maintain a resident pool of labouring families.

It could be argued that the tied cottage, as an institution which was likely to flourish in periods of labour shortage, was especially appropriate to the Later Middle Ages though this is not to say that it was unknown earlier. Even before the Black Death one finds references in custumals to boonworks owed to the lord from a person 'who holds a cottage from a yardlander', to tenants who paid 6d. for having 'more than one cotsettle', to works done by 'small cottagers [*cotterelli*] living upon the land . . . of the customary tenants', to 'cottars holding of the villeins' and paying churchscot to the lord.[80] A hypothetical construction of events might start with a situation in which sub-cottages began to be constructed on the lands of the main tenants. Who knows but that the proliferation of labour services said to have been a feature of the late twelfth century and early thirteenth may have encouraged some tenants to construct sub-cottages to be occupied by families which helped them to acquit some of those services?[81] At first, perhaps, sub-cottages went unnoticed in some manorial surveys, the result being rather bland documents with surprisingly few cottage

79 R. Britnell, 'Feudal reaction after the Black Death in the Palatinate of Durham', *Past and Present*, 128, 1990, p.33.

80 W. D. Peckham, ed., *Thirteen Custumals of the Sussex Manors of the Bishop of Chichester*, Sussex Record Society, xxxi, 1925, pp.33–4, and see also p.37; Somerset Record Office, DDCC 131911A; P. Vinogradoff, *Villeinage in England*, Oxford, 1892, p.213, n.2; B.L. Add. MS. 17450, f.191.

81 Elsewhere I have argued the case for employment of labour by thirteenth-century tenants in order to assist in heavy work-loads resulting from services on the demesne, though in that essay I had living-in servants in mind rather than tied cottagers: H. S. A. Fox, 'Exploitation of the landless'.

holdings.[82] Then, during the course of the thirteenth century and
the early fourteenth, lords perceived that they could increase their
own incomes and draw extra boonworks to the demesne by levying
small imposts on still anonymous sub-cottagers, such as those
mentioned earlier in this paragraph. Finally, the sub-cottager might
be drawn completely into the open and named in the lord's survey.
At Egham, Surrey, in the early fourteenth century, Chertsey Abbey
swept down on three sub-cottages when the holding upon which
they had been constructed was surrendered by its direct tenant, and
drew them into the abbey rental; at Hinton-on-the-Green,
Worcestershire, the compilers of a thirteenth-century survey were
concerned about 'new humble dwellings [*bordelli*] set up without
licence . . . [whose] rents ought to be inserted in this extent'.[83]

On the eve of the Black Death the stock of landless cottage
accommodation on a manor was in many ways a collection of
dwellings with heterogeneous social origins. Some were there to
provide for the kin of sitting tenants (who does not know a manorial
survey listing several cottager widows?); others were on slips of
ground taken out of the common highway or the common waste by
a landless person seeking an independent existence of a kind, a type
which we find newly erected at all times when population was
growing; yet others had been set up by the lord in order to provide
him with particular types of work on the demesne; others were in
origin what we have called sub-cottages or tied cottages, their

---

82 For perceptive comments on surveys apparently lacking in cottars see J. Z.
   Titow, *English Rural Society 1200–1350*, London, 1969, p.86.

83 E. Toms, ed., *Chertsey Abbey Court Rolls*, i, Surrey Record Society, xxxviii, 1937,
   pp.46, 58; W. H. Hart, ed., *Historia et Cartularium Monasterii Sancti Petri
   Gloucestriae*, Rolls Series, 3 vols., 1863–7, iii, p.61, though there is nothing in this
   reference to prove that these dwellings at Hinton were sub-cottages of precisely
   the type discussed here. See also B.L. Eg. MS. 3321, f.208 where a sub-cottage
   has been 'drawn out' (*extractus*) from the tenement on which it had been
   constructed; *Eynsham Cartulary*, ii, p.130 which orders an inquiry into two
   cottages 'without rent and service', apparently built on the tenement of John
   Scrag.

84 For cottages for kin, see above n.70. One sign of a demesne-orientated cottage
   is, on some manors, the lord's obligation to repair it. See, for example, P. D. A.
   Harvey, *op. cit.*, p.119, and N. W. Alcock, 'An East Devon manor in the Later
   Middle Ages, Pt. I', *Transactions of the Devonshire Association*, 102, 1970, p.173.

occupants originally dependent upon the main tenants.[84] Thereafter, following the Black Death, the balances shifted and we should expect to find fewer demesne-oriented cottages, fewer newly reclaimed cottages and, in regions where farming type demanded them (as at Stokenham, analysed in the previous section), a greater proportion of tied cottages. It must be left to other historians to trace the development of the tied cottage after the end of the Middle Ages and into the nineteenth century. But we can speculate that as the English population began to grow again in the early sixteenth century, and as the incidence of living-in servants in husbandry 'declined from a probable high point in the fifteenth century to a trough in the mid seventeenth',[85] so too was there a decline in the incidence of tied cottages, and for the same reasons: the growing numbers of poor adult labourers in need of work, so that contracts designed to bind workers to employers became less necessary. It is perhaps significant in this context that when arable was converted to pasture in the Midland counties during the sixteenth century, the farm-houses which thereby decayed as 'houses of husbandry' were often converted to housing for what the inquisition of 1607 calls 'pore men' or 'cottiers', who sound more like independent, and no doubt under-employed, labourers than servants of cottagers under a labour contract.[86] We can speculate, too, that historians should be able to discover tied cottages in the late seventeenth century and the early eighteenth, another period of relative labour shortage. Their task will not be made easy by the fact that now many cottages by the farm door have become so much part of the built assets of the holding that they are often included in surveys under some omnibus catch-phrase such as 'the appurtenances', or 'other houses necessary for husbandry'.[87] Nevertheless, some especially detailed seventeenth-

---

85 A. Kussmaul, *op. cit.*, p.97.

86 L. A. Parker, 'The depopulation returns for Leicestershire in 1607', *Transactions of the Leicestershire Archaeological Society*, 23, 1947, pp.244, 253 and many subsequent references. In the rare case where a decayed farmhouse was used by the depopulator for a *servant*, that term is used (e.g. p.271).

87 During the Later Middle Ages one finds cottages changing hands along with the farm holdings to which they had become permanently attached: for example, P.R.O. S.C. 2/168/61 (Yarcombe court of September 1491), D.R.O. C.R. 1071 (Alwington court of 1538). The first stage in the disappearance of the tied cottage

century written surveys do show that tenants owned cottage accommodation in addition to their own farmhouses. For example, on the manors of Philip, Earl of Pembroke, surveyed in 1631–32, a large holding at Barford sported a 'dwelling house of 5 ground rooms' and additionally 'a little cottage with a little garden'; even a standard yardland holding at Fugglestone had both a dwelling house and 'a small house of 2 ground rooms . . . at the end of the croft'.[88] Seventeenth-century maps, too, sometimes show a diminutive chimneyed building in a croft, close to the main farmhouse, though students of vernacular architecture will be well aware that these could have been detached kitchens rather than tied cottages.[89]

from documents would be its inclusion in catch-phrases such as 'appurtenances', 'outhouses' or 'house necessary for husbandry', for which see, e.g., C. R. Straton, ed., *Survey of the Lands of William First Earl of Pembroke*, Roxburghe Club, 2 vols., 1909, ii, pp.321–49; T. S. Willan and E. W. Crossley, eds., *Three Seventeenth-century Yorkshire Surveys*, Yorkshire Archaeological Society, civ, 1941, pp.82–143. A highly interesting transitional document is P.R.O. S.C. 11/163, a rental of Axmouth made in 1483. Here the attached cottages are listed not at the end of the rental (the normal place for cottages in medieval documents of this type) but in the body of the text following the entries for each farm holding.

88 *Surveys of the Manors of Philip Earl of Pembroke*, pp.53, 103 and, for other examples, *Three Seventeenth-century Yorkshire Surveys*, pp.9, 10, 16, 25, 39, 49, 51, 56 (including two references to sub-cottages converted from non-residential buildings, a kitchen in one case, a turf house in the other). One might expect to find tied cottages on some larger glebes, so see D. M. Barratt, ed., *Ecclesiastical Terriers of Warwickshire Parishes*, Dugdale Society, 2 vols., 1955 and 1971, i, pp.9, 26, 59, 121 and ii, 84, 87, 91, 169n. The county of Devon provides some manuscript examples: D.R.O. 1508M/ Lon./estate/valuations/4 and P.R.O. S.C. 12/22/19, surveys of the predominantly arable manors of Kenton and Kenn. See also E. Kerridge, *Agrarian Problems in the Sixteenth Century and After*, London, 1969, p.51.

89 See, for example, J. West, *Village Records*, London, 1962, plate 7; A. S. Bendall, *Maps, Land and Society: a History, with a Carto-bibliography of Cambridgeshire Estate Maps, c.1600–1836*, Cambridge, 1992, plate 17a; E. Straker, ed., *The Buckhurst Terrier 1597–1598*, Sussex Record Society, xxxix, 1933, plates xii–xiii; Northamptonshire Record Office, Finch Hatton 272. A Devon example, with some good drawings of cottages of this type is D.R.O. 1508M/maps/Kenton/1. There is independent, non-cartographic, evidence of sub-cottages at Kenton: see above n.88.

Conclusion

Researchers familiar with later medieval rentals and other manorial sources from their own particular regions of study will know of manors which echo those discussed in this essay. A central theme in what I have written is that the number of cottages on a manor, relative to the number of farm holdings, as well as the nature of cottage tenure, provide simple and very basic clues to the nature of labouring life in that place. Readers may be aware of manors with a suspiciously small number of cottages in the Later Middle Ages. I suspect that this is sometimes a first indication of the presence of living-in servants of husbandry: farmworkers' accommodation is not apparent in surveys of such manors, being hidden behind the façade of farm tenures. This may not always be the case, of course, because where there were many small farm holdings, say of between five and 10 acres, the surplus labour of their occupants may have been used on the larger holdings. But a shortage of cottages combined with the presence of many substantial farms, as at Ashwater studied above, can provide a good *prima facie* case for a servant-employing economy. Then again, readers may be familiar with manors in which cottagers survived in remarkable numbers during the Later Middle Ages. Why was this so? Answers may have to do, as at Sidbury, with plenty of opportunities for earning a living and of supplementing a labourer's wages: the classic example must surely be Castle Combe with its high proportion of cottagers among the tenants, its fifteenth-century cottage building boom associated with expansion of cloth making and its large population of immigrants.[90] Finally, I hope that I have alerted researchers to some of the documentary clues (where the cottager but not the cottage is hidden behind the façade of a rental) which may reveal the flourishing in this period of the tied cottage. My key example comes from Stokenham in the arable South Hams of Devon but there are hints of the same thing during the Latter Middle Ages on some other Devon manors and as far afield as Northampton and Oxfordshire. My interpretation may not stand the test of time but the clues are suggestive given the heavy labour requirements of large arable farms and given the struggle for labour which is a fundamental feature of the period.

90 E. M. Carus-Wilson, 'Evidences of industrial growth on some fifteenth-century manors', *Economic History Review*, 12, 1959–60, pp.119–204.

And, of course, we should expect to find manors with variations on and combinations of these characteristics.

Differences between manors and regions in the nature of farm-workers' accommodation has been the theme of my essay. These differences had many further ramifications. Let us look at the two extremes — Ashwater in North Devon with no cottages and many servants in husbandry; Sidbury in East Devon with numerous resilient, independent cottagers. We might expect the density of population at Ashwater to have been low. This would have been partly a result of large farm size (the independent variable here) and partly a result of absence of a population of married cottagers, because farmers preferred the labour of male living-in servants. Age of marriage delayed by servanthood, sex ratios skewed towards males, lack of a ladder of landholding: these too may have been contributory factors giving low population density. There is little surprise, therefore, in the finding that, by the early sixteenth century, population densities in North Devon were the lowest in the county and were already so by the end of the fourteenth century.[91] We might expect, at Ashwater, to find a population engaged predominantly in farming (as opposed to other occupations), and this was so throughout most of North Devon where rural cloth making was very poorly developed during the Later Middle Ages.[92] Again, the independent variable is the size of farms: large holdings practising an extensive type of pastoral farming did not tend to breed rural industries and, because servants were preferred as the labour force, there were few cottage families to practise a craft of some kind. At Ashwater we might expect that housing standards were good, for extensive cattle raising in the Later Middle Ages could turn a pretty penny and the wealth so derived could be invested in the luxury of improved

91 J. Sheail, 'The distribution of taxable population and wealth in England during the early sixteenth century', *Transactions of the Institute of British Geographers*, 55, 1972, p.119. My unpublished analyses of the poll tax returns for 1377 (P.R.O. E. 179/37–55) show that North Devon tithings generally rank lowest, in terms of taxpayers per square mile, when set against data for the rest of the county. Most of the Devon places excused from the parish subsidy of 1428 on account of feeble populations were in the North: *Feudal Aids*, i, London, H.M.S.O., 1899, pp.473–5. I am currently working on later medieval emigration from North Devon by individuals who failed to find a niche in this region.

92 H. S. A. Fox, 'Rural industry'.

housing.[93] In fact, a good majority of the surviving fifteenth-century farmhouses of Devon, substantial structures originally with open halls but soon fitted up with interior modifications for the elaboration of living space, are located in the North; the upper storeys could well have housed servants.[94] Conversely, we might expect relatively high population densities at Sidbury, with many smallholders and many cottage families, ease of family formation and a well structured ladder of landholding; rural industries and other non-agricultural occupations were well developed there, as we have seen; some accommodation was inferior, if only because cottage living tended to be cramped.[95] The reader familiar with nineteenth-century conditions will at once realize that the sets of contrasting characteristics just described are also those of the closed and open communities of the Victorian era.[96] Just as nineteenth-century commentators devised a typology of contemporary communities based upon attitudes to labour and to cottage building so too may the historian devise classifications of medieval communities based upon labour requirements and how they were met; Ashwater was in essence a closed community where labour was highly regulated, although closure here was the result of the policies of tenant farmers rather than a landlord. And with these

93 Calculations were presented in H. S. A. Fox, 'Late medieval farming economies in Devon: their relationship to building traditions', unpublished paper presented to a Council for British Archaeology conference, Exeter, March 1992.

94 Many of the examples in the surveys by N. W. Alcock, S. R. Jones and C. Hulland in *Transactions of the Devonshire Association*, 100–116, 1968–84, are from North Devon.

95 J. Sheail, 'Distribution of taxable population', p.119, where only some of the heavily populated vales of East Devon show up, on account of the fact that the author included the extensive wastes between them in his calculations of taxpayers per square mile. One might speculate that high population densities in East Devon during the Later Middle Ages were maintained partly through immigration to the region. In this connection it is interesting to find that just over half of the cottagers in the Silbury rental of 1394 bore surnames not recorded (for cottagers and tenants of farm holdings) 44 years earlier in the rental of 1350; many of these may have been immigrants and three in fact bore locative names. For the rental, see above n.34.

96 The typology has most recently been summed up (with due attention to its critics) in B. Short, 'The evolution of contrasting communities within rural England', in *idem*, ed., *op. cit.*, pp.19–43. The standard work is D. R. Mills, *Lord and Peasant in Nineteenth-century Britain*, London, 1980.

nineteenth-century parallels once again in mind, it is worth noting that it was in open Sidbury that the juggler and the prostitute were to be found; it was in Sidbury that labourers flouted the labour laws, their 'morals . . . corrupted' partly because the cottages were 'crowded together';[97] it was in closed Ashwater where farmsteads were 'separated from the rest of the world' that the social control of labour was most strongly developed. Slowly, and hesitantly, what Vinogradoff called 'the remarkable history' of the lower margins of medieval rural society is coming to life before my eyes.[98]

97 C. Vancouver, *op. cit.*, pp.97–8.

98 Cited in H. S. Bennett, *Life on the English Manor: a Study of Peasant Conditions 1150–1400*, Cambridge, 1937, p.65.

IX

———————— •✦✦✦• ————————

Stable Families in Tudor and Stuart England

DAVID HEY

IT HAS BECOME a commonplace of social history that in the Tudor and Stuart era the great majority of English people — men and women, country dwellers as well as those living in towns — moved from their place of birth at some stage of their lives. Ever since Peter Laslett and John Harrison's pioneering article on 'Clayworth and Cogenhoe' in 1963 we have been made aware that the composition of pre-industrial communities was constantly changing.[1] Two decades later the old idea that people remained rooted in the same spot had been abandoned so completely that David Souden and David Starkey could claim that: 'In almost any village of the seventeenth and eighteenth centuries, those who were born, lived and died in the same place in a district, were often a tiny minority. Families died out, names disappeared with what seems to us astonishing rapidity . . . high levels of movement characterized all villages. The villager who never moved was so rare as to be an oddity.'[2]

Yet when we turn to the work of Richard McKinley we find that in every county that he has studied surnames that can be shown to have a peculiarly local character are still most commonly found in and around their place of origin. This is readily demonstrated, for

---

1 P. Laslett and J. Harrison, 'Clayworth and Cogenhoe', in H. E. Bell and R. L. Ollard, eds., *Historical Essays, 1600–1750: Presented to David Ogg*, London, 1963, pp.157–84.

2 D. Souden and D. Starkey, *This Land of England*, London, 1985, pp.19–20.

example, in that numerous class of Lancashire surnames that are toponymic in derivation — the Aspinalls, Bickerstaffs, Greenhalghs, Singletons, etc. — but is it also true of many surnames that are derived in a different manner?[3] Even today, several centuries after the formation of surnames, distribution patterns commonly have a pronounced regional bias. How can we reconcile this evidence from surnames with that of the demographers? Or should it make us look anew at claims that our ancestors were constantly on the move?

It seems clear that in their use of purely quantitative approaches demographic historians have over-emphasised the importance of the statistics that undoubtedly prove the constant crossing of parish boundaries by a mobile population. Much of this movement did not affect the stability of the groups of families that formed the core of so many local societies. It can be argued that the character of a local community was determined not so much by all the coming and going but by the families that stayed put, even though at any one time they may have been outnumbered by those who had recently moved in. Where local historians have examined Tudor and Stuart rural parishes in detail, they have commonly emphasized the importance of the stable core. Thus, Professor W. G. Hoskins has written that the 161 households recorded in the hearth tax return of 1670 for Wigston Magna represented 82 different family names. Thirty-six of these families (44 per cent) had lived in Wigston for at least a century and 15 or 16 (20 per cent) had been there for 200 years or more. The Boulters had established no fewer than eight different households during the 100 years or so that they had lived in the parish. The Freers had eight branches after 200 years of residence. The Smiths, Vanns and Wards each had six branches, the Johnsons five, the Langtons, Holmses, Noones and Abbotts four and several others had three. These were the stable families that provided Wigston with a real sense of continuity. It mattered more that they stayed rooted in the place than that others were always moving in and out.[4]

3 R. McKinley, *The Surnames of Lancashire*, London, 1981, pp.110–35.

4 W. G. Hoskins, *The Midland Peasant: The Economic and Social History of a Leicestershire Village*, London, 1965, pp.194–204. A recent study by Anne Mitson has demonstrated the importance of groups of core families in South Nottinghamshire during the early-modern period; see C. V. Phythian-Adams, ed., *Societies, Cultures and Kinship, 1580–1850*, Leicester, 1993, pp.24–76.

Wigston was a nucleated village with no resident lord, a populous place at the heart of open-field England. Eighty miles or so to the west, the Shropshire parish of Myddle was a very different type of rural community. The farming was geared to raising beef and dairy cattle in woodland pastures, settlement was scattered and immigrants could still find land on which to squat; the poor were not yet a major problem. Only 91 households were recorded in the hearth tax returns of 1672. Yet here again certain families, notably the Lloyds, Goughs, Braynes, Groomes, Tylers, Juxes and Formstons, were remarkably tenacious in their attachment to the parish, often remaining in the same farm for several generations. Nathaniel Reve was probably expressing a common sentiment when he desired to be tenant of Bilmarsh Farm 'because his grandfather and father had been tenants to it before'.[5] A few of the gentry families, notably the Gittinses, were resident in Myddle for most of the sixteenth and seventeenth centuries, but it was the yeomen, husbandmen and village craftsmen who were most likely to stay and those below them on the social scale who were most likely to leave. Some farming and craft families remained in the parish for five, six or seven generations and in some other cases the turnover of surnames is explained by the failure of the male line and inheritance through an heiress.[6] Yet Souden and Starkey speak of 'the stable, ordered society that we have failed to uncover among the families of Myddle'.[7]

Small farmers in agricultural parishes were not the only ones who passed on their inheritance to their children and grandchildren. Stable families also formed the core of some industrial rural comunities. The parish of Norton in north Derbyshire, where scythe-making was an important activity, is a telling example. Between January 1560 and December 1653 the Norton register recorded 1,319 burials, 636 (48 per cent) of which related to 27 surnames; the other 683 entries (52 per cent) comprised 258 different surnames, with 125 of these appearing only once and 45 names

---

5 R. Gough, *The History of Myddle*, ed. D. Hey, Harmondsworth, 1981, p.131.

6 D. Hey, *An English Rural Community: Myddle Under the Tudors and Stuarts*, Leicester, 1974, pp.119–42.

7 D. Souden and D. Starkey, *op. cit.*, p.37.

appearing only twice. Here again, the contrast between the stable core and the mobile, short-term residents is marked.[8]

Table 1 — The most common surnames in the Norton Burial Register, 1560–1653.

Surname	No. of entries	Surname	No. of Entries
Parker	54	Kirke	21
Bullock	53	Rollison	21
Barten	44	Gill	19
Blythe	33	Cowley	18
More/Mawer	31	Atkin	17
North	28	Fox	15
Urton alias Steven	28	Bore	13
Poynton	26	Camme	12
Allen	26	Cooke	12
Bate	25	Barnes	11
Green	25	Gillott	11
Rose	25	Holland	11
Brownell	24	Owtrem	11
Biggen	22		

All but four of these families are represented in a seating plan of the church which can be dated by internal evidence to about 1640.[9] The pews were occupied by six branches of the Bartens, six Stevens, five Bates, four Mores, three Atkins, three Blythes, three Greens, three Rollinsons and 51 others.

The Parkers, Bullocks, Gills and Kirkes were parish gentry, though some of their members were involved not only in agriculture but in one branch or other of the local metal trades. John Parker of Little Norton had been described as a scythesmith back in 1459 and the Bullocks derived some of their wealth from the manufacture of axes and other edge tools. The Blythes, yeomen of Norton Lees, were middlemen in the scythe trade and it is likely that some of the other families who normally went under the description of yeomen or husbandmen may have been partly occupied in local crafts. The families described as yeomen in parish and probate records included the

---

8 J. Kingston, *Life and Death in Elizabethan and Early Stuart Norton*, dissertation for the Certificate in Local History, University of Sheffield, 1990.

9 Sheffield Archives, Oakes deeds, 1405.

Allens, Poyntons, Bates and Rollinsons. Those recorded as husbandmen included the Bartens, Norths, Greens, Mores and Hollands. The remaining 10 families listed above were unambiguously described as scythemakers, though of course they combined their trade with farming. They were amongst the most stable members of this particular community. The Atkins, Biggens and Gillotts were still making scythes in Norton parish several generations later, in 1787, when a trade directory was compiled.[10]

The hearth tax return for Michaelmas 1670 confirms the importance of this group of stable families, many of whom were already well established when the parish register began to be kept early in Elizabeth's reign.[11] The 118 entries for Norton included 48 householders with the 27 surnames recorded above, that is 41 per cent. It is interesting to note that the seven most prosperous householders in 1670, who were taxed on 18, 12, 11, 11, 10, nine and eight hearths respectively, were not amongst the 27 prolific families; they seem to have been relative newcomers to the parish. Eight of the families that were so prolific in earlier times were no longer resident there by 1670 and five families had dwindled to a single household. The Blythes (a family that had been at Norton Lees since at least the late fourteenth century) were represented by one household that was taxed on seven hearths; the other old families that were represented only once were the Gills (six hearths), Cammes (four), Rollinsons (four) and Roses (three). The families with several branches had standards of living that ranged from the modest to the middling. The six households of Gillotts had five, three, two, two, two and one hearths, the Parkers had five, two and one, the Urtons five, three and one, the Bartens four, three, three, two, one and one, and the Atkins four, two, two, one, one and one. But other long-established families had only the same modest means of many of the small farmers in Myddle. The Greens had two, one, one and one hearths and the three Norths and three Brownells each had only a single hearth. Taken together, the old-established families form a fair cross-section of the parish above the level of the poor cottagers.

10 Parish and probate records; D. Hey, *The Rural Metalworkers of the Sheffield Region*, Leicester, 1972, pp.8–9, 20–5; Gales and Martin, *A Directory of Sheffield*, London, 1787, pp.32–3.

11 D. G. Edwards, ed., *Derbyshire Hearth Tax Assessments, 1662–70*, Derbyshire Record Society, VII, 1982, pp.164–6.

The scythemaking families remained in Norton because their trade was profitable (they were the wealthiest of the local metalworkers) and because their investment in capital and craft skills was passed on from generation to generation. If and when the surname disappeared from local records it was usually because of the failure of the male line. When that happened the business was sometimes continued through a female line of the family. If the surname appears in neighbouring parishes under some other occupation, it is usually because a younger son moved away from home. Such lads rarely moved very far, except that the promise of London was as attractive to young people from this part of England as it was from any other.

Scythemakers are just one example of craft families that remained in the same place over several generations. Millers, maltsters, glassmakers and many other craftsmen who had invested their capital in fixed structures earned a living that was sufficient to persuade them that they had more to lose than gain by moving. It was notably the poor who sought an improved fortune elsewhere. This is not to say that the senior members of the stable families never ventured from home; as youngsters they may well have worked in a neighbouring parish before the farm or business became theirs. Much of the mobility that has been commented on by demographers relates to domestic and farm servants who travelled within a restricted area bordered by the nearest market towns.[12] But the evidence from these three contrasting rural communities shows that in some places at least a core group of families remained rooted in their parish decade after decade. It is time to look again at Clayworth, where Laslett and Harrison found that no less than 61.8 per cent of the people recorded in a listing of 1676 were not there 12 years later.[13] Does this impressive figure show that the seventeenth-century villager was forever ready to move his home, or does it conceal the sort of family stability that has been found in other parts of rural England?

12 A. Kussmaul, *Servants in Husbandry in Early Modern England*, Cambridge, 1981; P. Clark and D. Souden, eds., *Migration and Society in Early Modern England*, London, 1987, pp.11–48.

13 The lists are printed in H. Gill and E. L. Guilford, eds., *The Rector's Book, Clayworth, Nottinghamshire*, Nottingham, 1910.

Having demonstrated the great amount of mobility that occurred within the parish of Clayworth between 1676 and 1688, Professor Laslett wisely concluded that 'it might be easy to exaggerate the importance of the rate of *structural* change which these figures imply. A 60 per cent turnover of persons in 12 years is after all only five per cent a year . . . At Clayworth in 1688 something like 23 of the 91 households were new since 1676, and 10 of these were entirely novel: the 13 others may possibly show some continuity, or the movement of relatives into the village to take over existing establishments.'[14] This leaves a large number of households that were there both in 1676 and 1688. If we analyse the two lists in terms of households rather than individuals the picture that emerges is similar to that found in the parishes discussed above. Just under half the heads of households recorded in 1676 were still alive and living in Clayworth 12 years later. If we add to these the 18 who had been succeeded by a widow, a son or a close relation, we see that about two out of every three families were stable during this period. As some of the incomers may also have had a previous family connection, this figure is a minimum one. When we look at the two lists in this way the underlying stability of the community is made clear.

The hearth tax return of 1664 for Clayworth confirms this picture.[15] Though it is impossible to provide a firm statistic, we are safe in asserting that throughout the period 1664–76 at least two out of every three families remained in the parish. A wider view is made possible by the survival of the protestation return of 1642 for Clayworth, which lists all males aged 16 or more.[16] A few families may have had no adult males at that point in time; nevertheless the 78 recorded surnames probably included the great majority of households. The Revd William Sampson's list of 1676 includes 32 of these surnames; 44 of the 75 householders noted by the rector had surnames that were used by the previous generation. Sampson's list

---

14 P. Laslett and J. Harrison, *op. cit.*, p.177. On p.180, however, they note that at Cogenhoe (the other village in the study) 'the familial structure changed quite suddenly and not inconsiderably'.

15 W. F. Webster, ed., *Nottinghamshire Hearth Tax, 1664–1674*, Thoroton Society Record Series, XXXVII, Nottingham, 1988, p.27.

16 W. F. Webster, ed., *Protestation Returns, 1641/2: Nottinghamshire*, Nottingham, privately published, 1984.

of 1688 shows some further erosion of names over the next 12 years; even so 25 of the 78 surnames recorded in 1642 were still used by Clayworth families. The 90 householders in 1688 included 37 who had surnames that had belonged to families in the parish 46 years earlier. It is possible that some of the families with common surnames were unconnected, but a careful consideration of all four lists made between 1642 and 1688 suggests that the links were firm.[17] Two out of every five surnames found in Clayworth in 1688 had been present in the parish for almost half a century. We may conclude that a group of stable families formed the core of the community of Clayworth. Peter Laslett expressed his findings with suitable caution. Others who have followed the trail that he blazed have not been as circumspect. The villager of the seventeenth century who never moved was not a rarity, let alone an oddity.

If stable families can be found in a variety of rural communities during the reigns of the Tudors and Stuarts, what should we expect to find in the towns? Surely, in an urban context the resident population was always changing? There seems little doubt that the turnover of urban populations was more rapid than that in the countryside. Nevertheless, certain urban trades passed from father to son to grandson in the same manner as did some rural crafts. Where a particular trade dominated the economy of a town and entry to that trade was rigorously controlled, it is likely that some families remained rooted in the place over a least a few generations. The cutlers of Sheffield are a case in point. Families such as the Websters, Pearsons and Ellises can be identified both in the Elizabethan parish register and the hearth tax return for Ladyday 1672. Others with distinctive local surnames such as Creswick and Staniforth can be found throughout the Tudor and Stuart era, both in the town and in the neighbouring countryside. Moreover, those apprentice lads who entered the cutlery trades as immigrants usually did not travel very far.[18] Their pattern of movement is what we

17 The surnames are: Bacon, Bett, Bingham, Booth, Colton, Denby, Dickinson, Farnsworth, Gabbitus, Green, Greenfield, Hanson, Lillyman, Maples, Nettleship, Norris, Otter, Pearson, Raynes, Smith, Wawen, Whitehead, Woodcock, Wrawby and Wright.

18 D. Hey, *The Fiery Blades of Hallamshire: Sheffield and its Neighbourhood, 1660–1740*, Leicester, 1991.

would expect from Richard McKinley's conclusions on the ramification of surnames during this period.

The structure of families in urban communities is an under-researched topic, but the contrast between the comings and goings of a mobile population and the permanence of a stable core is as evident in some towns as it is in the countryside. Given the small size of most towns in the sixteenth and seventeenth centuries, this is what we might expect. In larger urban centres, some families remained attached not just to a certain town but to a particular district within it. In a classic study of this phenomenon Mary Prior has shown how 'a very tight knit community of boat-people who were united both by occupation and kinship' formed the stable core of Fisher Row, Oxford, while another group which included carters, drovers and seasonal workers who found cheap lodgings in the parish were always on the move.[19] Dr Prior came to the conclusion that the sense of community amongst the residents of this particular part of the town was not affected by the constant movement. What was important was the stability of a substantial group of native families who gave the place its distinctive occupational character.

Even in seventeenth-century London the same picture of a stable group of families forming the core of a local community emerges from a detailed study of the population. Dr Jeremy Boulton's analysis of Easter books and parish registers for Southwark has demonstrated the considerable residential persistence of many of the borough's householders.[20] Despite high mortality rates and the constant inflow of great numbers of young immigrants, Southwark's population structure was similar to that which characterized rural parishes. Forty-three per cent of the householders recorded in 1612–14 were still there 10 years later; many of the others may have passed out of sight merely by crossing the borough boundary. Much of the observable mobility was only short-range, as families sought to improve their accommodation. The common pattern was for a young married couple to start with a small house, to move to more spacious premises if they became more prosperous, and to move back to something

19 M. Prior, *Fisher Row: Fishermen, Bargemen and Canal Boatmen in Oxford, 1500–1900*, Oxford, 1982.

20 J. Boulton, 'Neighbourhood migration in early modern London', in P. Clark and D. Souden, eds., *Migration and Society in Early Modern England*, London, 1987, pp.107–49.

smaller in later life. Even metropolitan society, therefore, was organized into localized units whose core families and kin-networks provided a sense of community and of continuity.

People who moved in and out of the towns often did not travel very far. If urban historians widen their horizons beyond the boundaries of the town so as to include the neighbouring countryside, then the impression of unceasing mobility fades considerably. Here we come to the heart of the matter. In pointing to a population constantly on the move, demographers have usually been looking at evidence strictly focused on a town or a rural parish. But as Peter Laslett observed about Clayworth: 'Given that there was migration on a surprising scale in and out of these communities, it may nevertheless have been a very local migration.' One of the most important lessons that we have begun to learn is that although the parish was a unit to which men and women felt attached and which gave them a sense of separate identity, the wider neighbourhood or territory that people knew as their 'country' was of even greater importance in providing a geographic and social framework for human life.[21] If we look beyond the parish boundary to a more loosely-defined local society, then we may be able to reconcile the demographic evidence with that of the surnames studied by Richard McKinley.

Two tanning families of Sheffield illustrate this pattern of movement within a local context. Tanning was an occupation that tended to remain in the hands of the same family over the generations and younger sons were often provided with the wherewithal to set up business at a new site not far away. The Rawsons were Sheffield's most prolific family of tanners, with branches in several parts of this large parish and just beyond. At various times they were located at rural sites at Wardsend, Raisin Hall, Upperthorpe, Crookes, Pitsmoor, Grimesthorpe and also alongside the Ponds at the edge of the town. The Upperthorpe branch can be traced back to William Rawson, tanner, who died in 1550; his son, grandson and great-grandson were described as yeomen of Upperthorpe, but his younger son, James, moved to Raisin Hall to set up as a tanner. The tannery survived into the eighteenth century. Another branch was a junior line of the Rawsons who were settled at Brookside in the adjoining chapelry of Bradfield from at least the reign of Edward IV to that of

21 C. V. Phythian-Adams, *Re-Thinking English Local History*, Leicester, 1987.

Charles II. Robert Rawson (1621–66) was a younger son who married Mary, daughter of Edward Rawson of Walkley (a branch of the Upperthorpe Rawsons). Edward Rawson was described as a tanner in 1650–51 and his son-in-law became tenant of the 'Tan house of 3 bayes in the Tanyard' at Wardsend. Robert Rawson's trade was carried on by his son Thomas (1665-1728), his grandson Thomas (died 1766) and his great-grandson Thomas, who built Sheffield's first large brewery, in Pond Street, in 1780. Many more details of this family could be given, but enough has been said to indicate their web of connections and their continued presence in the parish.[22]

The other example from the families of Sheffield tanners is that of the Shemelds. The name appears to be of single-family origin and to have become hereditary in the adjoining parish of Handsworth, where Robert Schemyld', a smith, and Denise, his wife paid 6d. in the poll tax in 1379 and Adam Schemyld' paid 4d. The present distribution of the surname is emphatically local. Shemelds are recorded on the first page of the Sheffield parish register in 1560. Several branches became cutlers and scissorsmiths, but Humphrey Shemeld was a tanner at Grimesthorpe in 1643 and John Shemeld was practising the same trade there a decade later. Afterwards, other members of the family leased the Shude Hill tannery by the Ponds. In 1670 Joseph Shemeld was renting a dwelling house, malt house and 'tann office' in Sheffield with nine acres of land: this appears to have been the same property that was described in a new lease that he took in 1686 as 'a messuage, Malt-house and Tanyard, with pasture West of the river, and North of a lane leading to the Pond-mill'. Joseph's brother, Mercury, set up as a tanner at Billingley, a few miles to the north in the parish of Darfield, but both brothers remained staunch members of the Sheffield dissenting congregation. When Joseph died in 1687 he was succeeded by his son Benjamin, and eventually by his grandson, James. He and other Shemelds worked the Ponds tannery for most of the first half of the eighteenth century.[23]

---

22 J. Hunter, *Hallamshire: the History and Topography of the Parish of Sheffield*, ed. A Gatty, London, 1861, p.451 footnote; Sheffield Archives, ACM S374, S379, WC 1773, 1774, 1785, RC 155/2823, 158/8746, 8937, 9178.

23 Sheffield Archives, ACM S129, S376, S390, RC 156/4456, 159/12167, Sheffield parish register.

In Chesterfield, too, some members of the longest-established families, notably the Ashes, the Clarkes and the Heathcotes, made a substantial living from tanning. In 1563 Chesterfield was a market town with a population of about 1,000–1,200; the entire parish contained some 2,700 inhabitants.[24] The Heathcote and Ashe families appear on the first page of the parish register, in 1558, and are recorded on countless occasions thereafter. Tanning was not their only interest. The Heathcotes were also bell-founders who invested in the lead trade and cattle grazing and the Clarkes were the leading innkeepers. When a lay subsidy was levied in 1543 the seven richest men in the town included George Ashe (who paid £35), William Clarke (£30), Ralph Clarke (£20) and George Heathcote (£15). The Ashes and Heathcotes had been prominent townsmen much earlier, for in 1480 Richard Ashe, John Heathcote, mercer, and Richard Heathcote, brazier, had been members of the Common Council.[25] The Clarkes came a little later. During Elizabeth's reign, they were much involved in the town's struggles with the lord of the manor, the Earl of Shrewsbury, and in 1598 Ralph Clarke became the first mayor when the town was incorporated. In Charles II's reign 'Mr Richard Clarke Major' with 23 hearths headed the list of those who paid the hearth tax; presumably he was still running the town's largest inn. The return also noted two Mr George Ashes (each with five hearths), Godfrey Ashe (four), Alice Ashe (four), Mr John Ashe, apothecary (one), Mr Gilbert Heathcote (six) and Benjamin Heathcote (joint occupier of seven hearths). The continued importance of these families over a long period of time is evident.

Clarke is a common surname of multiple origins, so it is impossible to follow all the family connections, but Ashe and Heathcote are Derbyshire surnames that are toponymic in origin. They can both be identified with particular places even though they are derived from common place-names. Ashe was derived from a place in the parish of Brampton, just beyond the Chesterfield border, now known as Ashgate, and Heathcote was formed in the Peak District further west in the parish of Hartington.[26] Three centuries or so after the formation

24 J. M. Bestall and D. V. Fowkes, eds., *Chesterfield Wills and Inventories, 1521–1603*, Derbyshire Record Society, I, 1977.

25 P. Riden, *History of Chesterfield*, II, pt. 1, Chersterfield, 1984, pp.49, 51, 177–8.

26 K. Cameron, *The Place-Names of Derbyshire*, Cambridge, 1959, pp.220, 369.

Figure 1 — Distribution of Ash (+) and Heathcote (●) households in the Derbyshire hearth tax returns, 1662–70.

of these hereditary surnames their distribution can be plotted from the evidence of the hearth tax return of 1670 (Figure 1). The 17 households of Ashe were still concentrated in north Derbyshire, particularly in Brampton and Chesterfield. The 30 Heathcotes had spread wider from their base in the High Peak, but there is no doubting that the northern part of the county was their stronghold; only two Heathcotes were listed in the contemporary returns for Nottinghamshire. The restricted nature of their movement fits exactly the pattern observed by Richard McKinley in different parts of England.

Let us return to Souden and Starkey. One of their studies concerned the surname Braithwaite within the parish of Hawkshead. They wrote that 'The people of the north west frequently moved out of the poor region they were living in, and they were highly mobile at a local level within the parishes of the Lake District'. They conceded that 'few moved in before the important economic changes of the later seventeeth century, and very few before the nineteenth century. The large numbers with the same surname are some index of that. There were 2,000 registrations under the name of Braithwaite in seventeenth-century Hawkshead parish: during the eighteenth century their overwhelming primacy was diminished as Braithwaites moved away and other families moved in. Today a single Braithwaite family remains in the parish.'[27] If we look at that wider area of which Hawkshead forms part, however, we find that Braithwaites are still strong on the ground. The telephone directory of 1987 for Cumbria and North Lancashire (section 252) lists no fewer than 146 personal subscribers with that name. The surname is still one that is readily associated with north-west England. The majority of the Braithwaites have not moved very far.

The technique of plotting the distributions of particular surnames from current telephone directories and from earlier data bases such as the indexes of Civil Registration and the Mormon International Genealogical Index of Parish Registers, has been used effectively by J. D. Porteous in his study of his ancestors called Mell. Dr Porteous has concluded that the Mells 'appear to have been extremely loyal to the Humber-Trent region for well over 400 years'. Even in 1980, the 82 entries in telephone directories for this rare surname were

27 D. Souden and D. Starkey, *op. cit.*, p.43.

mostly to be found in Yorkshire and Lincolnshire, with a minor cluster in and around London; the name is almost entirely absent from western England, Wales, Scotland and Northern Ireland. The present distribution points to the likely home of the Mell surname. The John Mell, husbandman, who paid 4d. in the poll tax in 1377 at Thorganby, at the northern edge of the Humberhead Levels, is probably the ancestor of all who bear this unusual name.[28]

The plotting of the distributions of uncommon surnames at various points in time usually leads to conclusions similar to those reached by Dr Porteous and warns us to beware of those who say that the villager who stayed put was an oddity. The fact that the telephone directory of 1981 for Bradford contains 194 personal entries for people with the surname Hey while that for Northampton contains none at all suggests that my ancestors were reluctant to move far. This essay has concentrated on the Tudor and Stuart period but the stability of families often extends over a much greater time-scale. My great-great-grandfather moved into the West Riding township of Thurlstone, where I lived as a boy, about the year 1800; some of his descendants are still there. He was a younger son who had moved from Shelley, five miles to the north in the parish of Kirkburton, where his ancestors had combined the trade of weaving with farming a smallholding since at least the reign of Henry VIII. The surname appears exactly 300 times in the parish register of Kirkburton between 1543 and 1800; three branches of the Hey family still live in Kirkburton. Prior to Henry VIII's reign, the Heys lived a little further north. The Robert del Heye who paid the poll tax in Barkisland township in 1379 occupied the moorland farm that was known in later times as Hey House. A former teacher of mine once said jokingly that I should never argue from personal experience as it was not statistically significant, but I suspect that the experience of my own family was very similar to that of countless others.

The persistence of core groups of stable families in the 'countries' of England has obvious implications for the transmittance of local cultures. How else can we explain the peculiarities of local speech? Even today, despite the accelerated pace of lexical erosion and the

---

28 J. D. Porteous, *The Mells: Surname Geography, Family History*, Saturna Island, Canada, 1988. See also D. Hey, *The Oxford Guide to Family History*, Oxford, 1993, pp.40–61, and C. D. Rogers, *The Surname Detective*, Manchester, 1995, pp.7–80.

spread of received pronunciation, a person's speech can enable the informed listener to place him or her within a restricted area that corresponds to the idea of 'country'. If the turnover of local populations was as enormous as we have sometimes been led to believe, it is hard to see how characteristics of speech could remain so intensely local. The stable families of a community must have set the patterns to which newcomers — or their children — eventually conformed. Nor is it likely that without a core group of families a community would have preserved its distinctive traditions or would have seen itself as different from its neighbours.

People who had lived in a parish for all or most of their lives were the ones that contending parties turned to whenever a dispute over local customs or practices arose. Thus, in 1587 John Shemeld, a 70-year old yeoman of Hasland Bank in the parish of Sheffield, was called upon to explain how Ecclesall woods had been periodically coppiced during the course of his already long life.[29] Richard Gough spoke with great respect of the most ancient families in his parish of Myddle, of which his own was one of the most prominent. Gough's memories of his ancestors went back almost 200 years and his knowledge of his neighbours' family histories was remarkable. Though no one else has left us such a marvellous account, he was surely not alone in thinking of his local community in terms of the families that composed it. The fact that so many families had stayed not just in the same parish, but in the same farms for generation after generation, made it natural for him to think in this way.

---

29 J. R. Wigfull, 'Her Majesty's Manor of Ecclesall', *Transactions of the Hunter Archaeological Society*, IV, pt. 1, 1930, pp.28–45.

X

———————— ·◆ᵢᵢᵢᵢ◆· ————————

The Distribution and Stability of Surnames in south-east Surrey — 1664–1851

EVELYN LORD

THE PUBLICATION IN 1988 of the fifth volume in the English Surnames Series, *The Surnames of Sussex*, was one of great personal interest to me.[1] Not only is Sussex a county which I know very well, but it was also a county on which I had been working for several years. My examination of spatial and social interaction within and across the three counties of Surrey, Sussex and Kent, had drawn on Richard McKinley's previous work, but this volume was of direct relevance to what I was doing. Richard's speculations on surnames unique to one county and the ramifications of names across boundaries, had enabled me to form a working hypothesis on the role of boundaries. Therefore, I awaited eagerly the combination of Richard's thoughtful exposition on surnames for a county where I had some little vested interest; I was not disappointed. In his volume Richard gets to the crux of the problem that I had been endeavouring to solve — the role of boundaries in shaping local identity. I was especially concerned with administrative boundaries. How far was the individual's perception of locality shaped by these boundaries, and how far are investigations into the perception of boundaries shaped by the sources available? Richard writes: 'The use of counties as the basic units for carrying on the Surnames surveys is inevitable, because a high proportion of records which have to be used are drawn up by county.' He continues: 'Even so, it is of course the case that county boundaries are not in themselves a complete barrier to

---

1 R. McKinley, *The Surnames of Sussex*, English Surnames Series, V, Oxford, 1988.

the migration of surnames.'[2] This essay builds on the theme of the migration of surnames across the county boundary. It can only be a footnote to Richard's comprehensive and lucid survey of the surnames of Sussex. I hope that it will pay tribute to his scholarship, his mastery of his subject, and an instalment towards the debt which I owe him for the intellectual stimulation that his work and his presence in the Department of English Local History has given me and other students of the University of Leicester.

Surname Stability

English surnames have been studied in depth by George Redmonds[3] and Richard McKinley.[4] They have dealt with the history, origins and derivations of surnames on a county basis.[5] This essay does not undertake so wide-ranging an investigation, but will look at two aspects of surname studies. It will use names as a measurement of the stability of the population by calculating the turnover of names across two centuries. Secondly, it will look at surname distribution in relation to administration and natural boundaries. Unlike the English Surnames Survey, it is limited in time and uses only two main sources, parish register entries and the 1851 census returns (which are supported by other eighteenth- and nineteenth-century lists that have survived for the study area and which are used here). The baptismal register will be used in preference to the marriage or burial register, as it gives a wider sample of the total population of a parish. The registers and the census data will be correlated with the 1664 Hearth Tax return for Surrey.[6]

The location of the area being examined is the corner of south-eastern England where Surrey, Sussex and Kent meet. This essay concentrates on parishes in Surrey, but also looks at the migration of

2 *Ibid.*, pp.3–4.

3 G. Redmonds, *The Surnames of Yorkshire*, West Riding, English Surnames Series, I, London, 1973.

4 R. McKinley, *The Surnames of Lancashire*, English Surnames Series, IV, London, 1981.

5 See also R. McKinley, *The Surnames of Oxfordshire*, English Surnames Series, London, 1977.

6 H. Meekings, *The Surrey Hearth Tax of 1664*, Surrey Record Society Publication, xviii, Kingston, 1940.

surnames across the county boundary. Geographically, this is an area of contrasts. In the north is the high chalk upland of the North Downs. South of the Downs is a ridge of greensand that provided an east-west highway from Kent to Surrey. The three counties merge in the inaccessible Wealden claylands which once isolated Sussex from the rest of the world and gave the county its numerous distinctive characteristics.

One of the earliest pioneers to use surnames listed in the parish register to give an estimation of the population turnover of a parish was E. J. Buckatzsch. In a paper written in 1951, he concluded that, throughout the three centuries that he surveyed, relatively large numbers of families were leaving the parish and being replaced by others with different names.[7] This does not mean that there were none peculiar to one locality. Richard McKinley's latest work makes this clear. He writes that a significant characteristic of Sussex surnames is their degree of continuity,[8] whilst in *The Surnames of Lancashire* he wrote that:

> 'In most English counties, the surnames present up to the nineteenth century retain a distinctly local character, in the sense that the same surnames tend to persist in each county over long periods, and the effect on the composition of the surnames existing in most counties of the intrusion of surnames which have originated in other places, and which have been brought in by immigration, is generally slight.'[9]

This can be compared with Redmonds' findings in Yorkshire. In some parishes — Swillington, for example — there was considerable stability of surnames, but in others, two-thirds of the names were new every 50 years.[10] Rex Watson, who carried out a study of sur-name distribution in a group of Cambridgeshire parishes, concluded that, unless the parish had an unusually large population, it was the most common names that would remain in the parish over a long

---

7 E. J. Buckatzsch, 'The constancy of local populations and migration in England before 1800', *Population Studies*, v, 1951, pp.62–9.

8 R. McKinley, *Sussex Surnames*, p.429.

9 R. McKinley, *Lancashire Surnames*, p.441.

10 G. Redmonds, *op. cit.*, pp.116, 119.

time. As more individuals bore the name, the greater was the chance that name had of surviving.[11] This may not mean that the individuals who bore the same name were related in any way. Detailed micro-studies of parish genealogies suggest that it cannot be assumed that those bearing the same surname were related or even had a common ancestor — although in the case of an unambiguous locative name it is tenable that an ancestor who originated from that place was the common *ancestor* of the holders of that name. Furthermore, general statements on the nature of kinship links cannot be derived from surname evidence, especially as in England, surnames derived from the male descent line. The woman took her husband's name on marriage, whilst the children bore the father's rather than the mother's surname. This means that, although names can disappear from the sources, their bearers were still present in the parish. These strictures must be borne in mind when using names to estimate the temporal turnover of individuals and family units in a parish.

In order to look at this turnover, as illustrated by surnames, the baptismal registers for 10 parishes have been used as a sample and correlated with the 1664 Hearth Tax and the 1851 census. This is shown in Table 1.

Table 1 — Number of years that surnames present in the 1851 census had been in the same parish. Expressed as a proportion of surnames in the census.

Parish	Years						
	200	100	80	60	40	20	>20
Blechingley	11	11	19	na	na	14*	45
Burstow	4	10	9	4	4	3	66
Caterham	2	8	7	5	5	6	67
Godstone	9	10	6	6	3	4	62
Horne	9	16	4	6	5	5	55
Limpsfield	5	na	na	40	13	11	31
Nutfield	6	11	12	9	7	7	48
Tatsfield	0	2	0	4	0	0	94
Titsey	0	10	0	0	0	0	90
Warlingham	0	6	2	1	0	0	91

na = data not available.

* = based on 1813 militia list for that parish.

11 R. Watson, 'A study of surname distribution in a group of Cambridgeshire parishes, 1538–1840', *Local Population Studies*, 15, 1975, p.31.

This table shows that four parishes — Caterham, Tatsfield, Titsey, and Warlingham — show a high turnover of surnames, and perhaps a low stability of population. This is especially true of the last three parishes, where 90 per cent of the names had been in the parish for only 20 years. These parishes were small downland parishes. The three parishes that lie on the greensand ridge — Blechingley, Limpsfield and Nutfield — show a low turnover of surnames, and a high stability of population. The turnover of surnames in the Wealden parishes of Burstow and Horne lies between the high turnover on the downland and the low turnover in greensand parishes.

At this point, Watson's conclusions should be considered. It is possible that a parish with a small total population might have insufficient holders of any one surname to ensure its survival in that parish. A comparison was made with the most common names in 1750 with those surviving through until the census return of 1851. A common name was taken to be when there were more than four holders of that name in the parish. Table 2 shows this comparison.

Table 2 — Comparison of the proportion of common names (4+) surviving to 1851 with uncommon names.

Parish	Common Names	Uncommon Names
Blechingley	33	66
Burstow	19	81
Caterham	20	80
Godstone	38	72
Horne	59	41
Nutfield	29	71
Titsey	20	80
Warlingham	14	86

This table indicates that, in the sample parishes of the study area, those names most likely to survive were those held by a few rather than by many.

The final task in the analysis of the stability of surnames was to estimate the decadal rate of turnover. This was done by dividing the period 1750–1830 into 20-year blocks. (If a 21-year span is used in relation to the baptismal register, it means that those in the first period were likely to have passed out of the child-bearing phase by the second 20-year block, and so would not be counted twice.) The names in each 20-year period were divided into: those names which appeared in both the 1750s and the 1770s; names which occurred in the first period, but had disappeared by the second; and those names which appeared in the second period, but not the first. Those in the last category were new names. The rate of turnover is equal to new names + lost names, expressed as a percentage of all names. It is shown in Table 3.

Table 3 — Average decadal turnover of surnames in 10 sample parishes in south-east Surrey, 1750–1830.

Parish	1750–70	1771–90	1791–1810	1811–30	sp
Blechingley	40	na	na	na	3.42
Burstow	30	40	40	40	2.64
Caterham	30	40	40	40	2.70
Godstone	40	40	40	40	2.54
Horn	50	40	30	30	3.01
Limpsfield	na	na	40	40	2.07
Nutfield	40	30	40	40	2.64
Tatsfield	50	50	na	na	5.85
Titsey	50	40	na	na	5.46
Warlingham	40	30	na	na	3.54

na = data not available.

The result shows a remarkable conformity of over 40 per cent turnover of names per decade in all parishes. The standard error of sample in the last column suggests that the same figure can be used for the turnover of names of parishioners who did not appear in the baptismal registers between these decades. It can also be seen that the parishes with small populations — Tatsfield and Titsey — had a slightly higher rate of decadal turnover of surnames than parishes with higher populations. This shows a somewhat different trend to the small parishes examined in Yorkshire by Redmonds. He shows that the smaller the community, the greater the stability of surnames. Of course, the difference between Redmonds' sample parishes and those in Surrey lies mainly in geographical position. The parishes in Yorkshire were very isolated, lying away from large centres of population, and often physically separated from other communities by large tracts of moorland.[12] The small parishes in the Surrey

12 G. Redmonds, *op. cit.*, p.263.

sample were close to large centres of population in Croydon and London, and had good communications with the outside world.

The importance of communications on the rate of turnover of surnames is demonstrated by Godstone, a parish which lies on the greensand ridge, at the point where the east-west highway was crossed by the north-south turnpike from Lewes to London. By 1851, Godstone had a far higher proportion of new surnames than its greensand neighbours of Blechingley, Limpsfield, and Nutfield. The latter parishes, and Horne in the Weald, show a particularly high stability of surnames. Nearly a quarter of the surnames present in those parishes in 1851 had been documented in these parishes for over a hundred years. Although these parishes form a compact geographical block, Blechingley had, by the eighteenth century, diverged both economically and socially. This parish had developed as a service area, with a strong middle-class section. The opening-up of the Fuller's Earth pits in Nutfield, the parish which lies immediately west of Blechingley, had led to a diverse socio-economic scene, with a mixture of general labourers working in the pits and owner-occupier yeoman farmers. Horne on the Weald was purely an agricultural parish with a preponderance of small, family-run farms. It is likely, given these differing socio-economic situations, that, although the parishes shared a tradition of surname longevity, the surnames were different in each parish. The next section of this essay will examine the distribution of surnames in relation to administrative and natural boundaries.

Surname Distribution

It was H. P. Guppy's work in the late nineteenth century which drew attention to the fact that there were some surnames which were peculiar to one county rather than another.[13] Redmonds' work on the surnames of the West Riding confirmed this. He found that, even when a parish lay close to the county border, it was rare for surnames to be shared across that border. Thus, in 1851, at Bolton by Bowland, although there were 83 names which were new in the parish since 1812, only 21 of these came from Lancashire, which was closer to Bolton than its Yorkshire hinterland.[14] Furthermore, all

13 H. Guppy, *Homes of Family Names in Great Britain*, Baltimore, 1890, repr. 1968.

14 G. Redmonds, *op. cit.*, p.426.

the new surnames were traceable to an origin within five miles of the parish. Surnames, it is suggested, are likely to cross parish borders, but to remain within county borders. Indeed, it is unreasonable to expect that, given the population expansion of the late eighteenth and early nineteenth centuries, surnames would be limited by the parish boundary. In order to test this assumption, the parish boundary will be the starting point from which to assess the migration of surnames across boundaries. The main source for this is the 1851 census. Table 4 shows the proportion of surnames which were unique to one parish in the study area. This of course does not preclude the sharing of the surname with parishes outside the area of study.

Table 4 — Rank order of the proportion of surnames unique to one parish.

Rank	Parish	No. of names	No. unique	% Unique of all names
1	Blechingley	190	75	39
2	Godstone	258	73	53
3	Caterham	122	35	29
4=	Westerham	360	100	28
	Worth	119	33	28
5=	Nutfield	161	41	25
	Titsey	55	14	25
6	Warlingham	123	30	24
7	Edenbridge	230	52	23
8	Limpsfield	235	31	22
9=	Tandridge	150	31	21
	East Grinstead	127	27	21
10	Horne	109	20	18
11	Tatsfield	49	7	14
12	Burstow	256	28	11
13	Crowhurst	52	5	10

The Table shows that Blechingley has the highest proportion of unique surnames, although this parish does not have the largest population. (This might explain the high number of unique names: more population correlates with a greater variety of names.) Both Godstone and East Grinstead had larger populations than Blechingley. These two parishes were on the main London road. It is thus probable that the populations of these parishes were more mobile than that of Blechingley — hence a greater variety of surnames. This

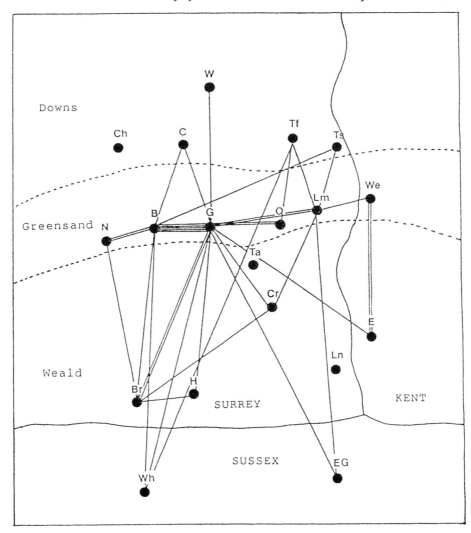

Downs

Greensand

Weald

SURREY

KENT

SUSSEX

B	—	Blechingley	EG	—	East Grinstead	Ta	—	Tandridge
Br	—	Burstow	G	—	Godstone	Tf	—	Tatsfield
C	—	Caterham	H	—	Horne	Ts	—	Titsey
Ch	—	Chaldon	Lm	—	Limpsfield	W	—	Warlingham
Cr	—	Crowhurst	Ln	—	Lingfield	We	—	Westerham
E	—	Edenbridge	N	—	Nutfield	Wh	—	Worth
			O	—	Oxted			

Figure 1 — Pattern of shared surnames with a cut-off point of 35 per cent.

was only true to a certain extent. The essential factor in determining the proportion of names unique to one parish was not the number of incomers, but the characteristics of those incomers. An analysis of the unique names in Blechingley shows them to be so because, not only were they held by incomers, but the incomers were new to the district, born outside the area, and with no relatives living locally. The incomers to the other parishes were more likely to have had local names, which were shared across parish boundaries. Table 4, therefore, measures in reverse: a high proportion of unique names indicates a low degree of localness. Most surnames, however, were shared across two or more parishes. Figure 1 shows the trends in the distribution pattern of shared surnames. It uses a cut-off point of 35 per cent shared surnames between two parishes. In other words, parishes that shared 35 per cent of their surnames are linked.

The figure shows that surnames were shared along the greensand ridge on an east-west axis, with lines stretching northwards onto the Downs, and southwards to the Weald from greensand parishes, but not between downland and Wealden parishes. The county boundary was of relatively little importance. Fifty-one per cent of shared names crossed the county boundaries. Thirty per cent of these shared names were found in all three counties of Surrey, Sussex and Kent, but this included the ubiquitous names of Smith, Brown, and Wood. Sixty-eight per cent of cross-county names were shared by Kent and Surrey, 20 per cent by Surrey and Sussex, and 12 per cent between Kent and Sussex. This reinforces the east-west bias of the distribution pattern, as well as confirming Richard McKinley's view that Sussex was an isolated county. Sussex surnames were more likely to be shared with the Sussex hinterland to the south of the study area than with neighbouring parishes across the county border.

A breakdown of the characteristics of the names peculiar to one county shows that they were likely to be topographical. Cross-county names show two trends. Names shared by Kent and Surrey tended to be locative in origin, whilst those shared by Surrey and Sussex were occupational. These patterns raise several interesting questions. First, are the names shared because they have spread from one centre or because they are part of a parallel evolutionary process? Second, if they are shared through diffusion, when did this take place and in what direction? One category of names that suggests migration rather than an evolutionary process is those of unambiguous locative origin. There are 13 such names shared between Kent and Surrey. All but four represent long distance movement from, for example, Ireland or Scotland. Two of the remaining four names can be traced to Sussex, with one of the remaining pair originating in Kent and the other in Surrey. In the case of the latter surname, the holder was born in Surrey, and had relatives still living in that county in 1851, and thus represents both migration over a short distance and recent mobility.

Names which were common both in Surrey and Sussex include one which Reaney attributed to a locative origin in Surrey: Bristow (which he presumes to have originated from Burstow in Surrey). One more, Apps, appears in early sources for Surrey, whilst Bish or Bysh, Feldwick, Jupp, Penfold and Steer all have early references in Sussex sources.[15] Richard McKinley discusses the last surname in *The Surnames of Sussex*.[16] One of the most common Surrey surnames, Killick, has no provenance in Reaney. McKinley suggests this may be a locative name originating from Kildwick in West Yorkshire or Childwick in Hertfordshire.[17] An alternative suggestion might be that the name has a more ancient origin. Reaney gives an instance of Kill or Cille as being a name found in Domesday.[18] It is possible that this name was once Killwick, being an inhabitant of Cille's dwelling. Names with the suffix '-wick' are common in south-eastern Surrey. The surname Howick was especially common in the area of Nutfield, Outwood, Burstow and Redhill. Other names common in Surrey have origins outside the county. Bashford, for example, may have its origin in Ashford, Kent, whilst Cole and Dartnell both have early references in that county.[19] McKinley suggested that the latter is a locative name from a lost village near to Penshurst in Kent.[20] Similarly, Reaney attributes a Sussex origin to the common Surrey surnames of Coppard and Dungate. He also places the origin of Sale or Sales in Sussex.[21] This name was common in Surrey and Kent in 1851, but not in Sussex.

15 P. H. Reaney, *Dictionary of British Surnames*, London, 1976, pp.10, 12, 53, 189, 250, 339.

16 R. McKinley, *Sussex Surnames*, pp.382–3.

17 *Ibid.*, p.426.

18 P. H. Reaney, *op. cit.*, p.190.

19 P. H. Reaney, *op. cit.*, pp.35, 50, 110.

20 R. McKinley , *Sussex Surnames*, p.117.

21 P. H. Reaney, *op. cit.*, pp.36, 50, 301.

The route from Kent to Surrey follows the greensand ridge, and it is possible that the greensand had a different *corpus* of names from those found on the Weald or Downland. The last test of surname distribution looks at surnames in relation to geographical zones. An analysis of surnames in 1851 shows that 26 per cent were exclusive to one *pays*, or geographical zone, but of these 90 per cent were unique to the greensand area. These names, 120 in all, were cross-referenced to the parish registers for the area. This further analysis showed that 41 of the names had at one time been present in the Weald and on the Downs, leaving 79 surnames exclusive to the greensand. These names were further cross-referenced to the 1664 Hearth Tax Return for Surrey. This source indicated that 5 per cent of the names were present in the greensand area at that date. The parish registers showed a further 29 per cent had been present on the greensand for at least 100 years, whilst 68 per cent had been there for over 50 years. Therefore over half the surnames exclusive to the greensand were well established in that area by 1851. Most of the surnames that could be traced back to the Hearth Tax Returns were derived from personal names or nicknames, usually the more unusual ones such as Lawrence or Osborne. McKinley shows the latter to have been common in fourteenth-century Sussex.[22]

This section has to be related to the section on surname turnover. It was shown in that section that the greensand not only had the highest proportion of unique names, but also had the lowest turnover of surnames per decade. This was in spite of its position at the centre of the communications network for the area. It suggests that this was an area with a stable population and a high degree of local identity.

In conclusion, I hope this essay emphasizes the debt we owe to Richard McKinley personally, and the English Surnames Survey in general. The study of surnames is a valuable resource for social, economic and local historians. The turnover of surnames in a parish can indicate the extent of a local indigenous population and the character of incomers to the parish. Furthermore, the distribution of surnames in space can lead us towards answering questions about the diffusion or evolutionary processes of change which in the long term can have important implications for the study of all types of social systems.

22 R. McKinley, *Sussex Surnames*, p.346.

XI

Surnames and Stability: a detailed case study

Suella and David Postles

The concept of the persistence of 'core' or 'focal' families in parishes, and even in kinship networks across groups of contiguous parishes, has attracted considerable attention in some quarters.[1] The implication behind the notion is that the continuity provided by these kinship groups allowed the perpetuation of local custom and notions of 'community', although 'community' is a problematic concept with its dark as well as nostalgic sides.[2] For some historians, social relationships in the parish in the late sixteenth century were contested and negotiated, consumed by 'power' with a small p which was contingent and characterized by resistance.[3] 'Community' is thus not always a consensual or imagined construct.[4] This permanence

---

1 M. Strathern, *Kinship at the Core. An Anthropology of Elmdon, A Village in North-west Essex in the Nineteen-sixties*, Manchester, 1981; M. P. Carter, 'An urban society and its hinterland: St Ives in the seventeenth and eighteenth centuries', PhD thesis, University of Leicester, 1989 ('focal'); C. Phythian-Adams, ed., *Societies, Cultures and Kinship 1580–1850. Cultural Provinces and English Local History*, London, 1993; M. Prior, *Fisher Row. Fishermen, Bargemen and Canal Boatmen in Oxford 1500–1900*, Oxford, 1982; see also above, the chapter by D. Hey.

2 G. Crow and G. Allan, *Community Life. An Introduction to Local Social Relations*, Hemel Hempstead, 1994, but more particularly N. Elias and J. Scotson, *The Established and the Outsiders*, London, 1965.

3 K. Wrightson, 'The politics of the parish in early modern England' in P. Griffiths, A. Fox and S. Hindle, eds., *The Experience of Authority in Early Modern England*, London, 1996, pp.10–46.

4 A. Cohen, *The Symbolic Construction of Community*, London, 1985 and *idem*, ed., *Belonging: Identity and Social Organisation in British Rural Cultures*, Manchester,

was not incompatible with the high levels of mobility into and out of such settlements, for the intensely localized nature of migration itself confirmed local norms in a confined 'country'.[5] Even the migrational patterns of the most mobile of life-cycle migrants, servants in husbandry, was tightly circumscribed, helping to define 'countries', and, indeed, in some of the remoter parts of England the employment of servants was an exchange between households within the parish.[6] The localization of surnames within parishes or groups of parishes has been used as a surrogate instead of reconstitution to illustrate long-term persistence of families.[7]

Two recent studies in particular seem to represent this school of thought which associates the local persistence of longevious families with the continuity of local norms and traditions. One suggests that a 'neighbourhood' area was delineated by the kinship network of 'dynastic families' in a group of adjacent parishes in south-west Nottinghamshire between *c.*1580 and 1700.[8] These persistent families were drawn from the middling sort, from the yeomanry or better husbandry, usually wealthier than their neighbours, and frequently held parochial offices, so that they comprised 'a group able to exert some influence in the community'; 'the dynastic families helped to create the character of the neighbourhood area', their stability promoting 'enduring traditions and characteristics'.[9] The other study adopts a wider approach than the single settlement, assessing

1982, by comparison with S. Wright, 'Image and analysis: new directions in community studies' in B. Short, ed., *The English Rural Community. Image and Analysis*, Cambridge, 1982, pp.195–217.

5 A. Everitt, 'Country, county and town: patterns of regional evolution in England', *Transactions of the Royal Historical Society*, fifth series, 29, 1979, pp.79–108.

6 A. Kussmaul, 'The ambiguous mobility of farm servants', *Economic History Review*, series 2, xxxiv, 1981, pp.222–35; M. R. Bouquet, *Family, Servants and Visitors*, Norwich, 1985.

7 D. Hey, above, is one example; for synthesis of some other work, G. W. Lasker, *Surnames and Genetic Structure*, Cambridge, 1985.

8 A. Mitson, 'The significance of kinship networks in the seventeenth century: south-west Nottinghamshire', in C. Phythian-Adams, ed., *Societies, Cultures and Kinship*, p.35.

9 *Ibid.*, pp.51–2, 71–2.

the social space around the urban centre of St. Ives, again characterized by the activities of core families. Accounting for some 60 surnames *in grosso*, this nucleus of families comprised four per cent of urban society, but, through their longevity in the area, encouraged 'continuity of communal feelings', so that 'we would expect that this core of families would be the repository of the traditional values of the community'.[10]

In this paper, we combine two approaches, reconstitution of families and isonymy, in a detailed local study of a single parish, Barkby, the demographic data collected and interpreted by Suella and the medieval nominal data by Dave Postles.[11] First, however, we wish to make some obvious points. The persistence of surnames is a minimal and not a maximal measure of the persistence of local people, since familial continuity may have occurred through females who are not transmitters, in normal circumstances, of surnames. The extent to which continuity proceeded through females depends very much on demographic circumstances: sex ratios and male replacement rates. The major question about using surnames is that it reflects only 'malestream' in another sense, since it ignores the contribution made by women, less overtly and formally than males, to the confirmation and regulation of 'community' norms and to local cultural and social developments which are only now being explored.[12] We are very conscious of this considerable failing of our nominal evidence.[13]

---

10 M.P. Carter, 'Town or urban society? St. Ives in Huntingdonshire, 1630–1740', in C. Phythian-Adams, ed., *Societies, Cultures and Kinship*, pp.110–12.

11 S. Postles, 'Barkby: the anatomy of a "closed" township', unpublished M.A. thesis, University of Leicester, 1979; Merton College, Oxford, Muniments (hereafter MM); Pochin MSS in the Leicestershire Record Office; Barkby parish registers deposited in the L.R.O. We would like here to record our debts to Roger Highfield and John Burgass of Merton College and to all the staff of the Leicestershire Record Office.

12 For our period, see L. Gowing, *Domestic Dangers. Women, Words and Sex in Early Modern London*, Oxford, 1996; for a later time, M. Tebbutt, *Women's Talk. A Social History of 'Gossip' in Working-class Neighbourhoods 1880–1960*, Aldershot, 1995.

13 P. Spufford, 'The comparative mobility and immobility of Lollard descendants in early modern England' in M. Spufford, ed., *The World of Rural Dissenters 1520–1725*, Cambridge, 1995, pp.309–31.

Returning to demographic criteria, we are equally conscious that the experience of Barkby, our selected example, will not be representative of many other places. Even within Leicestershire, the experiences of Barkby and, for example, some settlements with greater opportunities for by-employment, are likely to be quite different. In these terms, perhaps Barkby was closer to Bottesford than to Shepshed, although its influence of lordship was a contrast.[14] Located at the junction of river valley and Wold, Barkby was an agrarian parish with local resident lordship and limited economic opportunities for outsiders, approximating to a 'closed' character.[15] The conditions thus encouraged stability and continuity. Greater social and demographic volatility was occurring in parishes in N.W. Leicestershire more conducive to industries in the countryside and even industrialisation.[16]

The comparison was, indeed, even closer to home. Until the early nineteenth century, Thurmaston was divided between two parishes, north Thurmaston attached to the parish of Barkby. The fortunes of Thurmaston and Barkby diverged dramatically from the late eighteenth century as Thurmaston developed into a framework-knitting settlement of considerable size, whilst Barkby, just a few miles along the road, remained essentially an agrarian settlement, affording economic opportunity only to its own established families. There seems no point in suggesting that core families persisted or facilitated the continuity of notions of 'community', belonging and 'community' norms in all settlements. Certain types of parish were more favourable to the phenomenon which was not universal.

One final point of circumspection, which we wish to elaborate further below, is that the persistence of 'core' families was possibly *not* a timeless prospect. Rather we should prefer to conceive of the restoration of 'core' families and continuity in the sixteenth century in some areas — advisedly in some areas, since the Kentish Wealden

14 D. Levine, *Family Formation in an Age of Nascent Capitalism*, New York, 1977.

15 H. S. A. Fox, 'The people of the Wolds in English settlement history' in M. Aston, D. Austin and C. Dyer, eds., *The Rural Settlements of Medieval England*, Oxford, 1989, pp.77–101.

16 Ian Hunt of the Department of English Local History is researching this locational change.

experience was different, for example.[17] At this point, we encounter one debate about familial continuity in the late middle ages and another about the invention of customs and traditions in the late middle ages.[18] There is no doubt that within individual parishes there was immense discontinuity of family names during the later middle ages.

From the early sixteenth century, and even after enclosure in 1780, Barkby was dominated by two lordships, the resident Pochins, inhabiting the hall adjacent to the parish church, and the absentee Merton College. Landholding was concentrated in the hands of the Pochins, their tenants, the copyholders of Merton College and sundry freeholders. No opportunities were offered for immigrants, squatters or cottagers, so that, despite divided lordship, the parish presented to all intents and purposes a 'closed' 'community', although our use of the term 'closed' is imprecise and only a term of convenience for what is a complex construct.[19]

Population and surnames in the late middle ages

For the later middle ages, we are principally forced to rely upon the records of the College's manor, supplemented by records of central government (taxation), some material from the rentals of Leicester Abbey, but little from the Pochin angle or indeed from Langley Priory.[20] The analysis is therefore not comprehensive. The *lacunae*

---

17 M. Zell, *Industry in the Countryside. Wealden Society in the Sixteenth Century*, Cambridge, 1994, p.26.

18 Z. Razi, 'The erosion of the land-family bond in the late fourteenth and fifteenth centuries: a methodological note' and C. Dyer, 'Changes in the link between families and land in the west Midlands in the fourteenth and fifteenth centuries' in R. M. Smith, ed., *Land, Kinship and Life-cycle*, Cambridge, 1984, pp.295–312; R. Hutton, *The Rise and Fall of Merry England. The Ritual Year 1400–1700*, Oxford, 1994.

19 See, for example, S. J. Banks, 'Nineteenth-century scandal or twentieth-century model? A new look at "open" and "closed" parishes', *Economic History Review*, second series, xli, 1988, pp.51–73.

20 The principal sources used in this section are: MM 6556–6629. Compare C. Howell, 'Peasant inheritance customs in the Midlands, 1280–1700' [Kibworth Harcourt, Merton College] in J. Goody, J. Thirsk and E. P. Thompson, eds., *Family and Inheritance. Rural Society in Western Europe 1200–1800*, Cambridge, 1976, pp.123–4.

are serious to the extent that we cannot categorically be certain that when a byname or surname disappeared from the records of the College that it equally vanished from the parish. Conversely nor can it be proven that the appearance of a byname or surname in the College's records marked its introduction into the village. The possibility remains that people and bynames or surnames migrated between lordships in the parish, although the extent was probably inconsiderable. John Fraunceys, for example, was presented in the manor court of the College because he had settled in the lordship of the abbot of Leicester in Barkby.[21]

The data presented in Figure 1 derive from lay subsidies of central government, charters and the College's court and account rolls and rentals, sporadically from 1202 but more consistently from *c.*1270 through to 1544. Surnames introduced in the 1530s and 1540s thus have an ostensibly short duration in this figure, which is misleading. At the other chronological end, before the 1330s, the considerable instability of *cognomina* is partly the attribute of the volatility of bynames which had not developed into hereditary surnames in all kinship groups. The problem is demonstrated simply by the total number of *cognomina* generated — 291 — far too many for a manor of this size. What Figure 1 does illustrate is a fairly high level of continuity of some bynames and surnames into the 1350s followed by a rapid transformation of the corpus thereafter.

These changes are confirmed by analysis of the *cognomina* of tenants rather than all appearances in manorial and fiscal records, with some problems, however. The rentals of *c.*1300, 1311, 1312 and 1315 seem to represent a wider structure of the tenantry, including small tenants and perhaps some undersettles, since many fragmented holdings are listed. The subsequent rentals of 1354–5, 1450 and 1475, in contrast, contain more consolidation. Thus, whilst 60 holdings were enumerated in that of *c.*1300, only 28 were listed in 1354, 20 in 1450 and 19 in 1475 (although the number of tenants is even smaller because of multiple holdings in the late middle ages). Consolidation and engrossment in the later middle ages would not seem to account for all the difference in the tenemental structure.

From the rentals of *c.*1300–1315, some 54 different bynames can be accumulated. Although one tenant, Sampson, was listed without

21 MM 6570.

Table 1 — *Vital statistics by decadal periods*

| | Growth | | | | |
Decade	decadal	annual	Baptisms	Burials	Marriages
1586–95	29	2.9	114	85	26
1596–1605	21	2.1	93	72	28
1606–15	33	3.3	118	80	36
1616–25	53	5.3	120	67	34
1626–35	34	3.4	105	71	25
1636–46[ie]	38	3.8	96	58	20
1646–72[iie]	89	3.3			
1673–78	7	1.2	51	44	15
1679–90[iiie]	22	1.9			
1691–1700	26	2.6	89	63	21
1701–10	34	3.4	104	70	26
1711–20	7	0.7	87	80	27
1721–30	-57	-5.7	83	140	44
1731–40	41	4.1	113	72	39
1741–50	27	2.7	108	81	26
1751–60	23	2.3	122	99	36
1761–70	43	4.3	128	85	43
1771–80	31	3.1	118	87	39
1781–91	31	3.1	142	111	50

i – Based on figures for 1636–42.
ii – Based on a growth rate of 3.3 per annum.
iii – Based on a growth rate of 1.9 per annum.
e – Estimated.
* – The annual rate of growth for 1586–1642 was 3.36 and for 1691–1790 was 1.96.

a byname (but was once alluded to as *de Bark'*), his immediate descendants assumed the *cognomen* Sampson. Of the 54 bynames, 10 or 11 persisted into the rentals of 1354–5, about 20 per cent. Absolute numbers elude us, because *Faber* existed in 1300x1315 and both *Faber* and Smyth in 1354–5. About half of the 23 different surnames in the rentals of 1354–5 had existed on the manor in the earlier rentals, of which some are sufficiently distinctive to suggest that continuity resulted not simply from their commonplace nature but the survival of kinship (which, indeed, has been established by reconstitution from the court rolls): Arnold; Sampson; Playtour; Tante; and Styword.[22]

Although about half of the surnames of 1354–5 existed some 40 years earlier, only one or two, however, persisted from 1354–5 to 1450. Of the 16 different surnames in 1450, only Johnson (and possibly its variant Jakson) had occurred in the rentals of 1354–5, in the Latin equivalent of *filius Johannis*. Here again the actual transmission of the byname from Latin form to vernacular has been established by reconstitution from the court rolls. At least 14 of the 16 surnames of tenants in 1450 had been introduced into the manor during the previous century. By the next rental — in 1475 — merely four of the surnames of 1450 had survived: Braunston; Beregh' (Beverage); Jakson; and Bo(w)cher. Thirteen of the 17 surnames of 1475 had been introduced into the manor during the previous quarter of a century — perhaps a generation. This extreme discontinuity after 1350 is replicated in other places and may be one of the reasons for the invention of traditions during the late middle ages to exert some form of 'social memory'.[23]

Early modern demography and surnames

From the middle of the fifteenth century, dominant customary tenants became established in the manor through the consolidation and engrossment of multiple holdings, but their pre-eminence was individual, life-cycle and not dynastic. Towards the end of the century, stability of landholding was being re-established in kinship groups and a small nucleus of core families in terms of longevity and landholding resurfaced. Their position was consolidated during the early modern period, which is more widely the time of the formation of 'core' kinship groups represented in the persistence of surnames, their establishment associated with the demographic conditions of the period.

In 1563, the parish of Barkby comprised an estimated 288 souls

---

22 See generally D. Postles, 'Notions of the family, lordship and the evolution of naming processes in medieval English rural society: a regional example', *Continuity and Change*, 10, 1995, pp.169–98, esp. 189–90.

23 For this term, J. Fentress and C. Wickham, *Social Memory*, Oxford, 1992; see also P. Connerton, *How Societies Remember*, Cambridge, 1989.

in 44 families in the township of Barkby, 12 in the hamlet of Barkby Thorpe and eight in North Thurmaston. In the census of 1801, the parochial population had attained 576, comprising 389 in the main township, 72 in Barkby Thorpe, four in Hamilton (an essentially deserted hamlet) and 111 in North Thurmaston. Whilst the population of Thurmaston had expanded enormously over the time, Barkby had experienced a much lower rate of increase, below the general level for the county as a whole.[24]

Figure 2 presents demographic change for the parish in two ways: aggregative analysis from the parish registers and Bishop's transcripts (both commencing in 1561); and estimates at census points. Nonconformity does not complicate the calculations unduly, since the Compton census of 1676 made a return of 256 communicants but only 16 dissenters. Subsequently, the *Speculum* of the Diocese maintained that 94 of the total of 97 families communicated, but we are conscious of the lack of consensus about the complications of some of these types of static listings and the different notions about acceptable multipliers.[25]

Considering vital events, burials ranged from 16 to 29 per 1000, but baptisms remained at a remarkably low level, between 20 and 27 per 1000, with a mean of 25. Marriages fluctuated closely around a mean of 7·5 per 1000. Net growth accumulated very much more highly before 1686 than after: a mean of 3·36 accretions *per annum* between 1586 and 1642 compared with 1·86 from 1691 to 1790. Over the whole timescale, burials exceeded baptisms in 42 years, 30 of which occurred after 1686. A deficit happened in at least three

---

24 *VCH Leicestershire III*, pp.146, 166–7. For the background, E. A. Wrigley and R. S. Schofield, *The Population History of England 1541–1871. A Reconstruction*, Cambridge, 1981, esp. pp.207–15. We have not been able to consult E. A. Wrigley, R. S. Davies, J. E. Oeppen and R. S. Schofield, *English Population History from Family Reconstitution 1580–1837*, Cambridge, 1997.

25 N. Goose, 'The Bishops' Census of 1563: a re-examination of its reliability', 1994, (we have used the version at IHR-INFO: http://ihr.sas.ac.uk/ihr/sas/bishart2.html); A. Dyer, 'The Bishops' Census of 1563: its significance and accuracy', *Local Population Studies*, 49, 1992, pp.19–37; D. Palliser and L. J. Jones, 'The diocesan population returns for 1563 and 1607', *ibid.*, 30, 1983, pp.55–8; A. Whiteman, 'The Compton Census of 1676' in K. Schürer and T. Arkell, eds., *Surveying the People. The Interpretation and Use of Document Sources for the Study of Population in the Later Seventeenth Century*, Oxford, 1992, pp.97–116.

Table 2 — Child mortality by decadal periods 1606-1790

Decade commencing	Child burials	Total Burials	Child burials as per cent of total	Child burials as per cent of baptisms
1606	17	80	21.25	15.00
1616	14	67	2.80	11.60
1626	7	71	10.00	7.00
1636[–42]	7	35	20.00	10.40
1673[–79]	13	44	29.70	25.40
1691	25	63	39.60	28.00
1701	32	70	45.70	30.70
1711	37	80	46.20	54.20
1721	45	140	32.00	54.00
1731	34	72	47.00	30.00
1741	33	81	40.70	30.00
1751	46	99	46.00	37.70
1761	22	85	25.00	17.20
1771	22	87	25.20	18.60
1781	37	111	33.30	36.00

* – During the period 1606–42, the proportion of child baptisms to burials was 25.70 per cent and 31.20 per cent between 1691 and 1790.

years in each decade between 1686 and 1780, with severe difficulties in 1715–30 resulting from a total net deficit of 57. Accordingly, the level of population of 1715 was not restored until 1745. These years coincided with the heaviest levels of child mortality.

Global demographic change may also be calculated from estimates of population from the periodic listings (Table 3), which presents an ostensible contrast with aggregative analysis. For example, the increase indicated by aggregative analysis between 1586 and 1642 was 202, whilst the estimated population in the Bishop's census of 1563 was 288. Combined, these two figures suggest a resident population in 1641–2 of 500. In fact, the estimated population in 1641–2 (Protestation Oath) was 370 inhabitants. The dissonance between these two methods is represented in Figure 2, but was more apparent than real, since the difference is explicable by out-migration.

Continuity of some residence is reflected in the analysis of surnames in the township of Barkby, presented in Table 4; it should be emphasised that these data relate exclusively to the township of Barkby. Only 42 different surnames can be extracted from probate

Table 3 — Estimates of population from contemporary listings

Date	Raw data	Multiplier	Sub-total	Total
1563	B 44 families	4.5	198	
	BTh 12 families		54	
	NTh 8 families		36	288
1603	260 communicants	40 per cent added		364
1670	B55 houses	4.5	247	
	BTh 14 houses		63	
	NTh 15 houses		67	
	Ham 1 house		5	383
1676	274 communicants	40 per cent added		384
1717	97 families	4.5		437
1761	B 76 suit	4.5	342	
	BTh 12 suit		54	
	NTh 18 suit		81	
	Ham 1 suit		5	482
1772	B 89 suit	4.5	360	
	BTh 12 suit		54	
	NTh 18 suit		81	
	Ham 1 suit		5	500
1784	B 89 suit	4.5	405	
	BTh 13 suit		59	
	NTh 18 suit		81	
	Ham 1 suit		5	545
1801	B389			
	BTh 72			
	NTh 111			
	Ham 4			576

B – Barkby; BTh – Barkby Thorpe; NTh – North Thurmaston; Ham – Hamilton.

records, court rolls of the Merton manor (which held the court leet or view of frankpledge and thus comprehended at intervals the entire township), and parish registers, between 1555 and 1565. A subsequent compilation of surnames in 1666 has been derived from the Hearth Tax and parish registers. Of the initial 42 surnames of 1564, as many as 22 persisted a century later. A further listing of surnames has been constructed for 1772 from the lists of suitors to the court leet. Of the 74 surnames in 1772, 12 had existed in 1666 and seven in 1564. The continuous surnames over this bicentennial

Table 4 — Persistence and loss of surnames

1564	1666	1680–1772: introductions	1772
42 Surnames	22 survived from 1564	7 introduced 1680–1720	7 survived from 1564
	34 new additions	7 introduced 1721–30	5 survived from 1666
		3 introduced 1731–40	62 introduced 1680–1772
		5 introduced 1741–50	
		10 introduced 1751–60	
		8 introduced 1761–70	
		2 introduced 1772	
Totals:			
42 surnames	56 surnames	42 surnames	74 surnames

Table 5 — Fertile families, 1596–1605

Fertile couples	Total	No. of children
Married in Barkby	7	14
New families 1596–1605	21	45
Sub-totals	28	59
Families established by 1596	17	34
New surnames (longer stay: three years or more)	7	19
New surnames (transient: two years or less)	6	8
Total: children with new surnames		25

period were thus a very narrow and restricted corpus. In contrast, some 34 new surnames had been introduced between 1564 and 1666, whilst a further 42 appeared after 1680. Quantitatively, therefore, the newly-introduced surnames were much more significant than the established and continuous core.

It has, nevertheless, been suggested that the importance of the nucleus of surnames resided in their representation of core families and consequently communal values. It is important therefore to consider the actual demographic continuity of these families, through replacement by comparison with out-migration. Summarized below are data about child-bearing by the families of the township, principally divided into 'stayers' (core families) and immigrants.[26] The data, of course, relate to baptisms of children rather than births.[27] Newly-introduced surnames accounted for 25 to 60 per cent of families producing offspring at various times. Although some of these surnames remained for more than a single generation, they were a minority of persistent surnames. For all periods, the new surnames existed in the township for only a few years. Families representing established surnames were responsible for 25 to 50 per cent of childbirths at various times, despite being in a significant minority quantitatively. In some decadal periods, half the new families remained to produce children in the subsequent decade, as in the 1710s, 1720s and 1770s, which compared with only 32 and 24 per cent in the 1740s and 1760s.

Taking an illustrative decadal period, 1595–1605, 45 couples were responsible for a mean of 2·06 children (Table 5), but families with established surnames accounted for more than 50 per cent of the total. Six transient families produced only eight baptisms, a mean of 1·3, their productive life-cycle in Barkby curtailed by repeated migration. In contrast, the mean of children baptised from marriages with established surnames was much higher: 2·71.

Core surnames were thus associated with a large proportion of baptisms within the township. Demographic stability was maintained through out-migration, even by offspring from core families. Between 1585 and 1595, 114 baptisms were performed in the township and the fortunes of 104 of these individuals can be perceived to 1642, before the *lacunae* in registration, the sample of 104 issuing from 51 families. By 1600, 55, the issue of 28 families, still remained in the parish, but this number was reduced to 20 by 1620 (at mean age of 32 years). Of the 51 original productive families, 27 persisted in the township. Although the migration of individual offspring

26 See D. Souden, 'Movers and stayers in family reconstitution populations', *Local Population Studies*, 33, 1984, pp.11–28.

27 For the comprehensive data, see D. Postles, thesis, p.109 (Table F), which provides decadal details.

attained 80 per cent, by contrast more than 50 per cent of the productive families continued in the township. At least 30 children from continuous families left before 1620, about 25 per cent of whom married in the parish before departure, but 75 per cent left as singletons. Of at least 20 stayers from established and continuous families, five ostensibly did not marry and six (all male) were involved in exogamous marriages but returned to Barkby (thus uxorilocal marriages, it seems).[28]

Barkby thus illustrates one type of 'community' in which stability was restored in the sixteenth century by the continuity of core families, represented by the persistence of surnames. The relatively 'closed' nature of the township, its agrarian character, the reservation of resources to continuous membership of the 'community' to the relative exclusion of outsiders, deterred substantial immigration. Although substantial out-migration was a feature, core kinship groups remained in the township and parish. The exodus, combined with comparatively low reproductive rate and, after the 1680s, higher mortality, maintained a stable demographic régime.

Nevertheless, other 'communities' may undoubtedly have existed which did not share this experience and excessive generalization should be avoided. The transmission of localized norms, values and customs through core families is, moreover, a process which is not entirely clear and has yet to be elucidated for historical 'communities'.[29] A relationship between the persistence of surnames, core families and local custom, is assumed rather than proven and is at best an association. If the core families were also dominant families and not just longevious, problems ensue, for the analysis to date has not taken into account the increasing evidence that local social relationships were brokered, fragmented, contested, negotiated, and that in local societies 'relationships of power and authority, dominance and subordination are established, maintained, refused and modified'.[30]

---

28 See D. Souden, ' "East, west — home's best?" Regional patterns in migration in early modern England' in P. Clark and D. Souden, eds., *Migration and Society in Early Modern England*, London, 1987, pp.292–332.

29 J. Fentress and C. Wickham, *Social Memory*; Connerton, *How Societies Remember*; E. Muir, *Ritual in Early Modern Europe*, Cambridge, 1997, pp.1–17.

30 K. Wrightson, 'Politics of the parish', pp.18–22.

It is, indeed, possible that at some critical points dominant families exercised a form of 'social control' which may have been directed towards change rather than continuity and such families may not always have constituted simply the 'godly'.[31] It is possible too that this sort of social regulation of misbehaviour had a longer history through the later middle ages.[32] At this level, the association of local elites and the impact of state formation may have induced change in local *mores* rather than continuity, perhaps from the sixteenth century and the impact of the Reformation (although again in a brokered and sometimes contested manner, but crucially through the parochial élite), at least from the late seventeenth century.[33] The further difficulty then is to whom is attributed the influence in the continuity of local customs: to the genealogically continuous families or to the dominant families? As has been suggested, the latter may, at times, have been equally concerned to change local custom. Other than agreement that persistent surnames are a useful surrogate indicator of the continuity of some continuous families, the further relationships — with continuous local societies and their persistent customs and ways — are suggestive, but not affirmed.[34]

31 K. Wrightson and D. Levine, *Poverty and Piety in an English Village. Terling, 1525–1700*, Oxford, 1995, pp.197–220; M. Ingram, 'Puritans and the Church courts, 1560–1640' in C. Durston and J. Eales, *The Culture of English Puritanism 1560-1700*, London, 1996, pp.43–50; J. R. Kent, *The English Village Constable 1580–1642*, Oxford, 1986; K. Wrightson, '"Sorts of people" in Tudor and Stuart England' in J. Barry, ed., *The Middling Sort of People. Culture, Society and Politics in England, 1550–1800*, London, 1994, pp.28–51, esp. 36–40; K. Wrightson, 'The politics of the parish', pp.25–31.

32 M. K. McIntosh, 'Finding language for misconduct: jurors in fifteenth-century local courts' in B. A. Hanawalt and D. Wallace, eds., *Bodies and Disciplines. Intersections of Literature and History in Fifteenth-century England*, London, 1996, pp.87–122.

33 J. R. Kent, 'The centre and the localities: state formation and parish government in England, c. 1640–1740', *Historical Journal*, 38, 1995, pp.363–404.

34 We are grateful to Professor Alan Everitt who supervised the M.A. thesis on which much of this paper was constructed and Paul Ell and Linda McKenna for many kindnesses in the past.

XII

———————— ·•§§•· ————————

Name, Race, Terrain:
The Making of a Leicestershire Boundary[1]

Margery Tranter

IT IS UNLIKELY that when Richard McKinley was editing the cartulary of the Augustinian Priory at Breedon in Leicestershire he can have had even the slightest premonition of the many years his association with the county would continue. Subsequently, however, his work on the *Victoria County History of Leicester*, and especially that on the history of the forests, religious houses and extractive industries, involved him once more in the area surrounding Breedon, an area in which both the Anglo-Saxon monastery and its later successor owned considerable tracts of land. The historical problems considered here occur within that area and the analysis undertaken incorporates selected name-elements.[2] The middle Trent valley, the dissected

1 I am particularly grateful to Professor Charles Phythian-Adams for the interest he has shewn in the problems discussed here, for his encouragement over a long period and especially for reading and commenting on the preliminary draft of this paper. Dr Steven Bassett has also made helpful comments, while Mr Ralph Weedon spent many hours collating data and preparing base maps. The errors which remain are entirely my responsibility. Finally, it would have been impossible to have carried out the research without the help of a grant from the Leverhulme Trust

2 R. A. McKinley, 'The Cartulary of Breedon Priory', unpublished M.A. thesis, University of Manchester, 1950; 'Religious Houses' in *The Victoria History of the County of Leicester*, II, Oxford, 1954, pp.1–54; 'Forests of Leicestershire', *ibid.*, pp.265–70; 'Industries of Leicestershire', *ibid.*, III, Oxford, 1955, pp.30–46, 50–6.

upland area to the south and the valley of the lower Tame form a region divided between the counties of Derby, Leicester, Stafford and Warwick. To the west, and within Staffordshire, lies the territory associated with *Letocetum* (Lichfield). The major division between the carucated lands of Derbyshire and Leicestershire within the Danelaw and the hidated territories of 'English' Mercia in Staffordshire follows the valleys of the lower Tame, the Trent and the Dove, while the Trent itself appears to have functioned as a boundary between the North and South Mercians. In the eastern part of this territory, county, parish and township boundaries were intricately intermingled until they were rationalized in the nineteenth century. Clearly an investigation of all the factors which may have influenced the formation of political and social divisions within so large an area is outside the scope of the present paper; consequently attention will be focussed on one specific boundary in the east and will use the evidence of archaeology, soils and selected name-elements to relate racial groups to that boundary.[3]

The area to be discussed includes the section of the middle Trent valley which lies between the confluences of the Derwent in the east and the Tame in the west, and the dissected upland extending southwards towards the valley of the Sence. Thus it straddles the minor watersheds separating the tributaries flowing westward to the Tame from those draining north to the Trent or east to the Soar and includes the valley of the Mease. Since both the royal mausoleum at Repton and the important monastery at Breedon (known to be in the territory of the *Tomsætan*), are situated here, it must hold clues crucial to our understanding of the history and chronology of settlement in the 'heartland' of Mercia. Linked with the mystery of the origins of Mercia is the identity of those elusive peoples, the *Tomsætan* and the *Hrypingas* whose name is perpetuated in Repton. The extent of the territory of the *Tomsætan*, the possibility that it incorporated earlier

---

3 Pauline Stafford, *The East Midlands in the Early Middle Ages*, Leicester, 1985, p.137 and Fig. 53. Dr Stafford suggests that by retaining Tamworth and Lichfield in English Mercia the Danelaw boundary was drawn with sensitivity to Mercian feelings. Alternatively it can be interpreted as effectively cutting through the heart of 'Original Mercia' thus retaining the cult centre of the Mercian royal family at Repton in Danish hands; Bede, *Ecclesiastical History*, B. Colgrave and R. A. B. Mynors, eds., Oxford, 1969, p.294.

units, and the degree to which it was disrupted by the Danish invasions and the partitioning of Mercia are fascinating questions which, although of great importance, also lie outside the scope of the present inquiry. Nevertheless, the residual influence of earlier societies and of their political and economic links must not be ignored.[4]

The characteristics of the political, social and economic organization of late Iron Age Britain, and the effect upon the structure of the Roman invasion have been much discussed in the last two decades, and in this debate the nature of pre-Roman trade and the possible traces of proto-urbanism have been topics of leading importance. Contrasting the type of exchange which took place at varying levels of social relationships with that which accompanied the development of market trade, Hodder has written 'It is widely accepted that markets frequently grow up on tribal borders where bartering and haggling can occur within a profit-making context — outside the inner spheres of social relations', while Cuncliffe analysing the late hill-forts of south-east England sees them developing many of the characteristics of central places with defined territories, some becoming sufficiently complex to be classed as proto-urban.[5]

It is, of course, impossible to draw hard and fast boundaries for Iron Age tribal territories but the possibility that there may have been a broad frontier or buffer zone between the Cornovii of the west, the Corieltauvi of Leicestershire and Lincolnshire and the Brigantes of the north within the study area is strengthened by the existence of the hill-fort at Breedon. The inter-relationship of these territories, their possible limits, the significance of the two north-east/south-west Roman roads — the Fosse and Ryknield Street — which lay to the north and south respectively, together with the

4 Neither the *Tomsætan* nor the *Pencersætan* are listed in the Tribal Hidage although the neighbouring *Pecsætan, Wreocensætan*, and *Arosætan* are. For a recent discussion see N. Brooks, 'The formation of the Mercian kingdom' in S. Bassett, ed., *The Origins of the Anglo-Saxon Kingdoms*, Leicester, 1989, pp.159–70; Barbara Yorke, *Kings and Kingdoms of early Anglo-Saxon England*, London, 1990, p.102.

5 I. Hodder, 'Pre-Roman and Romano-British tribal economies', in B. C. Burnham and H. Johnson, *Invasion and Response: the Case of Roman Britain*, B.A.R. Reports, British series, 73, 1979, p.193; B. Cunliffe, 'Hillforts and oppida' in G. de G. Sieveking, I. H. Longworth and K. E. Wilson, eds., *Social and Economic Problems in Archaeology*, London, 1976, pp.343–58.

possible effect of Roman influence, may well have affected not only settlement and land use, but also the political role of the region in subsequent periods through to later medieval times.[6]

The location of this area should, therefore, be seen in the context first, of possible tribal boundaries; secondly, of the differences between the tribes of the 'Lowland' zone (who like the Corieltauvi had indigenous coinage) and those of the north and west, and thirdly, in relation to the division between the Civil and Military Zones of the early Roman occupation. The earlier view that the Fosse functioned as a linear frontier is no longer accepted by all Roman scholars and Salway has pointed out that its construction must have depended on control of the land to the north and west; he suggests that it was 'the spine of a very broad and well-garrisoned territory from the Humber to the Severn'. There is as yet little to indicate a military Roman presence in the area under discussion but the evidence for civil occupation is gradually increasing.[7]

As yet no real consensus as to the location of the frontier from which the Mercians took their name has emerged: Nicholas Brooks

6 The debatable status of this area is reflected in both the absence of coins attributed to the Corieltauvi, and in the paucity of Iron Age C pottery recorded. The hill fort at Breedon, for example, has yielded little that can be attributed to that period. K. M. Kenyon, 'Excavations at Breedon on the Hill, 1946'. *Transactions of the Leicestershire Archaeological Society*, XXVI, 1950, pp.17–69; J. S. Wacher, 'Excavations at Breedon on the Hill', *ibid.*, LII, 1976–77, pp.1–35. Moreover, under the Celtic system of clientship, changes in personal allegiance could, especially on the fringes of territories, lead to a change in political allegiance. The significance of the hill fort at Breedon, and especially the dating of its defences, should be considered in the light of both market and strategic importance.

7 P. Salway, *Roman Britain, The Oxford History of England*, 1A, Oxford, 1981, p.97. A silver tray measuring 50cm by 38cm, originally found in 1729 at Risley Park 2·5 miles from the Roman road from Derby to the Trent crossing at Sawley and subsequently lost, reappeared in 1991 and has been authenticated as Romano-British. The inscription records that it was a gift from a hitherto unknown British bishop, Exuperius, to Bogius whose name may be perpetuated in Boyah Grange. It has been postulated by Bassett that there may have been a British see at *Letocetum* (J. Blair, ed., *Pastoral Care before the Parish*, Leicester, 1992, p.33), and this piece of ecclesiastical plate, together with the discovery in 1995/6 of an unknown Roman site at Littlehay Grange one mile distant, emphasizes the civil and ecclesiastical importance of this part of the Trent Valley in the Romano-British period.

sees 'original' Mercia as comprising much of the modern counties of Stafford, Leicester and Nottingham together with southern Derbyshire and northern Warwickshire; Professor Dumville suggests that the Mercians expanded 'in three principal directions from their original settlement area around the river Trent: (i) north-eastwards into the Peak, Lindsey and Elmet . . . ; (ii) south-eastwards into the East Midlands and Home Counties; (iii) south-westwards into east-central and south-east Wales and north-west Wessex'; Margaret Gelling notes that 'Staffordshire has only a few [Anglo-Saxon] cemeteries along the Trent in the east of the county' and continues 'but since this county must contain the greater part of the entity which the Tribal Hidage calls "original Mercia", a considerable English presence must be presumed, even if it is not attested by pagan burials'. Thus, although there is an element of general agreement among these scholars, the divergence of opinion as to where the Mercian homeland originally lay is considerable. Much therefore hinges upon the identity of the people who were the 'original Mercians'. Brooks makes the suggestion that in origin they may 'have been a grouping of earlier peoples' and concedes that the whole of the area he has outlined could hardly have been the eponymous frontier of the Mercians. Noting that the principal Mercian sites, Repton, Tamworth and Lichfield are to be found in the middle Trent valley he continues 'it is surely in or near this Mercian heartland that we must locate the "March" from which the Mercians were named' and suggests 'it seems best to side with Stenton and earlier scholars in supposing that the Mercians were originally a "border people" because they were settled on the frontier with the Welsh Britons'. Thus these differing opinions leave the problem of the position of the frontier unresolved; furthermore, the relationship of the lands of the *Pencersætan* and the *Tomsætan* to that march is unclear.[8]

Three strands arise from the foregoing comments: first, there is the extent to which it is accepted that the 'Mercians' were, in fact, an amalgam of people, not all of whom need have been of Anglo-Saxon stock. Secondly, was the frontier they occupied one of

8 N. Brooks, *op. cit.*, pp.160–1; D. Dumville, 'Essex, Middle Anglia and the expansion of Mercia' in S. Bassett, *Origins*, p.128; M. Gelling, 'The early history of western Mercia', *ibid.*, p.195; N. Brooks, *op. cit.*, p.162.

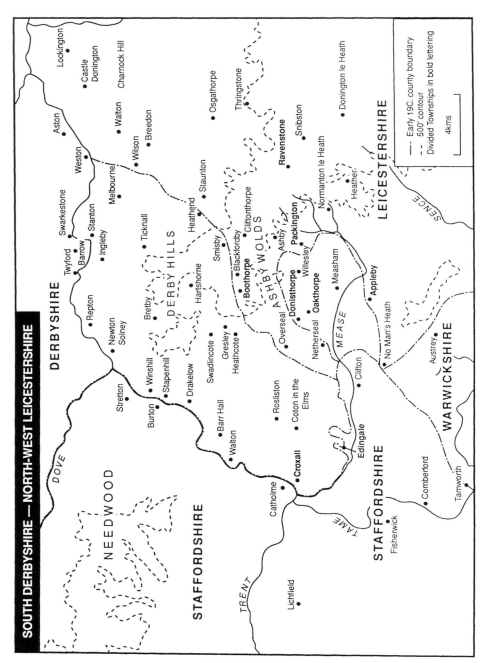

Map 1

confrontation — a westward advancing march separating rivals? Or thirdly, were they the people who occupied a recognized and long-established border zone which, in part at least, owed its significance to earlier tribal territories? These are difficult questions which cannot be fully explored here, but possibly an analysis of a limited area of the 'heartland' may contribute to the debate.

The land which lies between the Trent, Tame and Soar is at present divided between four counties — Derby, Leicester, Stafford and Warwick —in a comparatively straightforward way, but until the boundary changes of the late nineteenth century the partitioning of hundreds, parishes and townships was far more complex than appears on a current map. The most obvious anomaly is still evinced by the curious extension of Derbyshire south of the Trent (Map 1). The boundary between Derbyshire and Leicestershire leaves the river at the former ford at Weston-on-Trent and follows a south-westerly course across the higher central area following no obvious topographical features (Figure 1). South of this line the townships of Measham and Willesley, now in Leicestershire, formed an island of Derbyshire separated from the main part of the county by the parish of Nether and Over Seal (subsequently transferred to Derbyshire), and that part of the parish of Ashby de la Zouch known as Ashby Wolds. Ravenstone, Packington and Appleby, for example, were in both counties while Edingale and Croxall were divided between Staffordshire and Derbyshire. Most complex of all were the townships of Oakthorpe (divided between the Derbyshire parishes of Stretton, Measham and Gresley) and Donisthorpe (in Seal (Leicestershire), Measham and Gresley) (Map 2). The origin of this highly fragmented and fascinating pattern presents problems at present unanswerable and the following discussion will concentrate on the main north-east/south-west boundary between the counties of Derby and Leicester and the evidence of specific name-elements.[9]

It seems unlikely that this boundary had a defensive purpose as it wholly disregards topography; nor is there at present sufficient evidence to link its course with the short-lived diocese of Leicester.

---

9 The division of Donisthorpe was even more complex than appears on Map 2 since the Derbyshire portions were further subdivided between Measham and Gresley parishes.

Figure 1 — The county boundary near Staunton Harold.
The boundary crosses the field diagonally from the centre of the wood on the right of the photograph.

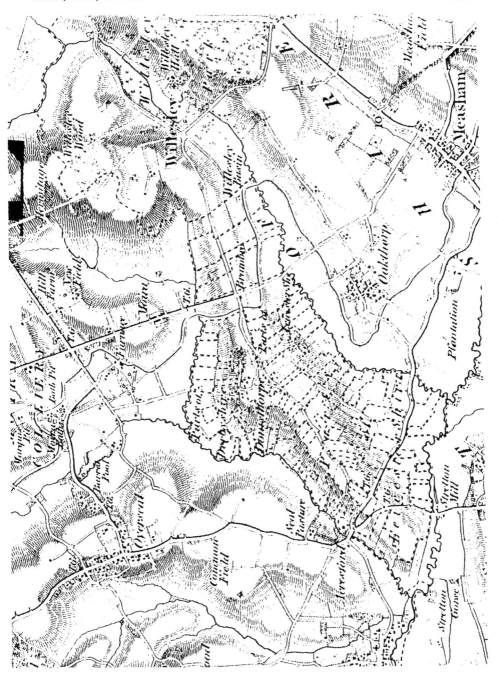

Map 2 — South Derbyshire–North-West Leicestershire.

Figure 2 — Breedon.
The church, formerly part of the Augustinian monastery, is sited within the hill fort.

Figure 3 — View north-north-east to the Lincoln Wolds from the Viking cemetery at Ingleby.

It seems probable therefore, that political, social and economic factors outweighed strategic considerations in defining the limits of the two counties. If the territory through which the boundary passed was originally part of a communal buffer, or trading, zone between early tribal territories incorporated later into the area controlled by the *Tomsætan*, the underlying physical characteristics of the terrain and the extent to which earlier land use may have inhibited subsequent settlement need to be examined.[10]

The geology is complex: all the valleys are floored with alluvium while those of the major rivers are edged with gravel terraces of differing ages. The solid rocks of the higher parts belong either to the Triassic (Keuper beds with an occasional inlier of Bunter sandstone) or to the Carboniferous series. The highly faulted shales and coal seams of the latter predominate in the south but outliers of Carboniferous limestone provide dominant landmarks, most notably at Breedon (Figure 2) but also elsewhere to a lesser degree. Millstone grit also outcrops occasionally to provide quarries of building stone more resistant than the soft sandstones of the Triassic. Cappings of boulder clay, glacial drift and fluvio-glacial sands and gravels overlie the solid rocks intermittently but are nowhere as deep as they are further east on the Leicestershire Wolds. This basic geology has been eroded and weathered into a more subtle and varied landscape than might be expected from a cursory glance at a relief map. In the north and north-west, river cliffs give extensive views northwards towards Sherwood, Lincoln and the Pennines (Figure 3); to Needwood to the west, and also overlook the series of important fords and shallows which occur along the Derbyshire section of the Trent between the confluences of the Derwent and Dove. To the south, the moors of Hartshorne and Coleorton overlook the valleys of the Mease, Soar and Sence. Although the maximum height of the upland is little over 600 feet the geological variety has allowed both major and minor streams to cut deeply incised valleys, creating a landscape of unexpected subtlety.

10 It is clearly not possible to examine the upland area through which the boundary passes as an isolated entity for the degree of exploitation will have been closely related to pressures emanating from settlement in the valleys. Moreover, the degradation of much of the upland and the paucity of available evidence necessitates comparison with sites on the fringes of the area.

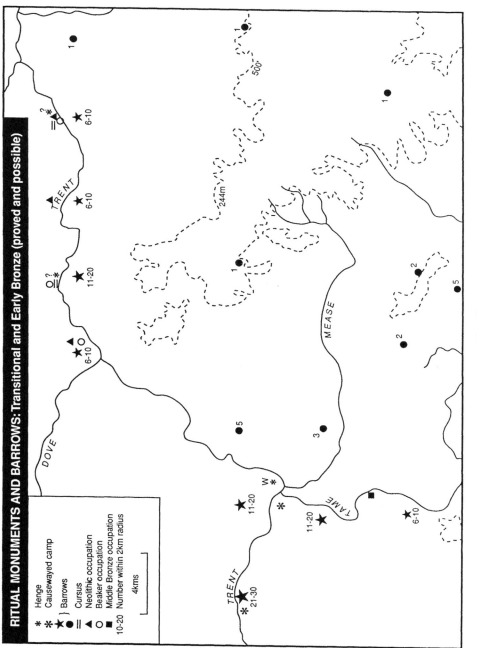

Map 3

Current land-use ranges widely: from mineral extraction — limestone, opencast coal and gravel — to commerce and light industry, from market gardening and cereal production to scrub and woodland plantations. Even after 200 years of enclosure the majority of soils are of low status and few areas come within the upper categories of the Soil Survey classification. Soil profiles, where available, reveal many areas of sandy soils with shallow A horizons and indications of iron panning, leaching and incipient podzolization; in the clay alluvial soils gleying is in evidence. An earlier landscape and land-use, however, must be reconstructed if the rationale behind the north-east/south-west boundary is to be understood, for the visual evidence of the present allows us only a veiled glimpse of the ninth- and tenth-century environment. Here the archaeological record can help. Inevitably the need for rescue archaeology or continuous observation in areas of gravel extraction and intensive excavation at individual sites such as Repton creates a bias in the record; additionally much evidence from the Coal Measure areas has been destroyed during centuries of extraction.[11]

Cropmarks revealed by aerial photography have shown that the middle Trent valley was more densely populated in the prehistoric period than hitherto suspected and that, like the Upper Thames, the valley was a focal point (Map 3). Two late-Neolithic cursuses with associated crop-marks and barrows have been identified on the north bank of the Trent and this ritual area continues westwards to the woodhenge and causewayed camps found near the confluence of the Dove and Trent. The siting of these monuments relative to the frequent fords across the Trent prompts two questions: whom did they serve and what were the territorial limits of those peoples?[12]

11 I am most grateful to Mr Malcolm Reeve for his courtesy in making the research maps and records of soil profiles held at the Soil Survey of England's regional office at Shardlow, Derbyshire, available to me.

12 The easternmost cursus runs for at least 5,700 feet (*c.*1733 m.) in a north-east/south-west direction in the parishes of Aston and Weston on Trent, J. May, 'An Iron Age square enclosure at Aston upon Trent, Derbyshire', *Derbyshire Archaeological Journal*, (*DAJ*), 90, 1970, p.10; the westernmost cursus extends into Findern, Willington and Twyford parishes. Now designated the Potlock cursus, its known length is *c.*1560 m. Personal communication from Dr Graeme Guilbert; P. M. Vine, *The Neolithic and Bronze Age Cultures of the Middle and Upper Trent Basin*, Oxford, B.A.R. British series, p.105, *passim.*

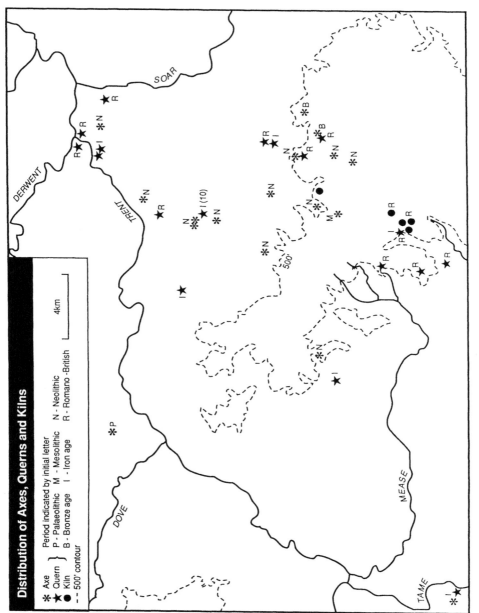

Distribution of Axes, Querns and Kilns

* ✻ Axe
* ★ Quern
* ● Kiln
* - - 500' contour

Period indicated by initial letter
P - Palaeolithic   M - Mesolithic   N - Neolithic
B - Bronze age   I - Iron age   R - Romano-British

4km

Map 4

The distribution of artefacts with prehistoric provenance raises further interesting points. Eleven neolithic axes, found at specific locations on the higher ground, suggest that its resources were then already being utilized. Although fewer axes of Bronze or Iron Age provenance have been found, there is greater evidence of occupation in these periods; finds of quern stones, for example, near Moira on Ashby Wolds, at Breedon and Castle Donnington, suggest that part at least may have been brought under arable cultivation, at least intermittently (Map 4).[13] It has been suggested that the dominance of cereals in the pollen analyses which have been obtained from rectangular enclosures in the river valleys are indicative of 'stable holdings with firm land divisions and extensive woodland clearance at a time of pressure on land'. When added to the sequence of occupation shown by lowland sites such as Lockington and the population density indicated by the numerous barrows, this implies that the demand for land may have exerted considerable pressure, at least periodically, on an exposed upland area of naturally light soils.[14] Clearance and continued exploitation of woodland could here lead to soils becoming degraded below a level which would

13 Map 4 is based on the Sites and Monuments lists for Derbyshire and Leicestershire. These include finds resulting from field-walking, excavation and aerial photography. Only artefacts and crop-marks which have been ascribed definite provenance have been included. The map therefore errs on the side of under- rather than over-representation. I am grateful to Dr David Barrett and Mr Peter Liddle for allowing me to use their computerized records.

14 C. O'Brien, 'Iron Age and Romano-British settlement in the Trent valley', B. C. Burnham, *Invasion*, p.301; The soil below the Bronze Age round barrow at Lockington was insufficiently eluviated to have produced a full podsol but was 'an incipiently podzolized brown earth' with a high phosphate content. The latter is compatible with human occupation or manuring and suggests that pre-existing woodland must have been cleared some decades prior to the construction of the barrow. I. W. Cornwall in M. Posnansky 'The excavation of a Bronze Age round barrow at Lockington', *Transactions of the Leicestershire Archaeological Society*, (*TLAS, TLAHS*), XXXI, 1955, Appendix 1, p.26; cropmarks indicate a native Iron Age village, possibly attributable to the first century B.C., adjacent to a Roman villa of relatively high status (SK 480294, 482294). The latter yielded material of second–fourth-century date. A tenurial distinction and possibly two differing economic systems has been suggested. P. Clay, 'A Survey of two cropmark sites in Lockington-Hemington parish, Leicestershire', *TLAHS*, LIX, 1984–5, pp.17–26; R. Hingley, *Rural Settlement in Roman Britain*, London, 1989, p.102.

allow for easy regeneration to the original cover. The occurrence today of gorse and bracken particularly on the steeper slopes underlines this possibility. Finds of querns and the identification of kilns, especially near Ravenstone, indicate that use of the upland both for settlement and for cultivation continued at least to some degree into the Romano-British period. Thus, although the archaeological record is slender, when added to the limitations imposed by geology and soils, it implies that the Anglo-Saxons encountered a modified landscape in which a climax woodland, if it ever existed, had long been succeeded by open woodland and heath.[15]

In the absence of early charters containing descriptive boundary clauses the validity of the hypothetical Anglo-Saxon landscape suggested can best be assessed through an examination of terms which they themselves used to identify places and settlements in the local environment; name-elements describing heath and woodland which were used in the formation of parish, township or minor settlement names give some indication of the then-existing landscape. Six elements denoting woodland occur in the area. Four, *lēah, scēgel, sceaga* and *wudu*, are of Anglo-Saxon derivation; two, *skógr* and *lundr*, have Old Norse roots. *Lēah* is found infrequently in names recorded before 730 and, although later it acquired the connotation 'meadow' is generally regarded as having the meaning 'woodland clearing' or possibly 'a settlement in a woodland environment'. *Scēgel, sceaga* and *lundr* are usually associated with small areas of woodland, while *wudu* is found mainly in minor names and field names.[16]

15 Three pottery kilns and one tile kiln have been identified at Kelham Bridge (SK 403116); querns at SK 403114, 310157 (Moira) and at Normanton le Heath; the site of the pagan Danish cemetery at Heath Wood, Ingleby, for example, is on Bunter sandstone. It is dry at all seasons and hence unconducive to deciduous woodland. At Swarkestone, north of the Trent, on sands and gravels, pollen analysis of soils beneath the barrows implies 'an open mixed woodland with hazel thickets and large grassy areas'. M. C. Pearson in M. Posnansky, 'The Bronze Age round barrow at Swarkestone', *DAJ*, 76, 1956, p.25.

16 Derivations in Table 1 are based on K. Cameron, ed., *The Place-names of Derbyshire*, (*PNDB*), English Place-name Society, 27–29, Cambridge, 1959; B. Cox, 'Place-names of Leicestershire and Rutland', ('Thesis'), unpublished Ph.D., University of Nottingham, 1971. Field-names have been excluded from the analysis because the greater detail available in the Derbyshire volume would

Seventeen names containing one of these elements are found in the area under discussion (Table 1; Map 5). Ten contain *lēah* and of these, three, Charley, Oakley in Croxall and Willesley are recorded in Domesday. Charley was an area on the fringes of Charnwood, Willesley a detached parish of Derbyshire possibly incorporating the Scandinavian personal name *Vifill* as its specific. Oakley is first recorded in 1002 and, although in the parish of Croxall in Derbyshire, was always part of Staffordshire. Interestingly it is approximately two miles from Coton in the Elms and may therefore refer to an isolated stand of oak in an area otherwise characterized by elm. A second Oakley is in Long Whatton and is recorded as *Acle* in 1254. It gave its name to a deanery and remains in use as a farm name. Of the remaining six *lēah* names Langeley (1180), Shortwood (Short(e)langele C.13), Holly Hayes (1369) and possibly Gresley (1125) are preceded by a descriptive adjective while Isley (1327) and Ramsley (1597) may contain personal names. Three of the remaining seven names contain Scandinavian elements and four OE ones. Seal and Woodcote are first recorded in Domesday and the rest are all attested before the end of the fourteenth century. Seal, Shaw and Lount refer to small woods, Gelscoe and Loscoe contain the Scandinavian element *skógr*, while OE *wudu* is found in Woodcote, next to Smisby on the county boundary, and Southwood which adjoins Heath End in Staunton Harold.[17]

OE *hǣð*, ON *heiðr* is the most common element in the area to suggest both poverty of soil and absence of woodland and forms the root of 10 of the 14 names or affixes listed (Table 1, pt. 2). Two, both recorded in Domesday, are of particular interest: Hearthcote which is situated

create an unacceptable bias in the data; M. Gelling, *Place-names in the Landscape*, London, 1984, pp.189–205, 208–9, 207, 227–9; and 'The chronology of English place-names', in T. Rowley, ed., *Anglo-Saxon Settlement and Landscape*, Oxford, 1974, p.96; B. Cox, 'Place-names of the earliest English records', *English Place-name Society Journal*, 8, 1973–4, pp.50, 60. Cox found only seven occurrences of *lēah* prior to 730, of which six appeared only in charters; A. H. Smith, *English Place-name Elements*, II, Cambridge, 1970, pp.18–22, 99, 103, 125, 127, 279–81; the field name *Hetle* (1208) in Hartshorne may indicate that *lēah* was used similarly in heath areas.

17 Mr Howard Usher has drawn my attention to the pronounced boundary bank on the edge of Southwood. Until recently the county boundary followed this bank.

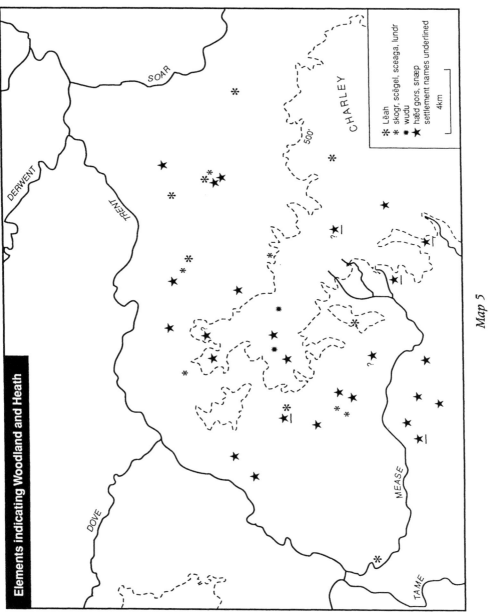

Elements indicating Woodland and Heath

* Lēah
* skōgr, scēgel, sceaga, lundr
* wudu
★ hǣd gors, snæp
★ settlement names underlined

4km

Map 5

Table 1 — Wood and Heath Elements

Name	Parish	Date	S	A	Early form	Element	Comment
Charley	area name	1086	S	A	Carnelega	carn+lēah	
Gelscoe	Isley	1244	S		Gelesco	skógr+Sc	farm
	Walton				Geylissco	Geílir	
Gresley	Gresley	1125	S		Gresele	?+lēah	
Isley	Isley	1327					
	Walton	1327			Isly Walton	*Isa+lēah	OE pers
Langley	Isley	1180	S		Langhelia	lang+lēah	
	Walton	1186			Langeleia		
Loscoe	Repton	1162	S		Loftescot	lópt +	farm
		1227			Loftessco	skógr	
Lount	Staunton						
	Harold	1347	S		le lounte	lundr	small wood
Seal	Over & Nether	1086	S		Sela, Scela	scēgel	small wood
Shortwood	Isley						
	Walton	c.C13		A	S(h)ortelangele	lēah	
Willesley	Willesley	1086	S		Wivleslei	Wifellēah	
Woodcote	Ashby	1086	S		Udecot	wudu	on b'dary
Oakley	Croxall	1002					
		1086	S		Acclea	ac + lēah	farm in Staffs.
Ramsley	Melbourne	1597		A	Roumsley	Hræfn + lēah	
Southwood	Ticknall	1162		A	Sudmude		
		1212			Suthw(o)de	wudu	adj. Heath End
Oakley	Long Whatton	1254	S		Acle	ac + lēah	deanery, farm
Holly Hayes	Coalville	1369	S		Halleheye	hall lēah hæg	farm
Shaw House	Coalville	1391	S		le Shawe	sceaga	
Brombrough	Donisthorpe	Ed I		A	Bromber- + walle	Brombeorg + wælle	thorn bush hill
The Shrubs	Repton	1200					
		1218		A	le Scrubb		
Heathfield	Ingleby	1648		A			Sc. cemetery
Hearthcote	Gresley	1086	S		Hedcote	haeð + cot	
Heath End	Staunton						
	Harold	1327		A	Litelheet	haeð	
Short Heath	Overseal	1342		A	Shertheth	haeð	
Rough Heath	Overseal	1806		A			The Rough
No Man's Heath[1]			S				ex. par.

1 — No Man's Heath was an extra-parochial area at the meeting point of the four counties of Derby, Leicester, Stafford and Warwick.

Name	Parish	Date	S	A	Early form	Element	Comment
Heather	Heather	1086	S		Hadre	ON heiðr	? repl OE hæð
Normanton le Heath	Normanton	1247 1299	S		othe heth	hæð	
Donington le Heath	Donington	1086 1347	S		Dunton s. Bruerum		
Sinope	Swannington	1520	S		Snape	OE snæ ON snap	boggy land poor pasture
St Bride's Heath	Stanton by Bridge	1620		A			
Drakelow Heath	Drakelow	1356	S			OE hæð	

S — settlement names; A — non-settlement names.

Brizlincote in Bretby which occurs as *Bersicot* (1100) *Bursinot* (1240) is suggested in *PNDB* as possibly representing ME *berse* 'forest enclosure'.

Table 2 — Names indicating heath and waste on 2½″ maps.

Name	Grid ref.	Location
Clifton Heath	SK21 2710	on Chilcote/Clifton boundary
Gorse Spinney	SK21 2718	third of a mile north of Chilcote
Linton Heath	SK21 2816	on Seal boundary
Heath House	SK31 3010	on Appleby side of boundary with Stretton en le Field
Barns Heath	SK31 3210	north of Appleby Magna
Gorsey Leys	SK31	of Moira on Ashby Wolds
Goseleys	SK31 3219	1½ miles east of Swadlincote, south of Hartshorne
Hartshorne Heath	SK31 3419	on boundary with Smisby
Heath Farm[1]	SK22 2520	on boundary of Drakelow and Stapenhill
The Gorse	SK22 2922	¼ mile south of Bretby
Waste Farm[2]	SK32 3223	between Repton Shrubs and Repton Common
Bondwood Farm[2]	SK32 3223	¼ mile south-east of Waste Farm
Hartshorn Bog[2]	SK32 3222	south of Bondwood Farm
Diseworth Gorse	SK42 4322	¼ mile south of Gelscoe on boundary with Belton and Tonge
Tonge Gorse	SK42 4322	¼ mile south of Gelscoe on boundary with Diseworth and Belton
Lockington Gorse	SK42 4526	under East Midlands Airport

1 — Occurs as Drakelow Heath in 1356.

2 — These are all situated on the boundary of Repton and Hartshorne.

in the parish of Gresley is found as *Heðcote* and Heather as *Hadre* from ON *heiðr* possibly replacing OE *hæð*. The addition of *en le heath* to Donnington and Normanton as distinguishing affixes recorded in the thirteenth century suggests that extensive heaths occupied many of the upland areas separating the valleys, and the extra-parochial status of No Man's Heath at the point where the four counties met, lends support to the suggestion. The place-name Ticknall — 'the nook or corner of the kids' — and the destructive effect of goats on woodland adds further weight to the evidence provided by the *hæð* names. The distribution of heath areas named on the first edition of the 2½″ maps (Table 2) emphasizes their persistence on the fringes of parishes and occasionally, as at Appleby, in association with administratively divided townships.[18]

The distribution of woodland and heath elements depicted on Map 5 highlights two significant points. First, names connected with poor pasture, including *hæð*, are widespread throughout the upland; secondly, with few exceptions woodland names are in close juxta-position to heath names. One example is Gresley where the name *Heðcote*, recorded earlier, has been superseded. The overall impression given by the distribution of these names strengthens the evidence of geology, soils and archaeology and supports the view that a predominantly open landscape, albeit with small areas of surviving or regenerated woodland, did in fact cover much of the area at the time of the Anglo-Saxon settlement. Furthermore, the persistence of 'heath' names on the edges of parishes implies that natural woodland regeneration may have been inhibited by the existence of degraded soils with a high acidic value. The resultant unrewarding environment is likely to have encouraged areas of inter-commoning — a 'no-man's land' — into which expansion could take place when necessary and which might provide a refuge in adversity.

Was this, then, a terrain which enabled small enclaves of racially or socially distinctive peoples to co-exist? The reaction of incoming settlers, whether of Anglo-Saxon or Danish descent, to the potential resources of the area will have influenced both the pattern of

---

18 K. Cameron, *PNDB*, p.637; B. Cox, 'Thesis', pp.498–9; Gillian Fellows-Jensen, 'Scandinavian settlement names in the East Midlands' (*SSNEM*), Copenhagen, 1978, suggests an OE *-er* derivative of *hæð* as applicable to Heather. The name is, however, pronounced 'Heether'.

subsequent settlement and relations between newcomers and their predecessors. The possibility that in this part of the Mercian heartland there may have been identifiable groups whose origins predate the advent of the Anglo-Saxons is difficult to establish but, in the absence of extant Mercian annals, the scanty references to the *Tomsætan* and the *Hrypingas* may be supplemented by a study of indicative name elements.

Table 3 lists names which suggest a non-Anglo-Saxon, non-Danish presence. Breedon, Barr Hall and the two Waltons, are settlement names which either contain a British topographical element or denote groups of non-Anglo-Saxons; Charnock Hill, Charley and *Penhull* also contain British topographical elements; the wapentake

Table 3 — Names reflecting a non-Anglo-Saxon, non-Danish presence.

Name	Parish	Alt./ft.	Earliest form	Date	Derivative
Breedon	Breedon	400	Briudun	730	PrW *brez
					Br. *briga
Charnock Hill	Isley Walton	275		1831	?Br. *carno
Walton	Isley Walton	275	Waletuna	1185	walh + tun
Walton	Walton on Trent	200	Waletuna	942	walh + tun
Barr Hall	Walton on Trent	200	Barr	1565	PrW *barr
					Br. barro
*Penhull	Drakelow	200	Penhul	lC14	?Br. penno + hyll
Charley		c.450	Carnelega	1086	?*PrW carn
					*Br. carno
St Bride's	Stanton by Bridge	400	St Brigide	1260	chapel dedication
Comberford[1]	Wigginton	180	Cumbreford	1187	cumbra
					?valley
					?Welsh
Walecros[2]	wapentake		Walecros'	1086	?walh + cros
					?Váli's cros
Bretby	chapelry of Repton	400	Bretbi	1086	Brettas, Bretar
Normanton	Normanton	450	Normenton	1209	Norðman
	le Heath		othe heth	1299	

1 — Comberford: this is sited opposite Tamhorn in an area of the Tame valley where recent archaeological work has revealed evidence of Romano-British settlement.

2 — Walecros: see n.19b, p.233.

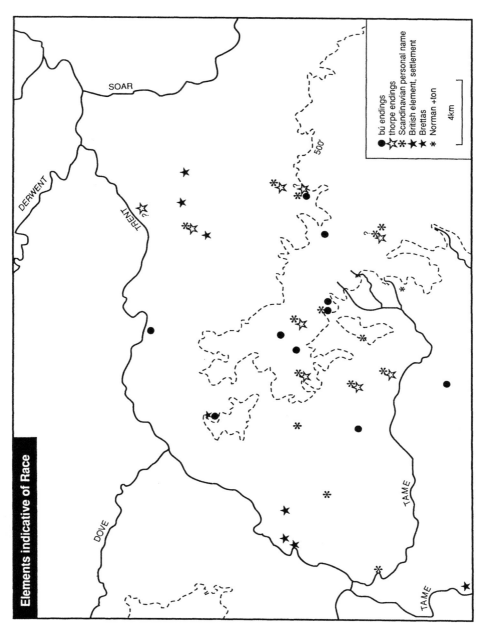

Elements indicative of Race

Map 6

bù endings
thorpe endings
Scandinavian personal name
British element, settlement
Brettas
Norman +ton

4km

name *Walecros* (later the area of Repton and Gresley hundred) has been ascribed a Scandinavian provenance but, given its location and the increasing evidence of Romano-British settlement in the area, it is possible that both that and Comberford refer to surviving British groups. The distribution of these names as depicted on Map 6 occurs in two main clusters; one, consisting of Walton on Trent, Barr Hall and *Penhull*, is wholly within Derbyshire while Breedon, Isley Walton and Charnock Hill, although in Leicestershire, are adjacent to the boundary; Charley is an area four miles north-east of Ravenstone. Thus at least seven names testify to a stratum of pre-invasion peoples whose presence may also be reflected in the dedication of the chapel of St Bride in the parish of St Michael, Stanton by Bridge and possibly also that of St Modwenna at Burton on Trent. Bretby and Normanton le Heath on the other hand indicate Britons and Norwegians respectively.[19]

Any early social structure that existed here will have been severely disrupted by Anglian penetration, the Danish invasions, the partitioning of Mercia, and subsequent Scandinavian settlement as well as by the campaigns of Edward the Elder and Æthelflæd. To extricate the effect of these events from beneath the overlay of succeeding centuries is well-nigh impossible. Nevertheless, an analysis of name-elements

19 a — Derivations given in Tables 3, 4, 5 and 6 are based on G. Fellows-Jensen, *SSNEM*; Olof von Feilitzen, *The Pre-conquest Personal Names of Domesday Book*, Uppsala, 1937. K. Cameron, *PNDB*; B. Cox, 'Thesis'; Olof S. Anderson, *The English Hundred-names*, (*EHN*), Lund, 1934-9.

b — K. Cameron, *PNDB*, III, pp.622, 633, 667; B. Cox, 'Thesis', Breedon, pp.346, n.42, Walton, pp.33, 366. For Charnock Hill, Cox comments that, as with some names in Charnwood Forest, this has a British look but only late forms survive. O. S. Anderson, *EHN*, p.36, suggests Váli + crōs by analogy with Walshcroft in Lincolnshire; G. Fellows-Jensen, *SSNEM*, pp.141, 162, 266, sees crōs as a Scandinavian loan-word linked with Norwegian settlement from Ireland and cites a Normanton in Walecros hundred. This, however, is Normanton-by-Derby which is in that hundred by virtue of its status as sokeland of Melbourne. The significance of the British names is enhanced by a reference to a 'vicus vocatur Wales' and of 'Walesend' which occurs in a sixteenth-century copy of an earlier survey of Barton under Needwood near Burton-on-Trent. Derbyshire Record Office, D3155/DL42/WH/886. These appear to be analogous with Wales in Yorkshire.

c — Bretby: K. Cameron, *PNDB*, p.623; G. Fellows-Jensen, *SSNEM*, pp.19, 39, 264; Normanton: B. Cox, 'Thesis', pp.524, 558, 559.

can reveal gaps through which one may catch glimpses of the tenth-century pattern. The implications of the scatter of names containing Scandinavian elements and their usefulness as a basis for estimating the numbers of incomers, whether in the army or as settlers has been the subject of much debate. For the present purpose, however, it is the distribution of the habitative suffixes *bý* and *þorp*, and of Scandinavian personal names associated with those and other endings which will be considered.[20] Since it is the overall pattern which is the focus of the present inquiry, references to the finer points of the discussions on the relationships of *þorps* as secondary or daughter settlements to those ending in *bý* are superfluous and for the purpose in hand it will be accepted that chronologically *þorps* are later, usually dependent settlements.[21]

The settlements with names compounded with *bý* are all found on the upland (Table 4a); eight are situated above 400 feet, Appleby is at 300 feet and Ingleby, although at 150 feet, faces north on the side of a river cliff. Three specifics contain topographical elements; Bretby and Ingleby indicate non-Danish people, Smisby indicates an occupation and two, Kilwardby and *Trangesbi*, contain Scandinavian personal names. Only three of the 10 names containing *bý*, all group specifics, Smisby, Bretby and Ingleby, are found on the Derbyshire side of the border. The evidence of these place-names is involved and the comparatively late date at which some are first recorded must be kept in mind. Superficially there appears to be a considerable

---

20 E.g.: a — G. Fellows-Jensen, 'The Vikings in England: a review', *Anglo-Saxon England*, 4, Cambridge, 1975, pp.181–206; and 'Scandinavian settlement in the Danelaw in the light of the place-names of Denmark', *Proceedings of the 8th Viking Congress*, Odense, 1981, pp.133–45.

b — P. Sawyer, 'Conquest and colonization: Scandinavians in the Danelaw and in Normandy', *ibid.*, pp.123–31.

c — N. Lund, 'The settlers: where do we get them from – and do we need them?', *ibid.*, pp.147–71.

d — K. Cameron, 'Scandinavian Settlement in the territory of the Five Boroughs: the Place-name evidence' in K. Cameron, ed., *Place-name Evidence for the Anglo-Saxon Invasions and the Scandinavian Settlements (PNESS)*, Nottingham, 1975, pp.115–38.

21 K. Cameron, 'II Place-Names in Thorp', in K. Cameron, *PNESS*, pp.139–56; N. Lund, '*thorp* names', *Medieval Settlement, Continuity and Change*, London, 1976, pp.223–5; G. Fellows-Jensen, *SSNEM*, pp.248–57.

Table 4a — Names with generic -bý

Place-name	Alt./ft.	Date	County	Geology/Soils	Parish links
Appleby	300	1086	Der./Leics.	Keuper sandstones	Divided parish
Ashby	450	1086	Leics.	Coal Measure shales	Includes Blackfordby, Boothorpe (part), Cliftonthorp, Kilwardby
Blackfordby	500	1130	Leics.	C.M. shales Keuper sandstones Boulder clay	Township in Ashby, includes part of Boothorpe
Bretby	400	1086	Derby	Keuper sandstones	Chapelry in Repton
Gunby	350		Leics.	Keuper and Bunter sandstones	Hill and farm in Seal
Ingleby	169	1009	Derby	Keuper and Bunter sandstones	Hamlet in chapelry of Foremark in Repton
Kilwardby	400	1130	Leics.	C.M. shales	Lies within the suburbs of Ashby
Limby		1520	Leics.	Keuper sandstones	Swannington
Smisby	550	1086	Derby	Keuper sandstones	Chapelry in Repton
Trangesgi		1086	Leics.	Keuper sandstones	
Thringstone	400	1200		C.M. shales	Thringstone

Table 4b — Names with generic -bý

Place-name	Specific	Topog.	Personal	Race/Occup.	Lang.
Appleby	Æppel	###			OE
Ashby[1]	Asce	###			OE
Blackfordby	Blæcford	###			OE
Bretby	Brettas, Bretar			###	OE ON
Gunby[2]	?Gunni				
Ingleby	Engla-			###	Scand.
Kilwardby	Calverte		kylfu-voðr Ketilfriðr		ON Scand.
Limby[3]					
Smisby	Smið, Smiðr			###	OE, ON
Trangesbi	Thræingr		Thræingr		OIcel.
Thringstone	Trangeston'				

1 — -bý may have replaced OE 2nd element.
2 — No early forms — ? analogous with Gunby St Nicholas, Lincolnshire.
3 — *Cf. le halle place*, 1520.

Table 5a — Names with generic -thorpe

Place-name	Alt./ft.	Date	County	Geology/Soils	Parish link
Boothorpe	450	1086	Leics.	C.M. shales	Seal, Ashby
Brasthorpe	475	1286	Leics	C.M. shales	
?Clifton-				Keuper sandstones	Ashby
Donisthorpe	300	1086	Derby/	C.M. shales,	
			Leics.	Bunter sandstone,	Seal, Measham,
				marls	Gresley
Oakthorpe	325	1086	Derby	C.M. shales,	Stretton,
				breccia, marls	Measham, Gresley
Osgathorpe	275	1086	Leics.	Red marls, boulder	clay
Ravensthorpe	475	1086	Derby/	Keuper sandstones	
Ravenstone			Leics.	Glacial sands,	
				alluvium	?Repton
Wifelesþorpe	200	972	Leics.	Keuper marls,	Wilson in
				Keuper sandstones	Breedon
Hubereþorp[1]		1200	Leics.		in Osgathorpe
Littlethorpe[1]		1632	Leics.		Ashby
Netherthorpe[1]		1616	Leics.		Ashby
Milnethorpe[1]		1462	Leics.		Castle Donington
Threingesþorpe[2]		1276	Leics.		?Thringstone

1 — Lost places.
2 — Possibly a scribal error for Thringstone.
Two suggestive field names — le Westhorpe 1347 and Thorpes 1406 — occur in
     Long Whatton.

degree of Scandinavian dominance in the area, but closer examination
raises some interesting points. Thus, for example, the Domesday
Trangesbi is recorded in 1200 as *þreingestūn*; Appleby is recorded
*c.*1002 as *Æppelby*, as *Aplebi* and *Apleberie* in Domesday.
Furthermore, the implications of *Brettas, Bretar*, in Bretby and the
interesting juxtaposition of the large Viking cemetery at Heath Wood
on the crest of the hill half a mile south of Ingleby with a settlement
containing a Scandinavian word for Angles raises speculation about
the relationship between the races; at the same time it lends support
to the suggestion that woodland was limited in the ninth and tenth
centuries.[22]

22 a — K. Cameron, *PNDB*, III, pp.623, 639, 658; Kilwardby: B. Cox, 'Thesis',
     pp.52, 337; G. Fellows-Jensen, *SSNEM*, p.57; *Trangesbi*: B. Cox, 'Thesis', pp.52,
     57; G. Fellows-Jensen, *SSNEM*, p.75.

Table 5b — Names with generic -thorpe

Place-name	Earliest form	Personal name	Lang.	Comments
Boothorpe	Bortrod	Búi, Bó	Sc, OD	by-name fr. búa
Brasthorpe	Brasþorp	Brasi	W.Scand	
		Brattr	Scand	by-name
Donisthorpe	Durandesþorp	Durand	O.Germ	Feilitzen notes
			C.Germ	nine in Suffolk
Oakthorpe	Acheþorp	Áki	OD	
Osgathorpe	Osgodþorp	Asgot	OD,O.Sw	Anglicized as
		Ásgautr	ON	Osgod
Ravenstone	Ravenestuna	Hræfn, Hrafn	OE, ON	
Ravensthorpe	Ravenesðorp			
Wifelesþorp	Wifelesþorp	Vífill	O.Sc	?Wilson
		?Wifel	OE	
Hubereþorp[1]	Hubert	C.Germ		
Littlethorpe[1]				
Netherthorpe[1]				
Milnethorpe[1]		Myl(e)n	OE	
Threingesþorp[2]	Threingesþorp	Thræingr	O.Icel	

1 — Lost places.
2 — Possibly a scribal error for Thringstone.
Other possibilities suggested by Fellows-Jensen are:
      Boothorpe E.Scandinavian *bō* 'farm'
      Wifelesþorp OD **wivael*, 'pointed piece of ground'; OE **wifel*.

It is immediately noticeable from Tables 5a and b that five of the 12 names containing *þorp* are of 'lost' places; Cox has suggested that *Brasthorpe* may be the modern Cliftonthorpe while *Milnethorpe* in Castle Donington may be represented by the cottages which lie at the foot of the 'Mylne' cliff by the ford. Two names show a fluctuation in the second element: Wilson is recorded as *Wifelesþorp* in 972 and Ravenstone occurs as Ravensthorpe in the Leicestershire Domesday entry. If *þreingesþorp* is not a scribal error for *þreingestūn*, it may either show a similar fluctuation or may possibly refer to a lost daughter

b — It has been suggested that the limit of the Danelaw may have been close to the southernmost part of Derbyshire; the cemetery at Ingleby would then represent an outpost of Danes. Camden Clarke and W. Fraser, 'Excavation of pagan burial mounds, Ingleby, Derbyshire', *DAJ*, 66, 1946, p.13. Ingleby adjoins Foremark which has a Scandinavian topographical name.

Table 6 — Township names containing probable Scandinavian personal names.

Place-name	County	Earliest form	Date	Derivation	Comment
Boothorpe	Leics.	Bortrod	1086	búi, bó	Divided township
Brasthorpe[1]	Leics.	Brastorp		?Brasi	
Croxall[1]	Derby/Staff.	Crokeshall	942	ON Krókr	Divided township
Donisthorpe	Derby/Leics.	Durandestorp	1086	C.Germ Durand	Divided township
Kilwardby	Leics.	Calvertebi'	1130	Kilvert from ON kylfuvorōr	in Ashby
Oakthorpe		Achetorp	1086	OD Áki	Divided township
Osgathorpe	Leics.	Osgodtorp	1086	OD, OSW Asgot ON Ásgautr	
Ravenstone	Derby/Leics.	Ravenestorp Ravenestun	1086	?Hrafn	Divided township
Rosliston	Derby	Redlauestun Rostlavestuna	1086 1189	?Hrodlaf	
Snibston	Leics.		1130	Snipr	
Swadlincote	Derby	Sivardinges- Su- Swartlin-	1086 1208	ON Svartling	
Thringstone	Leics.	Trangesbi'	1086	Thræingr	
Willesley	Derby	Wivleslei	1086	Vífill	
Wilson	Leics.			Vífill	
Wifelesthorpe		Wifelesthorpe	972		

1 — See n.25.

settlement of *Trangesbi*. Moreover, not only are four settlements, Boothorpe, Donisthorpe, Oakthorpe and Ravenstone divided townships, but additionally, four of the seven which can be definitely located are sited on Coal Measures shales, well-known for the thin cold soils to which they give rise. A further contrast between the status of the settlements bearing these names and those containing *by* is indicated by the greater preponderance of personal names forming the specific (Table 5b). Three 'lost' names, all first recorded after 1400, contain a non-personal specific. Of the remainder, six specifics appear to incorporate Scandinavian personal names, one may be either OE *Hræfn* or ON *Hrafn*, *Hubereþorp* is CGermanic *Hubert* and Donisthorpe, by analogy with the nine occurrences noted by Feilitzen in Suffolk is possibly from OGermanic *Durand*.

Fellows-Jensen, however, suggests ESc *bō* 'farm' as an alternative for Boothorpe and OD **wivæl* or OE *wifel* for *Wifelesþorp*.[23]

A total of 14 settlements in the area through which the county boundary passes include Scandinavian personal names; 11 of these lie on the Leicestershire side (Table 6). Five of the townships in what may be termed the 'heath' area — Boothorpe, Croxall, Donisthorpe, Oakthorpe and Ravenstone — were divided either between counties or parishes or both. A further salient point arising from the list of all Scandinavian personal-name elements is that three, Ravenstone, Thringstone and Wilson, are distinguished by apparent fluctuations in the second element.[24]

The spatial pattern depicted on Map 6 calls for some comment. First, within the study area only three *bý* names, all with specialized connotations, are found north of the border in Derbyshire; secondly, no *þorps* are found within that same area. Thirdly, as noted earlier, elements linked with Celtic settlement occur either within Derbyshire or adjacent to the border. Finally, of the townships bearing possible Scandinavian personal-name elements, only two, Swadlincote and Rosliston, are located wholly within Derbyshire; Croxall was partly in Staffordshire and Willesley, although part of Derbyshire, was detached from it.[25]

The evidence for non-Anglo-Saxon settlement presented by these name-elements highlights two distinct and differing patterns of population distribution within a topographically unified area. To the north-west occurs the major evidence for British survival, the greatest apparent racial diversity and less obvious Scandinavian influence. By contrast the south-eastern region is characterized by an

---

23 B. Cox, 'Thesis', Threingesthorp, p.359, Wilson, p.350; Ravenstone, *Domesday Book*, f.278a, b, 235b; O. von Feilitzen, *Pre-Conquest*, pp.29, 229. The nine occurrences in Suffolk were of *liberi homines*; G. Fellows-Jensen, *SSNEM*, Brasthorpe, p.124, Boothorpe, p.104, *wifelesþorp*, p.121.

24 See n.23.

25 In *SSNEM*, however, Gillian Fellows-Jensen suggests the following alternatives: Brasthorpe, ME 'brash' twigs, p.124; Croxall, OE topographical element 'croc' crook, p.375; Swadlincote, OE Sweartling, p.381. Dr Fellows-Jensen has commented that the few occurrences of *bý* in Derbyshire 'would seem to represent overflows from western Leicestershire and the Nottinghamshire uplands', *SSNEM*, pp.248–50.

absence of British elements, and by an apparently strong Scandinavian impact, (particularly that related to secondary settlements containing the element *þorp*). Against this, however, must be set the conflicting witness of settlements with both OE and Scandinavian forms. Appleby and Ravenstone were in both counties, Thringstone is recorded as sokeland of Repton in Domesday, Wilson is sited on the boundary between Breedon (Leicestershire) and Melbourne (Derbyshire). It is possible that the vacillation in the naming process shown here is associated with an Anglo-Saxon presence sufficiently strong to produce a linguistic balance. A comparable, detailed analysis of township names with OE specifics and generics, although not possible here, would test this theory.

When the topographical, pedological, archaeological and linguistic evidence presented here is collated, however, a sequence of broad land use and settlement patterns within the area can be postulated. Early prehistoric settlement appears to have been focused on the river valleys, especially of the Trent and Tame, and the whole of the upland at that time may well have constituted a marginal area — a communal resource — into which expansion from the lowland areas could take place as and when necessary. Although there is evidence that exploitation of the upland resulted in some degradation of the natural environment rendering it less attractive, this was not so severe as to preclude all settlement, particularly in the Roman and Romano-British periods. Indeed although the varied resources of the whole region, upland and lowland valleys, would have been complementary, those of the higher land alone could have enabled the survival of small groups in the face of incoming Anglo-Saxon pressure in the valleys. In the later Anglo-Saxon period the heaths may have remained as inter-commoning areas, albeit with assarting taking place with varying degrees of intensity. Subsequently, however, the pattern which had evolved will have been disrupted by the Danish invasions, the partitioning of Mercia and the presence of the Danish armies in Leicester and Derby.

In the light of these considerations the major boundary between Derbyshire and Leicestershire would seem to represent a socio-economic divide. The fragmentation of the county boundary suggests that earlier tenurial links were not wholly disrupted and the possibility that the north-east/south-west line incorporated elements of earlier boundaries, such as the *parochia* of the church at Melbourne or of the lands of the Saxon monasteries of Breedon and Repton, should not be discounted. The chronological relationship of the boundary to the partitioning of Mercia, to the military campaigns of Edward and Æthelflæd as well as to the formation of the shires is unclear, but it seems feasible that a need arose to formalize the use of an area of intercommoning. The degree to which the racial patterns described above were linked with underlying social causes, however, requires further more detailed assessment.